GOOD NEWS, BAD NEWS

The MIT Press
Cambridge, Massachusetts,
and London, England

GOOD NEWS, BAD NEWS

Edwin Diamond

First MIT Press paperback edition, 1980
Copyright © 1978 by
The Massachusetts Institute of Technology

This book was set in IBM Composer Baskerville by Techdata Associates
Inc., printed and bound by Murray Printing Company in the United
States of America.

Library of Congress Cataloging in Publication Data

Diamond, Edwin.
  Good news, bad news.

  Includes index.
  1. Journalism—United States. I. Title.
PN4867.D5   070.4'3'0973   78-4904
ISBN 0-262-04057-3
      0-262-54035-5 (paper)

To Jeffrey L. Pressman, a colleague in the Department of Political Science at MIT, who died in February 1977. Jeff Pressman counseled me in this project, arranged for some of its funding, and helped make the News Study Group part of the Political Science Department. His death diminishes all of us.

CONTENTS

PART II
News as Entertainment, Entertainment as News

PART III
Suspended Sentences

PREFACE

The Congress, the courts, the presidency, the military, the police, the universities, and other institutions of American society have come under increasing public scrutiny in recent years by critics in the press, for good reason. Belatedly the press institution itself is being studied by journalists and others. This is entirely appropriate; the watchdog must also be watched. The following report represents the efforts of one such "press watch," conducted by the News Study Group in the Department of Political Science at the Massachusetts Institute of Technology between 1975 and 1977.

Since 1972, the News Study Group has been doing research on political and press processes in the United States. In 1975, some of these studies became the basis of *The Tin Kazoo: Television, Politics, and the News* (MIT Press, 1975). *The Tin Kazoo* analyzed press coverage of major political events of the 1960s and early 1970s, including the Vietnam War, the Pentagon Papers, the Watergate scandals, and Richard

Nixon's fall, among other topics. The book also examined
some of the emerging forms of television news in the United
States. Since 1975, our group has been continuing its research
and analysis of television news and has widened its studies to
include newspapers and magazines. This work was made
possible in part by MIT and by various foundations, including
the Ford Foundation and the Sloan Foundation. Our principal studies centered on the 1976 presidential campaign and
the performance of the media. (We use the words *press,
media,* and *journalism* interchangeably here for the retailers
of news and public information in the United States.)
Certain aspects of the press-political relationship in the 1976
campaign are examined in part I. New trends and developments in the news are examined in the other sections of this
study. Part II discusses changes in television in the last few
years as new developments in technology, new shifts in the
audience, and new definitions of news have occurred. Part III
looks at changes in print journalism, principally in national
magazines and metropolitan newspapers, as similar forces
affect these news outlets.

ACKNOWLEDGMENTS

My first appreciation goes to the journalists who allowed us to watch them as they watched events. Almost all of these men and women tolerated this scrutiny and cooperated with us. As Andrew Glass of the Cox Newspapers said, "We can't very well expect politicians to be open to our questions and then not be open to question ourselves." Glass also added that being "press watched" is not necessarily a pleasant experience but that journalists should do what the politicians do—fight down the annoyance and smile and be reasonably cooperative.

Among journalists and political people of special help are R. W. Apple, Jr., Roone Arledge, Ken Auletta, David Broder, Maureen Bunyan, Gil Butler, Pat Caddell, Adam Clymer, Howard Cosell, John Deardourff, Barney Frank, Mel Elfin, Larry Fraiberg, Fred Friendly, David Garth, Steve Gendel, Jack Germond, Andrew Glass, Robert Gorman, Joseph Grandmaison, Lee Hanna, Lou Harris, Terry Ann Knopf, Aaron

Latham, David Laventhol, J. Anthony Lukas, Alan Lupo, Jon Margolis, Judith Martin, Martin Nolan, Alan Otten, Martin Plesser, Jerry Rafshoon, Richard Reeves, Robert Reinhold, Richard Salant, William Small, Sanford Socolow, Leslie Stahl, Richard Wald, Barbara Walters, Ray White, Curtis Wilkie, Jules Witcover, and Earl Ubell.

The people who made this work possible are the young men and women students who were members of the News Study Group over the last five years. Mainly these students came from MIT and from Wellesley College, but students from Harvard and Radcliffe also helped. I thank them all, especially Nicole Baker, Gretchen Clark, John Feingold, William Johnson, Nancy Lukitsh, Michael McNamee, Deborah Meyerson, Barbara Moore, Sasha Norkin, Claude Owre, Norman Sandler, Paul Schindler, and Kate Stout.

A number of faculty and graduate students at MIT aided this project by providing their own time and wisdom. A critic is fortunate indeed to have help from a group of men and women that includes Chris Arterton, Joseph Barnard, Walter Dean Burnham, Kay Israel, Ithiel de Sola Pool, Robin Reenstra, J. Michael Ross, Eugene Skolnikoff, and Myron Weiner.

All interpretations and conclusions here are, of course, my own. Some of the people mentioned here most certainly would disagree with one part or another of the analysis.

I also would like to thank the following friends and editors; parts of this book appeared in their publications: Clay Felker, *New York* Magazine; Lewis Laphan, *Harper's* Magazine; Gene Lambinos, the *New York Times;* Andrew Mills, *TV Guide;* and Ken Pierce, *Columbia Journalism Review.*

THE
NEW CAMPAIGN
JOURNALISM

PART I

PROLOGUE:
THE LESSONS OF 1972

CHAPTER 1

The 1976 presidential campaign officially began in "the snows of New Hampshire," where Theodore White has instructed us to look. Gerald Ford was photographed snuggling a campaign worker's baby; Ronald Reagan was recorded throwing snowballs—at the urging of camerapersons; and Jimmy Carter's "peanut brigade" arrived without gloves or overcoats. James Reston noted somewhat indulgently in the *New York Times* that the presidential primaries are "the last of the Chautauqua circuit, of vaudeville, and the road shows of America." In 1976, the "vaudeville" was quite different qualitatively from previous campaigns, partly because of the press's changing role in the act.

First of all, an apparent shift in political power took place. The traditional party nominating system was strained by the overload of new primaries, new campaign rules, and new candidates. Whereas in 1972 there were twenty-three primaries, there were thirty in 1976, beginning with New Hampshire in late February. In addition there were hundreds of district elections and caucuses to select convention delegates. There were literally hundreds of new rules governing everything from delegate selection to fund-raising practices. "It was possible to go to jail in 1976," said one campaign manager, "for doing things that were considered routine in 1972." And there was the large field of candidates, Republican and Democratic.

The overloads were the product of such well-intended measures as the Campaign Finance Act of 1974 and the changes engineered in the Democratic party rules at the 1968 and 1972 conventions. The resulting reforms were meant to curb the power of the big contributors and the party leaders; they succeeded—perhaps too well. In 1976, with the victory of the obscure, antipolitics candidate Jimmy Carter, we may have witnessed the beginning of what political scientist Walter Dean Burnham has described as "politics without parties."

The traditional political parties have been weakened by population shifts, by the breakdown of old coalitions, and by growing emphasis on mass media campaigns. They may finally be swamped by the wave of reform. Burnham and others believe that third and fourth parties are possible in 1980 or 1984. As the old parties flounder, the role of mediating among factions and building up one or another of the candidates has been shifting elsewhere. In the "bad" old days, a candidate had to reach a relatively small number of fat cat contributors and power brokers. Now each candidate must win over hundreds of delegates, potential campaign workers, and thousands of small contributors. To do this he must convince them that he is indeed a viable candidate by attracting the press's eye.[1] A magazine cover is one way; an appearance on "Face the Nation" or similar television programs, another. A generation ago a power broker like Colonel Jake Arvey of

Illinois could "make" an Adlai Stevenson. Now a Barbara
Walters interview or a *New York Times Sunday Magazine*
article can certify a candidate. More and more the press becomes a vehicle for the candidate who has studied the rules
and the nominating process.

Increasingly, too, the press can be cajoled to do more than
give or withhold printer's ink or broadcaster's air time; it also
analyzes and interprets events (something its critics have always been urging it to do). The more complex and crowded
the election process, the more interpretation there is. Interpretation may become power when the press can be per-
suaded to declare that Ronald Reagan ran strongly—or
failed—in New Hampshire or when Walter Cronkite concludes
an interview with Fred Harris by saying, "Harris is the most
radical presidential candidate, occupying a position on the
Democratic party's Far Left."

The new tasks of assessing and anointing political candidates are shifting to the press at a time when its own institutional forms are undergoing severe changes. The 1976 elections were the first post Watergate presidential election. Fatu-
ous as that may sound, it has some real meaning. Well before
the photo opportunities of New Hampshire, executives and
editors of national news organizations held earnest meetings
to plan their coverage of the 1976 campaign. Every four
years, editors and executives always convene meetings to pro-
claim their intentions of reporting the election in a fresh, distinctive, and professional way. In 1976 there appeared to be
greater resolve than usual.

Most reporters and editors acknowledged—as they prepared
for 1976—that the press had not done a very good job of
covering the 1972 presidential campaign. When pressed to say
what the media did well in their 1972 presidential election
coverage, these journalists usually cited the investigative work

of Carl Bernstein and Bob Woodward (although neither was doing only political or campaign reporting) and—with surprising frequency—the warts-and-all sketches of the press-campaign process reported in Timothy Crouse's book, *The Boys on the Bus*. After these names, though, the list trails off.

Reporters and editors usually mentioned three failures of performance. First, they had failed to recognize, and take seriously, the early rise of George McGovern; one reason this happened was the lack of appreciation of the then-new delegate selection rules (fashioned by, among others, George McGovern). While underplaying McGovern, the press overplayed the phantom candidacy of Senator Edmund Muskie. Most journalists—David Broder was a notable exception—took the Muskie press releases about the senator's endorsement strength at face value. Muskie "won" the nomination at the starting gate and McGovern was initially written off, in part because of the familiar horse race mania with Louis Harris and George Gallup calling the field like track announcers. As James M. Perry later wrote in *Us and Them: How the Press Covered the 1972 Elections:* "We leaped into print to award the nomination to Muskie, even before the first of 23 primaries took place. We read Dr. Gallup's famous poll and we leaped into print to write off George McGovern." Transfixed by the horse race, the press was late in covering many of the issues of the campaign—a second failure in performance. It was not until late May, for example, that McGovern's $1,000 "demogrant" proposal received any close scrutiny, and even then it was mainly due to Hubert Humphrey's prodding attacks in the last days before the California primary. The same was true of McGovern's military defense programs.

Finally there was the notorious failure to flush out Richard Nixon and the entire Nixon campaign. The huge sums of ille-

gally raised money, the activities of CREEP, the full dimen-
sions of the Watergate break-in and cover-up, Nixon's personal demeanor—all remained largely hidden. "We thought
that Nixon would eventually come out and campaign and we
would have access to him for questions," recalls Broder. This
failure was particularly galling not only because Nixon-
CREEP was *the* story but also because every political reporter had come under the influence of Theodore White by
1972. Reporters worked hard to dig out the color, the
quotes, and the scene setters ("snows of New Hampshire")
just as White had done in his presidential campaign narratives
throughout the 1960s. As a result, by the end of the campaign they knew what McGovern press secretary Frank Mankiewicz had done to McGovern campaign director Gary Hart
(or vice versa) but nothing about what Nixon-CREEP had
done to the country.

The determination to do a better job in 1976—"the media
want to get their manhood back," a friend once said—was admirable. Like analysis and interpretation, grit is a quality that
the critics value. In 1976, the press's manhood was stiffened
by another post-Watergate attitude, the strong antipolitics
mood of the country. Our own eyes and ears, as well as the
public opinion polls, informed us of the steady decline in
public trust of national leaders and governmental institutions.
Ever sensitive to trends, the press understood the message.

But how were they to cover politicians in a time of antipolitics? Not so long ago, the national politicians and the
national press were linked in the friendliest of embraces.
Crouse's book had a great impact because it revealed to a
wider public what insiders already knew: that the press and
the candidates needed and used each other. But even without
reading Crouse, a half-attentive public sensed the partnership
of newsmakers. "The audience could see them together at

news conferences and other public events," explained Gary
Hart, now a senator from Colorado. "In effect, they had their
arms around each other's shoulders." The correct stance
toward authority these days is more than arm's length; the
press wants distance between itself and the politicians. Post-
Watergate, these old friends act as if they don't even recognize each other. "Now a politician is considered guilty until
proved innocent," claims Frank Tivnan, the director of communications for Boston Mayor Kevin White's successful reelection campaign of 1975. Electoral politics itself is suspect.

The performance of the national news organizations in
their coverage of the 1976 campaign reflected the new press
stance.[2] One of the lessons of 1972 was that the press generally missed the significance of the early McGovern campaign.
One approach to prevent a repeat performance was to take all
of the candidates seriously in 1976. The *New York Times*,
with its customary thoroughness, began a comprehensive
series on the presidential candidates in late December 1975,
proceeding from the announced contenders to the unan-
nounced, such as Senator Hubert Humphrey. Jimmy Carter
appeared early in the series because the *Times* went down the
list alphabetically. Because another lesson of 1972 was that
political reporting had been distracted by the horse race psychology of the press, a number of strategies were devised to
get at what are invariably called the "real issues." CBS News
defined these as what public opinion polling showed was on
people's minds. Beginning in mid-November 1975, CBS News
broadcast a series of interviews called "Campaign '76—The
Candidates and the Issues." According to Walter Cronkite,
who did the on-camera interviewing, CBS "set out to find
what will most concern the voting public" and then sought
out the candidates to get their "hard answers to [these] hard
issues." Because the CBS News poll, a telephone survey of

1,126 persons of voting age during the week of October 6, determined that "the most often-mentioned issues" were inflation, unemployment, crime control, and the energy crisis, Cronkite asked each of the major declared candidates where he stood on those issues. One of CBS's premises, according to Robert Chandler, who was in charge of the network's campaign coverage, was that the public rather than the candidates ought to be able to define the issues.

NBC News was also committed to extensive polling. On the first Sunday of 1976, NBC aired "What America Thinks," a poll of attitudes on subjects such as President Ford's performance, abortion, drugs, and sex education in schools. NBC News returned to the American voters' concerns periodically during the year and also made use of the analyses of public opinion specialist Richard Scammon. During the 1972 campaign ABC News designated Columbus, Ohio, as an "ABC city" to be visited periodically so that ABC could broadcast regular reports on Ohioans' attitudes on the ABC evening news. In 1976, ABC hired the Louis Harris firm for analysis.

Newsday and the *Boston Globe* used the services of the Tubby Harrison group to poll during the election year. The *New York Times* linked up with CBS News to do its own polling, used an outside firm, and covered the continuing story of the polls in the campaign. The *Times*'s "precision journalism" specialist, Robert Reinhold, was sent to the University of Michigan to learn survey research techniques during the summer of 1975.

A number of news organizations also assigned reporters to follow the fund-raising activities of the candidates ("to find out where the money came from and where it is going," as one afternoon newspaper editor explained) because they had missed the funding story in 1972. And because the "real" Richard Nixon proved so hard to find in 1972 (and 1968 and

1960), analyses of the demeanor and character of the candidates figured in the coverage plans of several organizations. Maynard Parker, then *Newsweek* magazine's national affairs editor, tried to "convey a sense of the man and what he is really like and not just simply how he stands on abortion or détente." *Time* did a "first round introduction" of the candidates—"where Fred Harris has been, who he is and what his record is"—but held off on the personalities and private lives of candidates until after the primaries, "when the field begins to thin out." According to Robert Ajemian, the *Time* editor in charge of the overall coverage, "We have to avoid the 1972 pitfall of getting overly excited about someone like a Muskie and then seeing it all change."

The *Washington Post*, in a series of Sunday pieces that began in December 1975, examined "the past record and reputation of each candidate." According to David Broder, the *Post*'s chief political writer, character analysis came in as a minor note to "establish" the candidate's personality early in the campaign and thus provide a reference point for the rest of the coverage. For example, in an article on Senator Henry Jackson, the reporter Jules Witcover described the senator as a dogged workaholic and loner who never relaxes on or off the Senate floor. This comment was intended to put the frequently repeated charge that Jackson "lacks charisma" in a proper context; it showed, said Broder, that Jackson "has never been one of the boys." After these candidate portraits and scene-setting pieces on the primary states, the *Post* went on to describe the campaign in terms of the issues emerging and the candidates' organizations.

A number of news organizations looked at the role of the press in the campaign. The *National Observer, Newsday*, and the *New York Times* assigned reporters to write regularly about the political coverage on television, political advertising, and the use of consultants—the "media side" of the campaign. Other news organizations, such as NBC and CBS, watched and reported on how the press was watching and reporting the campaign, though they did not assign full-time correspondents to the story. There were other watchers watching the watchers who were watching the candidates. The Ford and Markle foundations and the Social Science Research Council made a study of the media-candidate "interface" its main research project of the campaign, funding some of the best political scientists in the country in a cooperative venture.

These topics—"money," "polls," "organization," "personality," and "media"—are known as *sidebar* stories, accompaniments to the day-to-day running story of what the candidates said and did. In 1976, the running story was suspect; after all, the press in its new-found sophistication clearly understood that candidates stage media events to attract television coverage every day and usually only repeat a standard speech or "position paper." "We are leaving the daily story to the wire services," a newspaper editor told me. "That way we can concentrate our own resources on other special stories."

One problem with this is that the sidebars may squeeze out the substance. In its renewed zeal to give the inside story and the "feel" of the campaign, the press learned about the temperature and upholstery of the studio where the candidate appeared, the last-minute details of who wrote his speech, and the gaffes in his delivery. In short, they covered everything except what the candidate had said.

The wire services were supposed to provide this daily bread and butter of the campaign, but they had also grown restive about merely covering what the candidates said and did. In a memorandum distributed by United Press International in early November 1975, H. L. Stevenson, editor-in-chief and vice-president, reported that UPI's Washington bureau was discussing "how to change traditional coverage patterns." When UPI's Newspaper Advisory Board surveyed one hundred client newspapers a few weeks earlier, board member Clayton Kirkpatrick, editor of the *Chicago Tribune*, had found that the client editors wanted "new approaches and new techniques" in UPI's political reporting. As Kirkpatrick reported,

Wrapups and interpretive stories are in strong demand. . . . Texts of speeches and official papers are seen by most editors to be of little value. Investigative reporting is highly prized. . . . It is not enough to follow candidates around taking down their speeches and putting them on the wire. Interviews with the candidate's staff, gathering in-depth reactions from crowds, reports on opposing candidates' positions on issues, wrapping up a few days of speeches in a single story, are devices that client editors recommend.

Where did this new journalistic aggressiveness leave the candidates and their plans? Every political campaign can be seen as a struggle for control between press and candidate in the sense that each has its own needs (for example, the "favorable" news versus the "real" news, the speeches versus the "in-depth reactions"). If we are to believe the press's own press notices, political journalism was more aggressive, more wary, and more independent of the candidates in 1976 than they had been in 1972. Successful politicians, however, successfully adapt to such changes.

If traditional politics are out and antipolitics are in, then some candidates will be antipolitical. Jimmy Carter, George Wallace, Ronald Reagan, and Edmund G. (Jerry) Brown all ran against the establishment in 1976—not a new stance, for Wallace and Brown had been making careers of antipolitics for years.

If on the other hand investigative reporting is in, then some candidates will serve up scandal. In the 1975 Boston mayoral election, incumbent Mayor Kevin White, who had served for eight years, faced what looked like an easy challenge from Joseph Timilty, a relative unknown. The major Boston newspapers and area television stations started out by providing carefully balanced coverage. In the final weeks of the campaign, however, an investigative reporter at one of the Boston television stations produced alleged evidence of a 1970 shakedown of real estate people by the city assessor—a White appointee. *New Times* magazine, based in New York, ran the same corruption story (it turned out that the Timilty campaign had sold the writer and the story to the magazine). The White counterattack proceeded on about the same level; the police commissioner was the apparent source of a story depicting Timilty as the candidate of organized crime interests opposed to the reform-minded, incorruptible mayor. The overall tone of the campaign is perhaps best conveyed by a cover headline of the *Real Paper*, a Boston weekly; WHITE LIES, it proclaimed. White won, but in a surprisingly close race.

"Woodward and Bernstein were fine investigative reporters and they did the country a great service," Frank Tivnan says. "But, journalistically, they have spawned a batch of poor carbon copy 'investigative reporters' in a business that is nakedly imitative." Tivnan is not an unbiased observer. Patrick Caddell, the Cambridge public opinion analyst and a Timilty campaign strategist (who later went to work for Jimmy Carter), saw what he judges to be a brighter side to the coverage: "There are certain standards we are beginning to expect in politicians and the press is becoming the arbiter of these standards." In Boston, however, the newly aggressive, investigative instances of reporters proved to be ultimately malleable in the hands of the skilled political operatives. It was a premonition of the presidential campaign of 1976.

A related problem was that the new political sophistication of the campaign reporters was not always tempered with new political wisdom. Some reporters have been known to disdain to read candidates' speeches and position papers because they were press releases and somehow tainted. But as diligent and hard working as the best political reporters are, they may just not know as much as the politicians inside the campaign. Mark Shields, a Democratic party strategist who emerged as a key Carter aide, made the commonsense observation that the press is like the military—always ready to fight the next war with the weapons of the last. Everybody wants to cover the "real issues," says Shields, but in 1974 a good part of the press thought the campaign was about social issues—the "three A's" of acid, abortion, and amnesty—when, as Shields points out, the real story was about illegal money. In the campaign of 1976, everyone was geared up to do money when the important story was somewhere else.

In one place, however, the lessons of 1972 took hold in 1976. The media were one of the real stories of 1976, although not in the terms most commonly discussed. For reporters to tell us that Fred Harris's camper trip across the country was a "media event" or that Jimmy Carter changed into blue jeans before making an important political announcement was merely to touch the surface of the candidate-press relationship. Down deeper was more vital material that had to be uncovered: how the press used its power.

THE PRIMARIES: WHAT THE MEDIA MADE OF JIMMY CARTER AND "OTHERS"

CHAPTER 2

In campaign '76, the big media—the three major television networks, the national newspapers, the news magazines, and the wire services—resolved that they would not be fooled again as they had been by Richard Nixon in 1972. They would be aggressive, avoid being manipulated by media events, avoid a horse-race psychology in calling the candidates' strengths, and cover the issues.

How closely did they live up to their resolutions? The News Study Group in the Department of Political Science at MIT started monitoring the press coverage of the 1976 presidential campaign as early as June 1975.[1] The group began by videotape-recording coverage on the network evening news of the major declared and undeclared candidates. They also paid attention to candidate appearances on panel interview programs like "Meet the Press," analyzed the coverage of the candidates in the *New York Times,* the *Washington Post,* and the weekly news magazines, and conducted interviews with candidates, campaign workers, press secretaries, editors, news executives, reporters, columnists, and political analysts. By early spring 1976, certain patterns began to emerge.

First, the group found that not all the candidates were treated equally in the eyes of the media. In the first months of the campaign, Ronald Reagan and George Wallace received more attention than all the rest of the candidates combined—with the exception, of course, of Gerald Ford. The Democratic candidates tended to be grouped together as "the pack," with the exception of Jimmy Carter, who managed to move away from the others and get distinctive attention. Part of the reason for Carter's success in this regard could be traced to a front-page story in the *New York Times* of October 27, 1975, recounting what the *Times* called his "surprising" strength among Democrats who would participate in the Iowa caucus votes. This strength—and the story—led to an appearance on "Face the Nation" a few weeks later, where Carter effectively disentangled himself from "the pack."

Second, the press often labeled candidates early in the campaign: "populist candidate," "Kennedy connection," "star," "dark horse," "bumbler." Although these labels may be a kind of journalistic shorthand for headline purposes, frequently they held and tended to shape deeper perceptions and ways of coverage. Fred Harris, for example, was the "populist candidate" who, by most accounts, was called "too radical" to win. Both in print and on television, Harris was presented as a "showman," "a gifted speaker," or "colorful." Relatively little attention was given to his programs "since he can't win anyway." Gerald Ford and Henry Jackson were similarly pigeonholed, as these samples show:

Gerald Ford

"Ford in Trouble" (*Newsweek* cover line)

"Accidental Jerry" (*Village Voice*)
"Congenital bungling" (Evans and Novak)
"New Doubts as to Whether He
Has the Brains to Be President" (Joseph Kraft)
"Incumbent Ford Is Just Another
Challenger" (*New York Times*)
"Bumbler and Fumbler" (Tom Wicker)

Henry Jackson
"Stern Humorless Lawmaker" (*Boston Globe*)
"Tireless, but Somber" (*New York Times*)
"Dullest Campaigner" (*Newsweek*)
"The Grind, Single-Minded" (*Washington Post*)
"Steadfastly Dull" (CBS News)

Third, the tendency to act like race-track announcers was
as prevalent as ever. The two candidates most affected were
Reagan and Wallace. In the summer of 1975, Reagan was introduced to the media consumer as a clever speaker-per-
former who entertained the foolhardy idea of challenging an
incumbent. By January he was called a "sure" winner. In the
news magazines, for example, the "calls" went like this:

"Does Ronald Reagan have a chance?" (October 20, 1975)
"A race that seemed open and shut for the President now
shapes up as a tough one." (December 1, 1975)
"Some Republican leaders are beginning to reckon with the
possibility that the President might withdraw from the race."
(January 5, 1976)

After the Florida primary (March) Reagan was called out;
after the North Carolina primary, however, he was a winner
again. The opinions about Wallace's chances also changed
over time, but in a different direction. In the early fall, he
was presented as a serious candidate, and attention was focused on his opinions and record. By January, he was no

longer considered "viable." In the columns and news reports, *slippage* was the key term. A major Wallace story in the *Washington Post* reported that he was not filling the auditoriums at his Florida rallies and was losing his southern base. (In Wallace's case, the *Post* was right in its judgment, but the calls for Reagan were off the mark.)

As our group became aware of some of these patterns, it began to look at the television panel interview programs from a fresh point of view. Programs such as "Face the Nation" on CBS, "Meet the Press" on NBC, "Issues and Answers" on ABC are usually criticized by commentators for being too short in length and too superficial to permit a line of thought to develop; the panel questioners are judged too soft. As the MIT group saw it, however, the panel programs, predictable as they were, emerged as one of the places where the candidates could counter their media labels and perhaps break out of the box to which they had been consigned.

Panel shows have highly constricted formats. On two successive Sundays in January 1976, "Meet the Press" assembled four Democratic candidates for thirty-minute programs, interrupted by program breaks for commercials. Nevertheless even this stuttering presentation, which also included four questioners, allowed the candidates to speak directly to the viewers in a more substantive form than usual on the regular network evening newscasts. Until the Ford-Carter presidential debates during the fall, the panel shows were the principal means most voters had for observing the candidates in live, direct, uncontrolled appearances.

Because the panel interview programs were the best form of direct unscripted communication between the candidates and the voters, the News Study Group concentrated on elements of the programs such as the amount of time that an individual candidate appeared on the screen; the manner in which he was presented to the public in terms of close-ups and mid-distance camera shots; the number and type of questions he was asked; the amount of time he was given to respond to each question; and the frequency of interruptions by the panel interviewers. These analyses were an attempt to ascertain, statistically, certain unexpressed attitudes toward the individual candidate. For example, the more questions asked, the more the candidate was being pressed—or so it seemed to the group. Relatively fewer questions show a less aggressive attitude.

The group's commonsense hunches proved right. Newcomers like Jimmy Carter and Edmund G. Brown, Jr., were permitted long answers. Controversial figures like John Connally, on the other hand, hardly were allowed to finish their sentences. George Wallace and Jimmy Carter tended to be asked to explain their "records," Jerry Brown to explain his "philosophy." Finally the panel interview programs were compared with the styles and the content of other television formats, such as the news conference and the news special. For example, the News Study Group observed Gerald Ford in three different televised settings within a few weeks of each other: a White House news conference, a "presidential conversation" with three CBS newsmen, and a "Meet the Press" appearance. The analysis affirmed what the group had expected: the news conference was consistently the most supportive of the president, the conversation the most neutral, and the panel format the most undermining of presidential authority.

The last area of coverage examined was substantive: the campaign issues. The group expected the issues to command the greatest share of attention (even though they knew that, according to one definition, an "issue" is something the other candidate does not want to talk about). But the lesson of

1976, by all accounts, was that there were *no* substantive campaign issues. In October 1975, a CBS News poll showed that the subjects most on people's minds were inflation, unemployment, crime control, and the energy crisis. The press dutifully prepared to talk about these concerns, but few of these issues ever came up in any sustained way during the primary campaign.

The candidates had other subjects in mind. Ronald Reagan wanted to defend the Panama Canal and the white man in Africa. He spent a considerable amount of time running against Henry Kissinger. These stands, of course, had a strong appeal to the conservative Republicans Reagan needed to win his party fight with Ford. But even in the general election the campaign was equally barren of substance of the kind that the media wanted to weigh. Carter campaigned on his character and trustworthiness; Ford relied on his role in "cleansing" the air after the Nixon nightmare, concentrating on presenting essentially his honesty and openness. The "agenda" of the campaign, such as it was, was set by the candidates, not by the press. David Broder in the *Washington Post* summed up the campaign spirit of '76 with these words: "There's a special Pulitzer Prize for Prophecy awaiting any journalist with clips showing advance knowledge that the two most powerful messages in American politics in this bicentennial year would be (1) 'Love to everybody from Jimmy and Rosalynn and little Amy'; and (2) 'To hell with tinhorn dictator Torrijos from Nancy and Ron.' "

Still the myths of American politics die hard. At the start of the presidential primary campaign in January 1976, the political "experts" by and large held the views that

(1) in the Democratic party primaries, the press would play a kind of kingmaker's role in the candidate selection process, with the king in all likelihood one of the party's high-recognition figures such as Hubert Humphrey or Edward Kennedy;

(2) on the Republican side, the glory and puissance of the "imperial presidency"—for example, the telegenic advantages of White House ceremonies and other media events—would enable the incumbent Gerald Ford to dispose quickly of challenger Ronald Reagan.

When neither of these scenarios occurred as the primary campaign eventually played out through the late winter and early spring months, the same experts should have been forced to reexamine certain assumptions about the role of the press in American electoral politics. Instead a fresh mythology was fashioned: Jimmy Carter, the Democratic party nominee, succeeded in his quest for the nomination in part because the press elevated him from the rest of the primary pack, giving him a special treatment that helped him with the voters. Carter's regular appearances on the covers of *Time* and *Newsweek* magazines, along with the numerous newspaper and television stories about his origins, are usually cited as examples of this extra attention. Ben Wattenberg, one of Senator Henry Jackson's strategists, complained at the end of the campaign: "The press was so intrigued with this peanut farmer number, with this born-again Christian thing, that it spent an enormous amount of time covering Carter to the exclusion of Jackson, who at the time he dropped out had almost as many delegates as Carter."

Similarly Ronald Reagan benefited from "good media" in his uphill fight against Gerald Ford, specifically from his polished performances on the platform—compared with Ford's bumbling appearances. The *New York Times*'s Joseph Lelyveld, a normally astute observer, reported that the Reagan campaign came back from early disaster as the result of a thirty-minute campaign speech that was televised throughout North Carolina the week before his first state primary victory. Reagan was able to stay in the race despite the

presidential advantages because of his skillful use of the,
media, or so the analysis went.[2]

It is not difficult to see why so many experts are seduced
by the picture of media power. The explosive growth of television set ownership that began in the 1950s now provides a
new way to reach voters. In the past the prospective voter
had to go out of the house to make some personal connection with the candidate. Now the candidate—or more precisely, an image of the candidate—comes into the voter's home
through a paid commercial appearance or on news or public
affairs programs. During the 1960s, the candidates had tried
to engage the voter in this new intimacy. In 1968, Richard
Nixon's campaign advisers exerted considerable energy to
create an image of candidate Nixon that would come across
well in living rooms. On election eve, 1968, Nixon appeared
on national television; Joe McGinniss in his account of the
Nixon election effort, *The Selling of the President*, described
how the telethon details were stage managed right down to
the way telephoned questions would be worded on the air in
order to conform to the questions Nixon wanted to answer.
As the program began, the producer, Roger Ailes, observed:
"This is the beginning of a whole new concept. *This is it.* This
is the way they'll be elected forevermore. The next guys up
will have to be performers."

But of course, that wasn't it. Our own work, *The Tin
Kazoo*, as well as other studies, confirms that the contemporary media consumer has received enough instruction by television itself to realize that the slogans of political commercials are often interchangeable—or meaningless. Viewers can
see through the artful staging of media events. The first ten
times a television spot, free or paid, featured a Kennedyesque
"action" candidate, with shirt collar open and shirtsleeves
rolled up peering at a suburban wetland, it was probably

quite effective ("He will protect the environment"). However, when that same basic idea is borrowed and constantly
recycled, few voters are likely to be influenced. People may
watch more and more television, but they believe less and less
of what they see and hear. The constant claims of advertising
and politics have made all of us media agnostics.

But the political "experts" have short memories. Every
four years, they start from zero. Thus few remembered the
lesson of 1968. Also, to be fair, in January 1976, the presidential campaign appeared to be shaping up differently from
previous campaigns. With the weakening of the traditional
political parties, a trend noted by political scientists over the
past fifty years, it seemed that the tasks of building up one or
another candidate was shifting from the party processes to
other centers of influence, principally the press.

At the same time the press itself was making significant
new commitments of time, talent, and money to the 1976
campaign. The three national networks, accused in the past
of cutting back on public affairs programming, decided to
give regular Tuesday night coverage to the primary election
results, treating the primaries as a continuing, unitary
process. Because of these changes, even those wary of the
claims of the power of the press in the political system
thought that the 1976 campaign would find the press playing
an expanded role in deciding who was a viable candidate
among the crowded field, and in "setting the agenda" of the
issues in the complex primary process. I was, in short,
prepared to say I could be wrong about the influence of the
press in the campaign.

As it turned out, there was no need for confession on the
part of the doubters. The press's great resolve to cover the
issues crumbled when the candidates chose not to talk about
them—or certainly none that the press had thought would be

the issues. Few, if any, of the issues the press had identified ever came up again during the primary campaign. In the same way, it was the campaign's dynamics, and not the press, that made Pennsylvania the critical primary in 1976 for the Democrats (as West Virginia had been in 1960), and it was Mayor Daley and not Walter Cronkite or David Broder who decided that Carter had captured the nomination after the Ohio primary. As the *Chicago Tribune*'s Jon Margolis remarked, "Who am I to say that Daley's analysis is wrong?" And in the same spirit, the great campaigners of the press—Humphrey, Kennedy, Nelson Rockefeller, George Wallace, Edmund Muskie, Birch Bayh—proved to be, literally, paper tigers, existing mainly in the press clips.

A diligent critic could fill this space, and more, with the misjudgments and bad predictions of the political commentators; Ralph Lowenstein of the University of Missouri had already accumulated a briefcase full of columnists' predictions and other published political nonsense as far back as the Massachusetts primary in March 1976. But the aim of such exercises ought not to be to embarrass the generally hardworking, sober, intelligent men and women who harvest the daily political news crop for newspapers, news magazines, and television. Richard Stout, who was press secretary of the Morris Udall campaign, has suggested one remedy: "Every political reporter, six months after the campaign, should be locked in a room with everything he wrote and forced to reread each article one hundred times."

The real point ought to be to put to rest the kind of cutrate McLuhanism that elevates the medium over the message (I call it cut-rate because McLuhan himself did not dismiss the importance of content in communications). For example, much has been made of Reagan's style in the campaign, but it was the substance of his charges about détente and Henry

Kissinger that most excited the conservative Republicans who turned out for him in North Carolina and Texas. Also, there is the example of the front-page story by R.W. Apple, Jr., in the *New York Times* in October 1975, which said that Jimmy Carter appeared to be leading in the Iowa state caucuses. Because Carter received such early and prominent attention in the single most important media bulletin board in the country, the myth has grown that Apple and the *Times* in some way made Jimmy Carter. But Carter himself told our News Study Group interviewers that all Apple did was be a "good reporter." The *Times* reporter went to Iowa and learned that the Carter forces had understood the importance of Iowa—where the caucus voting occurred *before* the New Hampshire primary—and that the Carter forces had been carefully working the districts. Apple, said Carter, only reported what had already happened. To use McLuhanist terms, in Iowa the message was the message: the achievement was Carter's, not the *Times*'s.

In a related example, the presidential campaigns of Terry Sanford and Lloyd Bentsen were "messages" of another sort. The president of Duke University and the senator from Texas were as known—or more properly, unknown—as Jimmy Carter when the campaign began. When Sanford, the only non-politician who ran in 1976, withdrew from the race, Jack Germond of the *Washington Star*, as well as other journalists, received calls from people asking why the press hadn't given more coverage to Sanford. As Germond explained to Gretchen Clark of the News Study Group: "The reason we didn't pay more attention to Terry Sanford is that the Democratic party wasn't paying very much attention to him, the political community wasn't paying much attention to him, and the voters at large weren't paying much attention to him."

As early as the fall of 1974, Germond had made a few trips
around the country with the senator "on the chance he might
become a serious candidate . . . but it soon became apparent
that he wasn't going to become a serious candidate, so we
stopped covering him." With Bentsen the message was the
message too.

I think that there may be three reasons why the press appears to be a center of power in the presidential electoral system. First, the press is out front; it is highly visible during a
campaign. Television lights up the scenes of politics, literally
as well as figuratively. The press is perhaps the biggest noise-
maker in a campaign (official noisemakers, like bands, seem
to play only when they see the television camera's red light
go on). Press men and women crowd the political stage as it is
perceived by the audience. One hot July day in Plains,
Georgia, the week before the Democratic convention, Jimmy
Carter was interviewing Senator John Glenn as a possible running mate. At the end of the day, Mr. and Mrs. Carter invited
John and Annie Glenn to tour a peanut farm seven miles
down the road. The Carter party, complete with Secret
Service men, pulled out quickly in three cars—followed by a
tire-squealing entourage of fourteen press cars. In the field
Carter showed Glenn the tender peanut roots; the press recorded the exchange and asked a few vapid questions (I include my own questions among them). Then, the motorcade
careened down the road once again. To the black tenant
farmers who watched the clouds of red clay dust, the press
may have looked like Hamlets, principal actors, rather than
Rosenkrantz and Gildenstern, meant to swell a scene or two.

Second, the stage center action that the press courtiers
share with their audiences may be all that the press really sees
in the campaign. Reporters must write about or film what
they know of the campaign. But what they know—what they

are allowed to find out—is only part of the campaign reality. They are excluded from the candidate's closed-door strategy sessions, from the fund-raising meetings with key contributors, from the polling operations mounted by the candidate's private public opinion analysts, and from the candidate's entire decision-making process (including the press secretary's decisions to manage and otherwise manipulate the news). Indeed by the time the press joins the campaign, the basic themes and strategies may have long since been laid down. Political reporter Jules Witcover of the *Washington Post* believes that the critical part of the presidential campaign occurs well before the official start with the primaries (in the case of Jimmy Carter, Witcover was certainly correct). Excluded from the real inside narrative of the campaign, the press must make do with what it has—as much out of ego as self-preservation. Journalists have to convince themselves and their editors that they deserve air time or newspaper space— and their continued expense-account trips. As a result, political writer Richard Reeves has observed, the press too often acts like a Howard Cosell hyping some forgettable ABC sports event "to keep the action and ourselves on the road."

Finally, the press is not unimportant in electoral politics. It would be foolish to argue that the media in general, and television in particular, have no effect on the selection of political candidates, their styles of political campaigning, and the outcome of elections—as foolish as saying that television "elected" Kennedy in 1960 or Nixon in 1968 or 1972. Of course, primary elections have to be distinguished from general elections. Primary results may be decided by small turnouts of registered, highly motivated voters—true believers like the Reagan voters in North Carolina. Media events and political coverage may be less important to these voters, but relatively more important to the citizens who don't get involved in the presidential political process until the final few weeks before the November election.

Quite clearly the big national news outlets can be important sources of information for these voters. Forty million Americans glance at *Time* and *Newsweek* and as many more television viewers watch the network evening news and may be exposed to thirty-second or sixty-second political commercials. The big media can help put the Panama Canal back on the map and inflate an unknown's "recognition factor," making him or her a familiar name, at least in the eyes of other politicians. The big media may also have long-term, cumulative effects on voting decisions. Some political advertising (free or controlled) may strengthen the resolve of the already committed voter or may influence the undecideds. Also once the politicians stake out the ground—making one state, like Ohio, "crucial"—and frame the issues, the press can spotlight that story. But even then the press's role tends to be reactive rather than active; it confirms rather than affirms.

THE PRIMARIES: WHAT THE CANDIDATES MADE OF THE MEDIA

CHAPTER 3

Once heads are cleared of the central confounding notion—that an omnipotent media, somehow, some way, sets the agenda or otherwise controls political processes—then we can sit back and appreciate the spectacle of what the press really does in a political campaign. The press is a vehicle, a stage, and all its members are supporting actors. Powerful in its own terms—50 million television news viewers and 62 million daily newspaper readers—it is nevertheless malleable in the hands of reasonably skilled political operatives.

In the course of the 1976 campaign, the MIT News Study Group examined three skillful, new, or innovative uses of media by the candidates during the primary contests: Ronald Reagan's "citizens' press conferences"; the "mini-doc" form, a five-minute paid political commercial; and the public "verification" of the Carter primary campaign strategy by attention given by the three national television networks. (This last was a two-way street in the press-candidate relationship; the press achieved some of its operational aims as well.)

Like the other candidates in New Hampshire, Ronald Reagan moved by bus through the snow-slicked roads and lowering New England skies. But he managed to get more mileage out of his appearances than anyone else. Each day his entourage would pull into a village where local Republicans had assembled. Reagan would shake hands, drink coffee, say a few words, and then hurry off to the next village meeting, shopping center rally, or factory gate or radio interview. At night in the high school gym at Keene or some other town, Reagan would hold a citizens' press conference, when he answered the questions posed by local residents. The governor usually was asked about the economy, and his answers, like most other candidates', always were just about the same; he talked, for example, about "ending deficit spending and balancing the budget." Reagan was at least smart about his own campaign budget—the questions and responses from the conferences eventually appeared as Reagan campaign commercials on the Boston television stations. New Hampshire has only one television station, and since the Massachusetts primary came just one week after New Hampshire's, buying time from Boston stations was something like an advertising package deal—buy one state and get the other free.

Reagan's material produced yet another bonus. The spots were made to look like news reports of the news conferences. The citizens' press conference commercials were shot by film crews working for Ball and McDaniel, the Reagan advertising agency. The crews stood alongside camera people from ABC, CBS, NBC, and local New England stations, recording a number of these meetings. The resulting film was edited down to a series of eight basic sixty-second commercials on such subjects as unemployment, jobs, social security, and defense. Audio tracks recorded at the conferences were used for the basic ten Reagan radio spots (in which he addressed the touchier themes of nuclear power and gun control).

Other candidates, of course, have used spots that resemble news spots but not with nearly the same adroitness. One of Congressman Morris Udall's media men claimed that the cinéma verité bobbing-camera style of political commercials would not work in 1976. Accordingly the Udall commercial makers and the Birch Bayh people shot their political spots showing the candidates in a television studio. The result was an undramatic, tightly framed, talking head. The ads for Henry Jackson eliminated moving film images entirely; a series of still photos of the Democratic candidates flashed on the screen, ending with Jackson's face and the voice of an announcer proclaiming the virtues of "the experienced senator." One or two of the Jimmy Carter commercials employed some of the cinema verité techniques reminiscent of the Kennedy and Nixon campaigns of the 1960s. The Gerald Ford television commercials, held back until the last week of the primary, were positively stately, showing the president working in the Oval Office on his State of the Union address with the tag line, "President Ford is your president. Keep him."

The Reagan people were doing a kind of verité with a vengeance. If you weren't concentrating like a political scientist when watching one of the Reagan television commercials, you might have thought you were actually watching a story on the nightly news. Seven of the eight citizens' press conference television commercials opened with the candidate, handsome and poised, standing at a lectern. An unseen narrator (known as a voice-over) intoned some variation of the line, "Here's another question for Ronald Reagan, asked the other day at a citizens' press conference." In the defense commercial, for example, the script went like this:

Voice-over: An important part of Ronald Reagan's campaign are the citizens' press conferences, which give the people a chance to ask the questions . . . (sound "bite" of question starts before voice-over finishes).

Question: As president, how would you deal with the congressional Democrats who are calling for still further cutbacks in defense spending?

Reagan: Well, here again, is where I believe a president must take his case to the people. And the people must be told the facts. The people will not make a mistake if they have the facts. But the one thing we must be sure of is, the United States must never be second to anyone else in the world in military power. (Applause, reaction shot.) But the purpose of weapons is not to go to war; the purpose of weapons is to convince the other fellow that he better not go to war. (Applause.)

Voice-over: Reagan, he'll provide the strong new leadership America needs. Paid for by Citizens for Reagan.

The required disclaimer at the end didn't distract from the news-event feeling. It also helped that Reagan's television-radio time buyer, Ruth Jones, a veteran in the field, bought spots within or adjacent to news and information programs. For example, the Reagan ad schedule for WBZ, the top-rated station in the Boston market, included spots on the "Today" show, the "Mike Douglas Show" (the lead-in to the early evening news), "The Tonight Show" (lead-out of the late evening news), and the "news adjacencies"—the station breaks between the local WBZ news and the NBC-Chancellor news. Reagan spent more than $100,000 for this TV time before the New Hampshire primary.

The man responsible for creating and executing the Reagan news event spots was Harry Treleaven, a veteran of the 1968 Nixon campaign. Treleaven and his client faced two related image problems in the New Hampshire primary campaign, one unique to Reagan and the other shared by all the candidates. Treleaven's first hurdle was the fact that Reagan was generally regarded by the voters as an actor. The middle-aged and elderly women who came out to meet the Reagan bus in a snow-covered restaurant parking lot in Fitzwilliam early in the campaign said that they wanted "to see the movie star." Political columnists also saw Reagan in this image. The *New York Times*'s James Reston wrote of the Reagan platform style: "He gives the impression that he is merely reading his lines. . . . [He is] an actor playing a role, and quite willing, maybe even eager, to go home when the play is done and particularly if the audience disagrees."

What better way, then, to get away from the actor image, with its aura of artifice and insincerity, than to present the candidate in a realistic, natural, serious setting? The Reagan image Treleaven says he wanted to project was that of a "hard-campaigning, straight-talking, former governor in the context of a campaign." The voters may have shown up in person to see the personality; but on television, says Treleaven, "They don't want to see a movie star in a slick production." If the sound overlap from a citizens' press conference was fuzzy, so much the better. Technical imperfections were deliberately left in the audio and film tracks to give the commercials the "look and sound of the news." In addition by stationing his film crews alongside the real television news crews, Treleaven ensured that his camera angles would be similar to theirs.

Treleaven's second problem was the strong antipolitics mood of the citizenry. Reagan's own conservative platform, as well as the attitude polling of likely voters that his organization had done, suggested the best topics for the commercials. The citizens' press conference format ideally matched the public mood. "The voters don't want to be conned by the usual political advertising," Treleaven said.

Viewed as an effort to deal with these two problems, the ads were well done. The citizens' questions were soft but not a great deal softer than the questions put to Reagan at genuine press conferences. And, in any case, Reagan was adept at handling questions; he had done a regular weekly news conference, televised live, when he was governor in Sacramento. He was professional in his timing, delivery, and platform manner. He was likeable. He never lost his warm smile and good humor, even when needled by the People's Bicentennial Commission squad, a group of young activists who had followed him around New Hampshire (their questions were edited out of the Reagan spots). He had his applause lines down pat. There were few gestures, no trappings. Reagan simply responded to the people's concerns. One spot, for example, showed a boy of no more than eleven or twelve saying, "I think taxes should be lower. I don't think all that money goes to good use." Reagan smiled and shrugged, allowed the applause to die down, and said: "I wish you were old enough to go to Congress, because you're talkin' sense."

The ads were so well done that it was possible not to notice the artifice of the antiartifice format and to overlook the question of whether making commercials that look like the news (an idea that has been around for a while) can fool casual dial flippers. But well done doesn't necessarily mean effective. Did television and radio spots bring any votes to the former governor when New Hampshire went to the polls? He lost by less than 2,000 votes out of over 100,000 cast on the Republican side. The Reagan camp was noticeably downcast when the results came in, and the news reports featured this sense of defeat. Perhaps a happy Reagan should have claimed a moral victory over the incumbent or feigned satisfaction with the "squeaker" results: *The president of the United States practically overthrown!* If only Reagan that day had been as good an actor as the man in the citizens' press conferences. . . .

On Monday, April 21, at approximately 10:55 P.M., EST, Senator Frank Church performed a neat bit of surgery on CBS's "Medical Center." The Idaho senator appeared on television screens across the nation and made an appeal for money for his presidential campaign. The time slot had been opened up when four minutes and thirty seconds of hospital-room dialogue and shots of dripping glucose bottles were excised from the show to make time for Church. The political appeal ran about five minutes—CBS permitted cuts of another thirty seconds out of station identification slides—and made political history of sorts. The CBS network, as well as ABC and NBC, had been trying to avoid selling Church and other Democratic candidates any time at all during the presidential primary races. The "Medical Center" surgery demonstrated just how a long-shot candidate can operate successfully on a giant, unwilling network. Not so incidentally it also showed how just a few dollars could be leveraged into a hefty campaign bankroll in the peculiar economics of television and politics in the 1976 presidential race. Within a week of the successful Church operation, the television time buyers for Ronald Reagan and Morris Udall had bought similar five-minute time slots. To understand this historic first, it is necessary to understand something about the business of buying time on television.

Because television is a strictly scheduled medium, the national networks and local stations generally prefer to sell thirty- or sixty-second schedules of time to political candidates, which fit into the commercial breaks in programs (about six to eight minutes of every thirty minutes). In election years thirty-minute periods in prime evening time may also be sold to candidates, though networks are reluctant to do so. They generally believe that such political broadcasts interfere with audience viewing habits, depress ratings, and otherwise cost the networks and local stations money. If they have to carry anything political, the sales people would rather offer the thirty- and sixty-second spots, which can be slipped in here and there in the commercials schedule—and sell for up to $70,000 a minute in prime time.

Most candidates, it seems, find the thirty-minute format unattractive to them as well. Viewers may get angered at the preemption of favorite entertainment programs, and many candidates don't have enough to say or do to fill the time (or would rather not be exposed that long). When the two Florida television stations owned by the Washington Post Company offered candidates thirty minutes of free prime time during the Florida primaries, there were no takers.

By the time campaign '76 began, the candidates' media managers were looking for some breakthrough in time buying techniques. The idea of a five-minute schedule apparently occurred to a number of people at the same time. Jerry Rafshoon, the creator of the Jimmy Carter media effort, says that the idea came to him while he was watching Carter on a panel with a group of other Democratic candidates. Although the others were good, Rafshoon says, he discerned a "magic" in Carter that couldn't be conveyed in thirty or sixty seconds. At least two minutes, and probably five minutes, would be needed to get the Carter message of trust and character across to viewers.[1]

The Church people were thinking the same thoughts. Frank Church announced his candidacy to a largely indifferent world on March 18, 1976. He had what political media people call a "low recognition factor": nine out of ten Americans told poll takers that they had never heard of him. He also had a small campaign staff and even smaller financial resources. On the plus side, the Church people considered the senator himself their greatest asset. "If the country could see him one-on-one the way Idaho voters do," said Bill Hall, the senator's press secretary and one of the chief assistants on the "Medical Center" case, "then we'd win the presidency."

The Church campaign staff hit upon a tactical plan in three steps: the senator would husband his resources by starting late; he would concentrate on the western state primaries, beginning with Nebraska in May; and he would use national television to increase his low identification score. Behind the Church campaign was the overall strategic assumption—woefully mistaken, it turned out—that no Democrat would arrive at the July New York City Democratic convention with enough delegates for a first-ballot victory.

What the Church people didn't factor into their plan was their own naiveté. On March 21, 1976, the Sunday after the senator had announced his candidacy, a Church campaign biography was aired on CBS. It was done in standard newsreel style: the senator as World War II officer, footage from previous Church campaigns, clips from Senate hearings, and a slide, flashed for four seconds at the end, asking for contributions to be sent to Church's campaign headquarters, Box 1976, Boise, Idaho. Staff volunteers had run down the film clips, Hall wrote the script, and Church edited the copy. CBS sold the candidate five minutes during halftime of a forgettable National Basketball Association game. In the Far West, where Church wanted a good hearing, the audience was minuscule; the game went on late in the morning. About $5,000 in contributions came in; almost half of the letters were addressed to the U.S. Senate, Washington, D.C.

The Church people had learned a lesson. On April 5, Stan Silberman and Hal Katz of Vitt Media International, the New York-based time buyers for the Church campaign, met with representatives of the three networks. Silberman and Katz

wanted to buy thirty minutes of week night prime time, preferably in the 9 to 9:30 EST slot. ABC, CBS, and NBC had
adopted a policy of not selling thirty-minute slots in prime
time to candidates during the primaries. The official explanation—as opposed to the real economic reasons—was that the
so-called equal time doctrine means that if a network sold a
thirty-minute time period to one candidate, then it would
have to sell a similar amount of time to all. "There just aren't
any half hours sitting around," said Bob Jamieson of CBS-TV
network sales. "The time has been contracted for." True
enough, NBC had made an exception for Ronald Reagan, selling him thirty minutes of prime time on March 30; Reagan,
NBC executives had reasoned, was the only candidate running against an incumbent president, and Gerald Ford, his
opponent, had routine access to television. Reagan got his
prime-time half hour when NBC preempted "The Dump-
lings," a situation comedy ranked sixty-fifth among seventy-
two shows in the Nielsen ratings and already marked for exe-
cution. For the record, Reagan also got a low rating (a 9.3 on
the Nielsen scale), but that still added up to an audience of
15 million. Contributors "overwhelmed" campaign headquarters in California with their checks and money orders.[2]

   Stonewalled by the networks, the Church for President
Committee petitioned the Federal Communications Commission for a declaratory ruling that the networks' refusal to sell
the senator the time he wanted was depriving Church of the
"reasonable access" to the public required by the Federal
Communications Act. Henry L. Kimmelman, national finance
chairman of the Church Committee, also argued that the networks' insistence on thirty- or sixty-second spots forced presidential candidates to use "the slogan-ridden forum of tooth
whiteners and clothes brighteners." There aren't many
times when a political candidate can accuse someone else of
sloganeering.

The FCC moved with its usual glacier-like speed when faced with conflicting pressures from the broadcasting industry and the Congress. But two developments made the access issue moot. First, the regular television season ended on April 20; the ratings "sweeps" stopped and the networks went into re-runs. (The sweeps are the weekly Nielsen samplings that help determine how the television viewing audience is divided among the three networks, and therefore how much advertisers will have to pay for commercial spots in the season ahead.) From May until a new season begins in September, the prime-time programmers need not worry excessively about the ratings scorecards. Second, with the development of the five-minute format, the candidates and the networks had a way they both could come out ahead. CBS cut out the fat from the plot of "Medical Center"; not a rubber glove was laid on the eight precious commercial minutes sold to hawk Geritol and other products in the show. In fact CBS made extra money, charging Church $14,815 for the program time, plus another $550 in "cutting costs," a surcharge for the surgery done to the "Medical Center" episode.

Church also did well. He prerecorded the talk in two quick takes on his way to the Senate one morning. The public television station in Washington billed him about $300 for the facilities he used. All told, he spent under $20,000 for five prime-time minutes (compared with the $70,000 he might have had to pay for one prime-time advertising minute). The Nielsen figures indicate that he may have captured an audience of 20 million with his surprise appearance at the end of "Medical Center." In addition Church got substantial wire service and radio news coverage on at least two news cycles. First, they carried stories that the networks had turned him down (little David versus the Goliaths of broadcasting), and then they carried the accusations, in his televised talk, that Gerald Ford was a weak president.

Most important of all, Church ended his talk with a strong plea for funds. By the beginning of May, some $50,000 in contributions, more or less attributable to the program, had come in to campaign headquarters. The Reagan campaign claimed a similar payoff; his thirty-minute appearance cost $100,000 and brought in an estimated $500,000. When the Congress unsnarled the campaign finance laws a few weeks later, the contributions were doubled with federal matching funds. The arithmetic shows that the five-minute "mini-doc" program can be almost free national advertising; it may also be a vehicle for a serious discussion of politics. Church used his talk to air his views about multinational corporations and the CIA and FBI. His positions may have been well known in Washington, but they were not household topics elsewhere. The format allowed time for more than the hard sell of the short form thirty- or sixty-second spot. Also Church was able to maintain audience interest without running the room-emptying risk of the thirty-minute long form. At least one viewer said she watched because "I kept thinking it would be over in a minute."

The week after the Church appearance at the end of "Medical Center," Congressman Udall went on ABC in the five-minute format. His appeal for funds took the format a step further by including not only a postal address but two toll-free telephone numbers "with operators standing by twenty-four hours" to take contributions.

Almost all the thirty state primaries held in 1976 occurred on Tuesdays—Texas, on a Saturday, was the notable exception—and the three national television networks made a kind of television series of them. This coverage paid off in some surprising ways for the networks and in a rather unexpected way for Jimmy Carter.

The first surprise came in the audience figures for the primary nights' coverage. The accepted wisdom has been that news and public affairs programs on television are little watched: viewers prefer entertainment shows. Also 1976 was supposed to be the year of antipolitics. The political spirit of '76 was widely pictured as drooping and negative. However, the Neilsen ratings showed that the special coverage of the state primary elections on television drew significantly larger audiences than did the networks' usual late-evening programming. For example, in the period between February 24 and April 6, when primaries were held on six of seven Tuesdays, the networks' late-evening programs averaged these ratings: "The Tonight Show" (NBC), 6.8; movies (CBS), 5.4; "Wide World of Entertainment" (ABC), 5.8. The average ratings for the coverage of the results of the primaries, which preempted the first half hours of these entertainment shows, were NBC 8.8; CBS 7.1; ABC 6.0. Each rating point is equivalent to something like 1.2 million viewers, so in terms of votes a combined audience of 18 million was tuned to Carson and the other shows, while some 25 million viewers watched the primary coverage.

According to network executives, none of the usual explanations of audience behavior—such as the ratings strength of the preceding shows—can account for this upsurge in late-evening viewership; on NBC, in particular, the prime time lead-in programs were exceptionally weak in the 1976 season. (A cynic might argue that from the point of view of the home audience primary nights were not better TV but merely shorter TV, ending at midnight rather than at 1 A.M.) The best explanation seems to be that the networks succeeded in conveying some of the manic energy of a political campaign by translating it into television production values. Certainly ABC, CBS, and NBC made coverage of the primary returns fast paced and visually attractive—in a word, entertaining. Whether television made the primary nights equally informative is another matter.

A lot of imagination and money (upward of $5 million) were expended during the spring by the three networks on their primary coverage. NBC News spent as much ($2.5 million) as ABC News and CBS News combined; not so coincidentally, it led the ratings competition.[3] NBC commissioned the set designer Fred Harpman, whose Hollywood credits include "Planet of the Apes," to build a $50,000 set with lush carpeting and a red, white, and blue "Decision '76" logo. In the same bicentennial vein, ABC called its primary nights "Political Spirit '76," while CBS settled on "Campaign '76." Henry Mancini composed appropriately patriotic-sounding theme music for NBC, and two flatbed trailer trucks transported the whole set around the country from New Hampshire to Florida to California. NBC also did more on-scene broadcasting than its rivals did on primary nights—"to give the feeling that we are there and we are involved as reporters," according to Lee Hanna, NBC News vice-president.

Some of these efforts, however, were just that—show. The busy-looking desks that appeared in deep-focus shots behind the anchormen were sometimes just window dressing; on the night of the Michigan and Maryland primaries on May 18, one CBS newsperson, who appeared on camera to the left of Walter Cronkite, seemingly hard at work harvesting election news, was actually typing up the list of the staff's hotel assignments for California. Yet the overall effect was often impressive. On the night of the Pennsylvania primary, when NBC did an evocative broadcast from Independence Hall, one of the Philadelphia newspapers thought the occasion merited a three-column, page-one picture.

A more substantial advance in television's primary night

coverage, however, came in the nature of the information
presented rather than in the style. All three networks relied
on public opinion polling techniques and computer technology in their primary night coverage. Although the use of polls
and computers by news organizations is no novelty, never
have they been employed so extensively as they were in the
1976 campaign.

Since television began reporting presidential politics some
three decades ago, viewers have turned to it to find out who
won. In recent years the networks provided the answer, late
or early on election night, by using "key" or "tag" or "bell-
weather" precincts to project the winner. Although the networks still do projections of the "who"—and still fumble
some of them—they have added new techniques in an attempt to give the "how" and the "why," to say with assur-
ance what motivated voters. Questions usually treated intuitively by the analysts of the media—thumbsuckers, in the
trade—can now be addressed with some degree of precision
on election night. These new techniques theoretically make it
possible to know, perhaps as early as midday, voter turnout
by age, sex, race, education, and religion; voting choices of
self-described liberals, conservatives, and independents; "cutting issues"—such as inflation, the Nixon pardon, the Panama
Canal, or busing—that may influence turnout and choices;
and voters' assessments of the candidate's abilities—his or her
perceived qualities of leadership, competence, honesty, and
consistency.

By broadcast time, Roger Mudd of CBS was able to say,
with authority, as he did after the Pennsylvania primary, that
Carter won "all strata of the electorate" by age, sex, religion,
race, ethnic background, and in terms of presidential qualities, issues, education level, and political philosophy. Mudd
also reported that Jackson surpassed Carter in only two voter

categories—people over sixty-five and Jewish voters. Or Mudd
could write, as he did sitting at his typewriter in the CBS
Studio on West 57th Street, two hours after the Michigan
polls closed, "Mr. Ford came across to the homestate folks as
the more honest, nine to one, as the stronger leader, two to
one, as the more competent, three to one, and is the more
likely to win in November, three to one . . . the so-called Reagan issues, welfare, détente, defense spending and the size of
government, all belonged to Mr. Ford in Michigan today."
Mudd knew all this because CBS—and NBC as well—combined the older technique of sampling key precincts with a
newer technique of "exit polling," interviewing voters as they
leave the voting booths in key precincts. In CBS's case 1,840
randomly selected Michigan voters in twenty randomly selected precincts from an original base of ninety key precincts
were interviewed. In the NBC system about the same number
of randomly selected voters were interviewed from an original base of one hundred key precincts. The CBS interview
consisted of about thirty questions; the interview took less
than fifteen minutes to complete. The NBC interview involved as many as sixty-six questions. ABC News did nothing
like this at the start, and its primary coverage—and ratings—
lagged. Before the Wisconsin and New York primaries, ABC
hired Louis Harris to do preprimary day polling and on-air
analysis. His interviewers visited some 1,500 likely voters in
their homes, conducting a sixty- to eighty-minute interview
on the weekend before the primary. Harris tended to ask the
same questions as CBS and NBC and got much the same information. He was paid a reported $500,000 for his firm's
services to ABC.

Harris's findings were available to ABC News before election day (he called the Pennsylvania finish to the decimal
point). At CBS and NBC field interviewers phoned in their

findings at designated intervals during primary day, and the
newsroom had a line on the who, how, and why by lunch-
time. "We may know the outcome," explained Robert
Chandler, the vice-president in charge of CBS's election coverage. "But all Walter or Roger will say on the evening news
is something like 'Ford is leading in Michigan.' "

The exit polls made more information available than either
CBS or NBC chose to use on primary nights. Television
newscasts make certain assumptions about the attention
spans of viewers; producers constantly worry about pacing.
The show must move along—to the vote boards, to the live remotes from the candidates' headquarters, to the taped interviews with the winners and the losers, to the recaps by the
anchormen, and to the sponsors' messages. As a consequence
Mudd at CBS, Harris at ABC, and John Hart at NBC may be
confined to two-minute segments. Information from computer printouts as thick as the Manhattan phone book is
squeezed into two- or three-word headlines. Alexandra Norkin of the News Study Group played and replayed videotapes
of all three networks' primary night coverage from New
Hampshire through California. After fifty hours of viewing,
she concluded,

In trying to tell the viewer why a candidate won or lost, the
networks rely on no more than three or four reasons—"Did
well with blacks and retired persons, captured anti-Washing-
ton vote, won middle of the road." Then in the recap, the list
may be reduced to one factor: "Well, it looks like the black
vote won the election for Carter today" . . . "The politics of
easy promise looks finished" . . . "The Jackson defeat in
Pennsylvania spells the end of the power of labor." The problem is not that the explanations are wrong but that they are
too simplistic.

One irony in all this is that television news may have missed
a chance to run all over its competitors. If television really

decided to move the election night story forward—and give Mudd or Hart or Harris as much as five minutes for analysis rather than two minutes, aided by imaginative graphics—how much would be left for the newspapers the next day? Or the news magazines the next week? As it is, both CBS and NBC had arrangements with newspapers permitting them to use the exit poll material that television collected but only skimmed. NBC shared its findings with the *New York Daily News, Newsday*, and half a dozen other papers. CBS News shared costs and poll findings with the *New York Times*, and the *Times* often filled an inside page or two with meaty material on the days following a primary. Print has undeniable advantages over television, at least as long as television thinks anything longer than three minutes will lose viewers.

There is still a large margin of error in polling and computer analysis, in print or on television. As computer people say, GIGO (garbage in, garbage out). Precinct projection techniques have been used for a decade; yet ABC and NBC both badly miscalled the Democratic contest in Wisconsin, giving the state in the hours before midnight to Morris Udall. At CBS Warren Mitofsky and Robert Chandler wisely held back—and then called for Carter well after midnight. The exit polls are only as good as the humans involved—the surveyors who frame the questions, the field hands who conduct the interviews, and the interpreters. Some questions were poorly designed. Others were plainly loaded. In Michigan, for example, 65 percent of Democratic voters said they agreed with the following statement (intended to plumb the religious issue): "My main source of comfort and guidance in life is my *faith in God*." A more neutral way to word the question would be: "What is your main source of comfort and faith in life?"

The interview form can also affect results. In Massachu-

setts NBC used a professional polling group to work the Boston area, and a pick-up group to do the rest of the state—with
predictably uneven results. Police chased some NBC interviewers out of polling places, where they had set up tables,
and into the snow, where people felt less disposed to answer
questions. Harris ran his show almost exclusively, but NBC
and CBS interpretations filtered through layers of public
opinion experts, including Richard Scammon at NBC and
Peter Hart at CBS. In Massachusetts John Hart reported that
school busing was a major factor in the Jackson vote; Roger
Mudd said the economy was. In Pennsylvania NBC said Carter's "ethnic purity" remark cut into his black support; CBS
and ABC said the remark didn't hurt him with blacks.[4]

The networks' new commitment to political coverage done
in an entertaining and information-rich way may have had indirect effects on the political outcomes. NBC, CBS, and ABC
could have stayed in New York City and broadcast the primary night results from headquarters, saving air fare, hotels,
and meals for fifty people. Instead the networks chose to
lend their presence to the primaries; they also treated them as
a continuing, unitary process. As one consequence the coverage of the spring series of primary nights helped to explain
and legitimize the delegate-selection system. The Carter strategy was to "run everywhere." The "month of primary Tuesdays" added up to the rise and triumph of Jimmy Carter,
who looked unbeatable in the computer-generated shorthand
of the television screen ("moderate, has black support, anti-
Washington feeling"). Never mind the defeats he suffered
toward the end of the process. By May he had momentum
and could not be denied the prize. The weekly appearances
of Cronkite, Chancellor, and Reasoner, together with their
patriotic bright sets and imposing vote boards, demonstrated
that the primaries were important. Otherwise why would the
networks be there?

Of course, one reason ABC, CBS, and NBC were there was because of their own battle for ratings. Presidential campaigns also "elect" a news leader among the networks. But, as the networks pursued their "voters," they also spotlighted Jimmy Carter's own voter efforts. It could very well have been viewed as something of an immoral, if not illegal, act if the anti-Carter forces had put together some coalition to stop Carter after he so clearly, and publicly, triumphed on the televised primary nights.

THE CAMPAIGN:
THE ALMOST-GREAT
DEBATES

CHAPTER 4

Just before Gerald Ford and Jimmy Carter began their third and final televised debate on the campus of William and Mary College in Williamsburg, Virginia, on the evening of October 22, Ruth Clusen of the League of Women Voters pronounced an off-camera benediction on the 1976 presidential race. Clusen was president of the league, the organizer and sponsor of the Ford-Carter meetings. It had been a very uninspiring campaign, she said, picking her words carefully, but the league-sponsored meetings had brought it a certain vitality.

If anything, this was an understatement; the *New York Times* later called the Ford-Carter race petty and issueless. Thanks to the league, the Ford-Carter meetings—plus the vice-presidential debate between Robert Dole and Walter Mondale arranged by the league—were the bright centerpieces of the otherwise dull and plodding efforts of the candidates, the most visible manifestation of the contest. But like so much else connected with the press-politics relationship, they have sustained their own myths.

Everyone agreed in advance that the televised debates between Gerald Ford and Jimmy Carter would be "historic,"
"crucial," "a showdown"—the big event of the 1976 campaign. After all John F. Kennedy had beaten Richard Nixon
in the first—and, until 1976, the only—televised debate series
between presidential candidates, and then went on to a
razor-thin victory in the November elections.

About 70 million voters had watched the Kennedy-Nixon
debates; in 1976, an estimated 100 million voters—there were
more of us, and the voting age had been lowered—tuned in
the Ford-Carter debates, certainly more than enough to elect
the next president. The eagerness of Ford's challenge for a
television meeting—he called for the series in his acceptance
speech—and the equally quick Carter response quite clearly
showed how important the candidates considered debates.

Yet the motives of politicians and the decisions of voters
may not be as obvious as they appear to be. With television
and politics, there may be somewhat less than meets the eye
and somewhat more that is hidden—and requires teasing out.
The viewer-voter, for whose benefit the Ford-Carter debates
were held, had to keep in mind some distinctions between
the illusions and the realities of politics.

The first illusion was that the meetings would be real debates rather than "highly staged performances," to use Douglass Cater's apt description of the Kennedy-Nixon series. In
1960, Nixon and Kennedy had insisted on using panels of reporters to ask the questions. According to Cater, who served
as one of these interrogators, the candidates "felt it would be
better for image purposes to let the reporters play the
heavies." So instead of face-to-face argument and direct ques-
tioning and rebuttal, Kennedy and Nixon gave mini-speech
answers to predictable queries.

In 1960, there was a great debate—about the details of presentation, the cameras' angles, the studio lighting, the temperature (the Kennedy people knew that Nixon perspired easily and wanted to keep the air conditioning low). All of that happened off camera among the campaign managers. As for what was actually said, as opposed to how it was said, it is painful to recall that the big issues of the 1960 meetings were Quemoy and Matsu, the need to "get the country moving again," and President Truman's bad language (Nixon pledged "to restore dignity and decency to the White House"). Not much real history was made.[1]

The Ford-Carter meetings have receded from memory more rapidly. Can anyone a year or two later recall a topic from the meetings, with the possible exception of Ford's "East European gaffe" (that some Eastern European countries were free of Soviet communist domination) in the second meeting?

The second illusion was that the televised debates—perhaps they should be called performances—exerted the critical influence on the outcome of the election. The four Kennedy-Nixon encounters provided a kind of full employment act for academics; no fewer than thirty-one different scientific studies—most of them public opinion surveys (did you watch? who won?)—were published about the meetings within two years. Considering all the build-up that was lavished on the Ford-Carter meetings, these studies make sobering reading. For example, the mythology holds that John Kennedy "won" the meetings. The surveys suggest that viewers perceived that Kennedy won the first meeting, that the second and fourth meetings were too close to call, and that Nixon won the third meeting. For the overall series, Kennedy was given the victory. But even here there is some fine print to read:

• Those who listened on radio gave Nixon higher marks in the first meeting than those who watched on television.

• Kennedy supporters tended to think Kennedy had won, Nixon supporters tended to think Nixon had won, and independents tended to say they couldn't decide who won.

• More viewers—25 percent—did say they tended to change their vote to Kennedy after the first debate—but so did 25 percent of the nonviewers.

MIT research assistant Larry Levine, who helped do this survey of the surveys, concluded that Kennedy was gaining in the polls prior to the first debate and that his popularity would have continued to rise with or without the debates. The Kennedy-Nixon meetings, Levine suggests, "may actually have helped strengthen the voter's own commitment to his or her previously desired candidate." This was most true for Kennedy supporters and least true for Nixon supporters, with the independents falling in between. The television confrontation was important but not crucial.

In the case of Gerald Ford and Jimmy Carter, much the same pattern occurred. Carter started on Labor Day, the official beginning of the campaign, with a commanding lead in the public opinion polls. But he soon made a series of perceived blunders and false starts—the ethnic purity remark, the confusion about his income tax proposals, the *Playboy* magazine interview—that cut into his strength. His campaign strategists came to see the approaching debates as a reinforcing or reassuring mechanism rather than as a conversion mechanism. Carter's demeanor in the debates was intended to shore up his support among traditional Democratic voters by assuring them that Carter was not unsteady, untested, or "weird" (he had, after all, talked about lust in the heart). After the *Playboy* interview in particular, Carter's standing in the polls steadily ebbed. His public opinion specialist, Patrick Caddell, conducted almost daily polling in the days after the *Playboy* interview contents became known. Caddell used a graphic word—*hemorrhaging*—to describe what was happening to Carter's strength. The second debate, on October 7, was like a healing tourniquet; it stopped the hemorrhage by reassuring already leaning Democrats for Carter.

The third illusion may be that, despite the lack of content, despite the staging, the real candidates still stand up and are judged. We know now of the time, effort, and thought Kennedy and Carter gave to looking competent. We know how Nixon—after losing his cool, literally, in that first hot studio and with his Lazy Shave makeup accentuating the haggard lines brought on by campaigning—collected himself for the later meetings.[2] We know now how Gerald Ford practiced his convention acceptance speech and prepared for the debates for hours, with his coaches and his videotape-playback machine—like a weekend tennis player correcting his serve.

In the Ford campaign the managers debated whether the candidate should appear as "good old Jerry" or as "Mr. President." In the mirror-image argument at the Carter headquarters, the question was whether to stay with his populist image or to shift to a more presidential style. Both Ford and Carter made their character and competence a major issue of the campaign. But where did the well-rehearsed performance end and the real person begin? And were viewers perceptive enough to see through the artifice?

I must confess what may be my very own illusion here. I thought that the real Carter and the real Ford came through on television and that some voters were able to make certain judgments about the men. The first Ford-Carter meeting was ninety minutes long, which allowed more time for questions and answers than the usual "Meet the Press" formats (and

more time than the Kennedy-Nixon meetings). The panel format meant that reporters were expected to play the heavies
again. After reporters asked one candidate a question, the
other candidate was allowed to reply, and then there was opportunity for a counterresponse. The moderators were the
key to a genuine exchange of ideas. Both Ford and Carter
strayed from the questions, for different reasons. Ford was
used to the House of Representatives "colloquy," where
speakers talk past each other in presenting their set packets
of information and rhetoric. Carter, for his part, tried to talk
to the Democrats in the audience, convincing them of his
"leadership qualities." Representatives of the League of
Women Voters had admonished the moderator to cut off excessive wandering in the candidates' answers and get as much
candidate-to-candidate exchange as possible.

Though it did not work out that way, the meetings were
undeniably live and (somewhat) unrehearsed. Frank Stanton,
president of CBS during the Kennedy-Nixon meetings, de-
fended them at the time: "To judge the character of a man,"
he said, "you should catch him in the act of being alive, responding to a situation." The televised Ford-Carter meetings
provided that opportunity. It is the unexpected, the opportunity for something spontaneous and human to happen
without intervention or interpretation by the reporter, that is
the promise of live television. That is why live event television is the best television: professional sports, convention
floor coverage, a breaking news story, interviews on public
television's "The MacNeil/Lehrer Report," even the interplay
on Johnny Carson.

The reality, as opposed to the illusion, of the Ford-Carter
meetings was that they were the best chance for many voters
to see the candidates "in the act of being alive." On this
count alone, the meetings were worthwhile. Aristotle thought

that the Greek city-states should number no more than 5,000 citizens so that everyone could know the magistrates. In the United States, even when the population was relatively small and the franchise restricted to white, propertied males, it was still not possible for every voter to take the measure of a presidential candidate in person. Now the new federal election law, which restricts the money that candidates can spend, means that there are fewer dollars around today for even the controlled image making of the political commercial; the Ford and Carter campaigns combined weren't able to spend as much on television time and media advertising as Nixon alone did in 1972. The televised meetings between the candidates filled this strange new gap. As stilted and staged as the candidates' responses often proved to be, they still had more information content in them than the artfully constructed thirty- or sixty-second spots of the commercial advertising form. Whatever sloganeering we heard came from the candidate, not from his advertising agency.

But if we are going to be realistic about what to expect from candidates in television meetings, then we ought not to romanticize the television audience either. They don't watch the way the critics and the historians do, with notebooks open and ballpoints poised. Voter surveys indicate that those individuals who decide how to vote late in the campaign are usually those with the least interest in politics and public affairs. These people may also be the heaviest television viewers; they usually don't vote at all.

On the other side the real fans of politics, as well as those who care about certain issues, such as abortion, gun control, or Mideast policies, need no reminders to get involved in campaigns. To the right of center, they voted and/or worked for Reagan, Ford, or Wallace in the primaries. To the left, they turned out for Udall, Bayh, Jackson, Harris, or Carter. These political "actives" make up their minds, by and large, by Labor Day. The politically passive—misnamed "independents"—have not. (Of course, there are real independents— people of conscience who study the record and vote issues, rather than the party of their fathers or mothers. These are people like the members of the League of Women Voters.)

When the first televised confrontation between Gerald Ford and Jimmy Carter began, there were three audiences in attendance: the already committed, or leaning, voters, for Ford or Carter; the undecided passives; and the undecided independents. Depending on how Ford and Carter came through on the screen, the committed went out from the television meetings either more or less willing to canvass, to ring door bells, or, at a minimum, to show up to vote and to turn out friends and family. For the passive, the Ford-Carter meetings were one more momentarily exciting prime-time programming package in a television season that promised whole evenings of big-event dramatic series and blockbuster movies.

When the set goes off, the memorable clash of ideas may quickly be forgotten by most viewers. But for the truly independent voter trying to make up his or her mind, the Ford-Carter meetings served as one more key bit of information to add to the extraordinarily complex mosaic of facts, opinions, feelings, family upbringing, and social class that go into the voting decision. Like good consensus politics and good prime-time television, there was something for everybody when Ford and Carter met.

There remains perhaps one other media-politics myth to deflate. In all the commentary about the Ford-Carter and Dole-Mondale debates, a striking point was overlooked. The level of audience attention to the meetings was independent of the contestants, the subject matter, the debate style, and all the surrounding media excitement. Viewers did what they usually do: they watched television qua television—rather than watching the candidates making "history." For the candidates the size of the television audience was about the same as it is on any other autumn evening during prime time. Around 38 million television households, almost two of every three television households in the country, were tuned to the meetings; the estimated audience had from 83 to 93 million viewers, depending on how many noses Nielsen and the networks figure are in front of each set. There was a dropoff for the last two debates, but it was about what might be expected on a Friday night, when many turn to other forms of entertainment. The individual members of the television audience change from night to night, like the individual stars in the Steady State model of cosmology. As with the Steady State universe, old stars die and new ones are born, but the total remains the same. Carter-Ford and Mondale-Dole may have attracted some viewers new to week-night prime-time television—young professionals, political activists, college students required by their professors to watch, for example. The candidates may also have driven some viewers away from television for the night; in those areas outside the major markets of New York or Los Angeles where independent stations exist, viewers have no choice except to watch ABC, CBS, NBC, PBS, or nothing. But overall, television watching evens out. As New Yorkers drop off during the evening—from 73 percent of television households at 9:30 P.M. to around 54 percent at 11 P.M.—Los Angeles and Bay Area people come home at 6:30 P.M. from work, wash up, eat, and turn on television.

The name of this phenomenon of people watching television rather than programs is "audience flow," a concept well known to veteran programmers like Paul Klein of NBC. In the Nixon-McGovern campaign, when anyone tried to tell the experts about the great nightly flow of television habit, it was like trying to tell a fifteenth century church congregation that the world is heliocentric. The pre-Copernicans, however, cannot account for some undeniable facts: the first Carter-Ford debate was, obviously, big box office—it was first, it centered on domestic matters, and it had the media build-up. The second debate was, just as obviously, a big turnoff. The first meeting had been pronounced boring by the press judges, the subject was foreign policy (no longer sexy, since Vietnam), and it was, after all, the second debate. Who can remember the name of the second aviator to fly the Atlantic or the second man to set foot on the moon? Yet about the same number of people watched debate 2 as debate 1, give or take 2 million viewers (within the margin of sampling error).

If most people tend to watch television rather than "history," it must be because of something about the act of viewing itself. It takes no Copernicus to determine that television entertains most people. The prospect of a show brings people to their sets, with varying levels of disappointment and pain each night. Because the audience is watching spectacle anyway, the candidates should have concentrated on putting on "good television," projecting images rather than statistics. The opportunities for good "entertainment" at the presidential debates were limited by the news conference format agreed upon by the candidates and the League of Women Voters. In the French national elections a few years ago, Valery Giscard d'Estaing and François Mitterand met on television and were seated across a small table, with only an inobtrusive moderator present. They argued back and forth. It was a dramatic face-to-face confrontation—and good television. Giscard won the debate, and the election.

Something similar happened with Ford and Carter. In the first debate, Carter was stiff. He later claimed he had been awed by the authority of the presidency standing next to him in the person of Jerry Ford. The press and the polls gave the first debate to Ford. By the second meeting Carter and his managers had seen the need to concentrate on aura rather than memory feats. To the extent that Carter did, he won the second debate. Robert Dole tried to be conversational and entertaining in the vice-presidential debate (out of instinct, I think, rather than direct knowledge). He seemed to win that debate, although Mondale had the better, more "serious," arguments.

I was in the auditorium at the final Ford-Carter meeting. The *Boston Globe*, which had asked me to phone in my assessment of who "won," wanted my words within fifteen minutes of the time Ford-Carter went off the air. Here is what I dictated and what the *Globe* ran in its October 24 edition:

The man from the Associated Press called it the "tie-breaker"—the race had narrowed and the Ford-Carter Debate III would be the last chance for the candidates to make their appeals to the undecideds.

If the AP man was right, then Carter won the last debate, took the overall series 2 to 1, and stands on the verge of a victory—though perhaps a narrow one—in the election.

Carter won Friday night by being audacious. He did not play it safe, as the experts expected.

Early on, he brought up—voluntarily—the *Playboy* interview. He said in hindsight he should not have given it and called it a mistake. A little later, he passed up a chance to comment on Ford's connection to Watergate—something like a confident district attorney saying "no questions" to a witness. Still later, he volunteered his views on abortion.

These were gambles—and they paid off. So did Carter's answer on aid to the cities, when he reminded viewers that Ford had told troubled New York City to "drop dead."

Both seemed to grow visibly tired, at least to me seated in the audience a few yards away. At times they both lacked fire and seemed to be going through the motions. Carter did finish strong. He offered the vision of a partnership of the President, the Congress, and the people working together.

Ford, on the other hand, just could not seem to rise to a final unifying statement of purpose. He said, in effect, if you like me, vote for me.

I'm happy with this assessment, except for one omission: I should have added, "And Carter put on the better show."

THE CAMPAIGN: PRESIDENTIAL IMAGES AND REALITIES

CHAPTER 5

Jimmy Carter may have won the election but he lost the campaign. Everyone on Madison Avenue knows that. Even if the more conservative polling figures are used, Carter came close to squandering a fifteen-point lead. Many media specialists credit the "brilliant" Ford media campaign, principally the Ford television commercials, for making the race close.

The presidential campaign of 1976 was not the first time that the experts have become beguiled by the cleverly crafted, telegenic appeals of the spot-makers. Television commercials are an art form, and they have their admirers. During the 1972 presidential campaign, Thomas Patterson and Robert McClure, two Syracuse University researchers, looked at television's coverage of the Nixon-McGovern campaign and concluded that voters could get more information from the candidates' commercials than from the network evening news. These findings were meant to be as much a criticism of television news as praise of television commercials.[1] In 1976, the Syracuse researchers concentrated on television news' coverage. Had they continued to look at the candidates' commercials in a systematic way, they might have been surprised at what they would have seen. Such a study would have been an antidote to the claims made on behalf of the media campaign.

The winner's campaign—Carter, after all, did get more votes than Ford—was the work of Jerry Rafshoon, an irreverent, bright, able, and outspoken advertising man.[2] Rafshoon and Jimmy Carter were together right from the start. In 1966, Rafshoon had joined Carter's first unsuccessful race for governor of Georgia. Carter was the first, and only, political client of Rafshoon's Atlanta-based advertising agency. Rafshoon has been a member of the inner circle—the Georgia Mafia. Beginning with the Iowa caucuses and the New Hampshire primary, Rafshoon used a country-and-western theme in his Carter commercials. He put the candidate in blue jeans and work shirts and had him walk the peanut fields while a guitar picked out a down-home sound. Technically he used a lot of movement: jump cuts, marching bands, cutaways, faces in the crowd. It was the sixty-second world of the commercial. The candidate moved about in the Rafshoon ads, pressing flesh, kissing cheeks, and pulling up peanut roots. The aim was to introduce Carter to the American public as a trustworthy, competent candidate. In the standard, five-minute, Rafshoon-produced Carter biography shown during the primaries and in the general election, the words *love, home, family, land* and *hard work* occur a half-dozen times. When Rafshoon got Carter off the farm in his commercials, he typically showed him campaigning or speaking in three-quarter profile to an audience or at a news conference off camera: "Now listen to me carefully. I'll never tell a lie. I'll

never make a misleading statement. I'll never avoid a controversial issue. Watch television, listen to the radio. If I ever do
any of those things, don't support me."

These twin themes of the Rafshoon spots—on the farm, on
the campaign trail—became the basic building blocks of the
Carter media campaign. As Rafshoon explained his campaign
to *New York Times* reporter Joseph Lelyveld, "It's Jimmy."
The commercials reflected the man. Carter had so much confidence in Rafshoon's work that he consented to whatever
themes and styles the ad people produced and didn't ask to
see them before public screening.

Rafshoon's self-confidence deserted him only once. Just as
the Carter campaign had difficulties making the jump from a
small, tight, Georgia-based primary operation to a large general election campaign, so too did the media operation have
trouble with its transition to a national strategy. In early October, about midway through the campaign, Lelyveld
brought Rafshoon together with Tony Schwartz, author of
The Responsive Chord and a political commercial maker with
a very high opinion of himself. In 1964, he produced an anti-
Goldwater commercial that showed a little girl picking a
daisy and counting down from ten to one as a nuclear bomb
exploded. The spot was shown just once on television; protests led the Johnson people to cancel it. That was one more
public showing than certain other Schwartz classics in "negative" commercials were allowed. In 1972, Schwartz did the
napalm baby spot for George McGovern: a news clip showing
a Vietnamese mother running and cradling her child, whose
burned skin hangs loose like a torn shirt; a jet engine roars on
the sound track. The anguish on her face is as searing as the
wounds on the child's body. The voice-over, Schwartz's own
five-year-old son, asks: "Does a president know that planes
drop bombs?" Then came the message: Vote McGovern. Mc-
Govern's people vetoed the ad as too strong.

The Carter people commissioned both radio and television commercials from Schwartz, and the candidate came by twice in mid-October for recording sessions at Schwartz's studio on West 56th Street in New York. The news that Schwartz had been summoned by Rafshoon in the middle of the campaign was interpreted as a sign that the Atlanta media operation was in trouble. In a story in the *Times*, Lelyveld noted that "the call to Mr. Schwartz is being knowingly and sardonically viewed as a tacit acknowledgment of the campaign's failure to fashion an effective communications strategy this fall."

Actually it was Schwartz who failed. He made twenty-five commercials for Carter, done in two general styles. In one series Schwartz took the candidate off the farm and out of his work shirt and put him in a dark suit and tie. He turned Carter's head directly to the camera in a closely framed shot with the candidate looking the camera—and the viewer—squarely in the eye. The words were soft—about the need for jobs, the problems of the elderly, the chance for new leadership. The message was not so much anti-Ford as it was an attempt to enhance Jimmy Carter. There were also some symbolic spots. Actor E.G. Marshall was the voice-over for stills of Franklin Delano Roosevelt and John Fitzgerald Kennedy and then Jimmy Carter. "What happens if people ask why we left out Lyndon B. Johnson?" Schwartz asked Rafshoon. "We'll tell them we forgot," Rafshoon supposedly replied.

The second series Schwartz did was the so-called negative spots. Rafshoon rejected ten of these. In one a New York actor, shown head on, quotes in biting tones a Republican party comment about "necessary unemployment." In a second unused commercial, an off-camera voice lists all the Ford "against" positions—against Medicare, against job training, against school lunches, against food stamps, against day care.

The voice-over asks: "Who'd believe a nice man like Gerald Ford would vote against or oppose all these?" A third no-show was a variation of the "against" commercial. The spot opens on a white sheet of paper titled "Résumé for Gerald Ford." The page turns and the résumé lists all of Ford's "against" positions, once more a series of ten or twelve items. Finally, the voice-over says: "Mr. Ford, you can expect to hear from us November 2." A fourth no-show took off on the theme of the "two Jimmy Carters." The first Jimmy Carter, in black and white, is the flip-flopping "fiction" depicted by the Republicans; the other, "real" Jimmy Carter, shown in color, is the leader of principle and vision. Finally, there was a group of highly evocative thirty- and sixty-second photographic commercials. One of these picture ads opens on a wide view of the Manhattan skyline seen from the East River There are the sounds of the harbor, shots of the bridges, wheeling gulls. The voice, Carter's own, asks, "How can anyone say to this great city, 'Drop dead'?" In a variation, the pictures of Manhattan scenes are accompanied by the distinctive cultural sounds of the city—a string quartet, the hint of a *salsa*, a bongo beat, a *hora*, Italian music. All these Schwartz spots were rejected; so was one showing photographs of the Russian suppression of the Hungarian uprising in 1956 and asking, "Can the president of the United States be ignorant of this?"

There is disagreement about why the Schwartz "attack" commercials did not run in the last two weeks of the Carter campaign. Carter's people say they preferred positive ads that pointed up their man's abilities; they went, they say, to Schwartz in the first place for ads aimed at the undecided voter. The "intimate" style of the accepted spots played to this idea of getting to know the candidate better; the others did not.

Hamilton Jordan, the Carter campaign manager, says, "Schwartz really didn't understand Jimmy." It is clear that Rafshoon did not want ads that stressed the inabilities of Carter's opponent as much as ads stressing his man's abilities. As for the two Jimmy Carters idea, everyone was talking about Carter's being "fuzzy on the issues," and Schwartz's approach was to deal with it directly. That, however, was just what the Carter people didn't want to do; they were not going to spend their own money to remind voters of their candidate's alleged flip-flops. (In 1972, the most memorable of the Nixon attack commercials pictured George McGovern as a two-faced weather vane, adjusting positions to the prevailing winds; this itself was a version of a 1968 "attack" commercial Humphrey used against Nixon.)

A plan to mount a more aggressive campaign appealed to a movement within the Carter camp led by Patrick Caddell, the Carter public opinion specialist. According to Caddell, when Carter's lead began eroding in mid-October, he and other advisers went back to the candidate with fresh polling data, indicating that the Nixon pardon issue was "our best issue with the younger voters and independents" who were leaning to Ford. "The pardon issue was vetoed by the candidate himself," Caddell told a meeting of the American Association of Political Consultants the Saturday after the election. According to Caddell, "Carter didn't want blood all over the floor," that is, a divided and bitter electorate.

There was no Jerry Rafshoon in the Ford campaign. Instead there were three different ad campaigns led by three different creative directors. The Ford people spent about $11 million on television and radio advertising, a lot of it in the last ten days of the campaign. Too little, too late? Or too much? On these two points the Ford campaign may have turned, depending on who is telling the story.

When the President Ford Committee (PFC) organized its
media operations in the fall of 1975, it borrowed a page—but
not, mercifully, the book—from the Nixon campaign of
1972. Nixon's CREEP organization had an "in-house" media
operation, known as the November Group, to create, buy
time for, and distribute all campaign advertising. The Ford
committee set up a similar operation, using staff on leave
from Grey Advertising, Leo Burnett, McCann Erickson, J.
Walter Thompson, and other first-rank advertising agencies.
The Ford in-house operation was known as Campaign '76,
Media Communications, Inc., and it was housed on L Street
in Washington, up the street from the *Washington Post*. The
chief executive officer was Peter H. Dailey, a Los Angeles ad
man who had held the same job at the November Group.
Bruce H. Wagner, on leave from Grey Advertising, was the
executive vice-president. Winkler Video on Third Avenue in
New York did all the production of the television and radio
spots. Dailey-Wagner eventually became known as team one;
two other "teams" were later to take the field for Ford in the
campaign.

The Dailey-Wagner team fashioned, in Wagner's words, an
"assumptive" strategy for Ford's media campaign. It would
emphasize the strengths of the presidency and of Gerald Ford
and would not mention his opponents in the primaries or in
the general elections. "Our plan was to be positive and presidential and to stick with those themes," Wagner said.

If you happened to live in any of the contested primary
states, you might have seen, briefly, Campaign '76's "Oval
Office" commercials: President Ford listening to aides, smok-
ing his pipe, wearing a vested suit, striding through the White
House, gravely listing his accomplishments, presiding at
cabinet meetings. The tone was documentary, the colors regal
blue and rich gold, the story boards carefully researched to

talk to the concerns that Campaign '76 polling surveys had
shown to be on the minds of the electorate. About $1.2 mil-
lion was spent on the assumptive commercials through
May . . . and then the whole campaign was dumped uncere-
moniously right before the California primary. The Ronald
Reagan candidacy had refused to die, even though the political correspondents had written its obituary after Reagan's
New Hampshire and Florida defeats. In fact for a time in the
spring of 1976, it looked as if Reagan might go to the Republican convention with more delegates than Ford. Only
Reagan's failure to field a slate of delegates in the Ohio primary, his chief strategist Lyn Nofziger told me at the time,
prevented a sure convention victory. No one in the Reagan
camp had thought about Ohio carefully enough to see its
pivotal votes.

By California the Ford people were shaken. "When it got
down to the short strokes," Wagner says, "the White House
panicked." Wagner diplomatically won't say who the panicky
ones were. The White House ("they") did an end run around
Campaign '76—"Suddenly a separate loop developed in our
advertising," Wagner says—and brought in Jim Jordan of the
advertising firm of Batten, Barton, Durstine & Osborn.[3]
Jordan made three so-called slice of life commercials for
Ford, using professional actors and actresses—and some of
the most heavy-handed techniques ever seen in national political advertising. In one commercial a pretty young woman
tells another pretty young woman that she is working for the
election of President Ford:

First Woman: "Did you know he's cut inflation in half?"
Second Woman: "In half? Wow!"

In another one a father holds up his son to see President
Ford, the man who makes us all feel proud again. The actors

are clearly in a studio; the Ford footage, just as clearly, comes from news film. The splicing is clumsy; not even the four-year-old would be fooled by it. The third commercial put two handsome, lean-jawed actors, better cast in Brut ads, in yellow hardhats and spliced together some Ford news film footage to make it seem like the hardhats were watching Ford walk by their construction site. They talk about how Ford has managed to get working men just like them back on the job again. These three ads were shown in California the Tuesday before the June 8 primary. Forty-eight hours later they were ordered back. Michael Owen, the producer who worked on all the Ford ads at Winkler Video, says, "Those workers wouldn't convince anyone in a bar in Queens." Bruce Wagner reported, "There was a lot of bad comment about slice-of-life as soon as they got on the air . . . the audience is smart. Ad men have to respect it. You can't try to jerk people around."

Still another loop developed in Campaign '76. The White House commissioned a California-based advertising firm to make the Rhodesia commercial, an ad that quotes a Ronald Reagan remark about the possibility—hypothetical—of sending American troops to Africa. A middle-aged woman talks about how the campaign issues are becoming clearer: "Governor Reagan can't start a war; President Reagan can."

The Rhodesia spot had one day's exposure before it was killed. That was enough for Dailey and Wagner; they both resigned. The Campaign '76 staff shrank from around thirty-five to a five-person holding operation. June, July, and half of August went by with the Ford media operation essentially moribund.

The week of the Republican National Convention, Bailey, Deardourff and Eyre, a Washington-based firm, took over. John Deardourff is a youngish, bright, attractive campaign specialist who usually takes on young, bright, attractive, moderate Republican candidates. His commitments when the President Ford Committee called him included Kit Bond and John Danforth in Missouri, James Thompson in Illinois, and Pierre DuPont in Delaware. Deardourff spent a week in Vail, Colorado, with Ford and his White House staff after the convention, getting to know the candidate. Together with Bob Bailey, he developed a "media planning document" for Ford. The campaign would emphasize two major positive themes: Ford's character and decency and the progress the country had made since Nixon and Watergate. "Things *were* better, the bitterness was gone," Deardourff maintained. The general plan was later sharpened to diminish the amount of actual open campaigning Ford would do. Campaign director Stuart Spencer said he wanted to "maximize" Ford's good points and "minimize" his liabilities. He would keep the President off the stump and in the Rose Garden. Mainly Ford would appear in controlled television situations—to decrease the opportunities for Ford's misstatements, mispronunciations, malapropisms, and other stumbles and pratfalls. "We faced it," a White House man told me. "Ford is not a great speech maker; he is not great in news conferences. We had to find a setting in which he was comfortable."

Deardourff and Spencer spent more than half of their $21.3 million federally mandated funds on a radio-television campaign blitz between October 10 and November 1 aimed at the "big eight" states—such as New York, California, and Pennsylvania, where there are 228 electoral votes—and at the so-called second tier states—like the Carolinas, Virginia, Wisconsin, and Oregon.

The media blitz used two types of commercials—"national concepts" shown on network television and regional ads with specific appeals for different parts of the country. The na-

tional concepts were upbeat; their theme was expressed in
the Pepsi-Cola-like jingle, "I'm Feelin' Good About
America." When Ford appeared, he was always in controlled
situations—speaking from Air Force One, for example, or
taking soft questions from Joe Garagiola on "The Jerry and
Joe Show," shown on statewide networks in the last week of
the campaign. (Joe: "How many leaders have you dealt with,
Mr. President?" Jerry: "One hundred and twenty-four leaders
of countries around the world, Joe.") The regional ads used
local politicians to speak for the president—John Connally in
Texas, Strom Thurmond in South Carolina, Governor Ray in
Iowa (Nelson Rockefeller was considered for New York but
not used). Deardourff estimates that 75 percent of the television ad material was "very positive." the ads were extremely
good as television—that is, high in "production values."

Deardourff did do some tough material in the form of
"man in the street" sequences. "I want a Georgian for president," a woman says in one of the commercials, "but not
Carter." The Deardourff team also prepared some strong
attack commercials—"I don't like the word negative," he
says—in the final days of the campaign. One was the "crawl
title," which borrowed from a familiar oil company commercial ("We thought you'd like to know . . . "). White type on
the black screen is accompanied by a brisk off-camera voice:
"Those who know Jimmy Carter best are from Georgia, so
we thought you'd like to know." Then comes the crawl, a
series of white type on black:

The Savannah, Georgia, *Press* endorses Ford.
The Savannah, Georgia, *News* endorses Ford.
The Marietta, Georgia, *Journal* endorses Ford.
The Albany, Georgia, *Herald* endorses Ford

And so on, for more papers than anyone imagined were published in Georgia. (They were mostly small town papers; the

major Georgia paper, published in Atlanta, endorsed Carter.)

The crawl title didn't get out until the last four or five days of the campaign and even then did not get circulation to match its punch. One reason was the general delay in the Ford blitz; also the commercial makers said they had to wait for the newspapers to make their endorsements.

Bailey, Deardourff and Eyre made several spots that weren't aired. One showed Ford talking to a group of pre-teens; a well-scrubbed eleven-year-old asks, "What will you do about unemployment?" A pretest of the commercial, Deardourff says, showed that people didn't believe it was spontaneous. At least one very tough ad was also rejected: the Carter personal taxes ad. When the story board for the personal taxes commercial came through to Winkler Video, Michael Owen knew that the material required special hand-ling. "I just kept it separate from the others," Owen recalls. "It was a rough ad." The personal taxes commercial does seem to leap out of the pack of "feelin' good" material. It begins with a Rafshoon production, a commercial for Jimmy Carter in which the candidate is talking about taxes. "The tax laws are a disgrace . . . to the human race," Carter intones, as the words *actual Carter commercial* are superimposed on the picture. Carter talks about tax loopholes for millionaires. Then comes the voice-over: "Jimmy Carter and his family took advantage of the tax loopholes to reduce their taxable income below that paid by a family of three earning $15,000 a year."

There are several versions of why the personal taxes spot was not used. According to Deardourff the Ford campaign managers phased out anti-Carter material in the final days of the campaign because they wanted to end on a totally posi-tive note. The Ford operation also had focus groups—small, demographically representative assemblies of potential voters. When the personal taxes ad was shown to a focus group in a Cleveland motel—a pretest—some group members found it confusing; the tax laws already were complex for most of them and the "commercial-within-a-commercial" technique further unfocused them.

The Ford campaign ended up spending more on media than the Carter people did—roughly $12 to $13 million to Carter's $10 million. The Ford people spent their money at the end— they really didn't get organized until then—while Rafshoon went for a more even buy throughout the general elections, partly because, as a Carter staff person explained, "We were concerned about our man dropping out of the public sight in the period after the Republican Convention."

In many ways the Ford and Carter media campaigns were mirror images. If you watch the Ford and Carter five-minute campaign biographies side by side, you would think they were done by the same filmmaker. The marching bands and the other production values are in both. There are also the artful half-truths in the text, the carefully misleading jux- taposition of images, and the outright falsehoods. Peanut warehouseman Carter walks the fields in work clothes as if he were a farmer . . . football center Ford is extolled while the screen shows a fleet halfback running for a touchdown . . . neither man says anything about substantial matters, but both look forceful.

What if Deardourff had started earlier? Or had used his tougher ads? The Ford polling operation, done simultaneously with the airing of "The Jerry and Joe Show," indicated that the program was being well received by the television audi- ence—and by potential Ford voters. Does that translate into any votes? Would more "attack" commercials have helped tilt the balance to Ford in some of the closer states? Did

Rafshoon's evocations of the land and family stem the outward flow of Carter support at the end? Did his decision to remain faithful to the original tone of the Carter campaign forestall defeat?

Believers in the "old politics"—and I am one of them—tend to place more emphasis on the pocketbook, on political organization, and on tradition (how your parents voted) in election outcomes. The demographics of the vote on November 2 suggest a victory of the traditional New Deal coalition. Many believers in the "new politics" of media campaigns place more weight on the influence of free media—candidate appearances and the campaign accounts that appear on the nightly news and in the newspapers. "Paid media is supplementary," says Bruce Wagner. "It is a refinement of the campaign that reaches only a relatively few people. Of course, in a close election, where every ounce of effort must be magnified, the commercials *have* to influence a few percent of the vote." On election day, 1976, 2 or 3 percent was enough.

Deardourff and I talked after the election. He declared that he would not have done anything different if he did his media campaign all over again. "It almost worked," he said. "Hell, it *did* work, considering where we were. Our polls showed that the Nixon pardon was our biggest burden and in the end we couldn't shake him with all our advertising." In the end, then, an old politics issue weighed heavier than all the new politics media dazzle—by the testimony of the man who produced most of the dazzle himself.

THE ELECTION: PUTTING THE PRESS IN ITS PROPER PLACE

CHAPTER 6

The people who helped win the election for Jimmy Carter smoke more cigarettes than those who helped almost win the election for Gerald Ford. But the Carter campaign people used the word *perception* less than the Ford people, as in the phrase, "The public perception was that we lost momentum after the candidate's Eastern European mistake." (Campaign strategists actually use the word *momentum*, too.) These bad habits, however, were about the only serious lapses of taste when the winners, the losers, and the also-rans—strategists for Ronald Reagan, Henry Jackson, Hubert Humphrey, Morris Udall, Edmund G. Brown, Jr., and Birch Bayh—gathered at the Institute of Politics at Harvard University in early December 1976 to relive the glorious days of the 1976 presidential campaign. From the snows of New Hampshire in January through the television blitz of election eve, Hamilton Jordan, Jerry Rafshoon, John Deardourff, Robert Teeter, Patrick Caddell, Ben Wattenberg, and others all discussed what they did and why, putting their cards on the table. They told each other in effect: *when you led with that card, we were waiting for it and had decided how to counteract it. . ...* It was like listening to some good Las Vegas blackjack players arguing about the percentages of taking another card or standing pat.

The rules of the particular game at Harvard that weekend made all the sessions off the record. The institute, part of the John F. Kennedy School of Government, is publishing an edited version of the sessions, just as it did for campaign '72. (One of the lowlights of that conference was CREEP head Jeb Magruder telling everyone about the Nixon operation's sophisticated use of telephones, a discussion that came just a few weeks before the activities of the White House plumbers were revealed.) Still, it is possible, without breaking the rules or scooping the book, to give a sense of the campaign *interactions* (another buzz word of '76) among the chief strategists as they talked shop.

Perhaps the most striking impression when fifteen or twenty campaign strategists gather in a room together is that they all—winners and losers—look alike, although there are a few differences. The Ford people tended to be younger than the Humphrey or Jackson people, the Reagan people seemed the brightest, the Carter people the wittiest (winners can afford to be funny), the Wallace man the most charming, the Udall woman (the only woman at the table other than one woman moderator) and the Jackson men the most issue oriented. But beyond these differences the strategists seemed to have more in common with each other than with their candidates. It was not so much us versus them at the table, but all of us campaign people versus them (the candidate). Perhaps this is true of all technocrats: the process is the thing. Albert Speer could just as well have organized the English defense forces and production lines in the Battle of Britain.[1]

Hamilton Jordan and Jerry Rafshoon had problems getting through to their man Carter at times, just as Bob Teeter and John Deardourff had troubles getting through to their man Ford. In part this failure of communications in the quintessential wired environment of the campaign may be the result of a kind of "spaceship mentality." The candidate travels by jet plane, hermetically sealed, from media market to media market; he gets out of the plane, gives a speech, hears the cheers, gets back in, and jets, sealed again, to the next stop. It is literally hard to get a message through to him, to tell him that some of those local applause lines may be costing him points in the national polls. In a sense the candidate is flying by his own internal gyroscope during the high of a campaign. He may be thinking, "I don't care what the damn polls are showing, I know what works for me." Not only is he older than his aides, he also thinks he is wiser . . . and he is hearing all those cheers from the committed who turned out to see him.

Not so surprisingly the technocrats of political strategy generally saw eye to eye on the general themes of the '76 campaign. In almost every talk I had with the winners and the losers, they gave the press coverage fairly good marks. Perhaps reporters were too slow to pick up on certain substantive stories, perhaps they ran too long with others—fluff, for example, like the *Playboy* interview. But overall, the campaign managers claimed, the coverage evened out. "You lose one, you win one," the Reagan man said. All this goodwill from the political operatives was in sharp contrast to a meeting across campus the next night when a panel of press people, including *Playboy* interviewer Bob Scheer, had harsh things to say about the campaign coverage.

Political campaign people may have a certain avuncular attitude toward the press. Still when the insider technocrats talk, as opposed to communications experts on the outside, the press tends to be put in its proper place. The key to good campaigns is not media but money—where and how to spend it. Among those who should know, the hero of the Carter campaign—next to Jimmy, of course—was its comptroller, Robert Lipshutz. And if there was a heroine, then it was Lady Luck—that is, all the factors that money can't buy, like sunny weather on New Hampshire primary election day (it helped Ford) or an early edition of the *Milwaukee Sentinel*, with its Dewey-eyed 1948 headline: "Udall Defeats Carter." The wire service photo of Carter holding up the paper, Truman-style, made page one of the *New York Post* the next day, driving out the otherwise bad news for Carter that he had lost New York State the same night. He squeaked by in Wisconsin. "Someday," Jody Powell told a friend, "someone should write a book about what campaigns are really like."

When the Institute of Politics publishes its book, the technocrats of the next presidential campaign will have a blueprint for spending the $21.3 million the federal government gives the major party nominees. The candidates of 1980 and 1984, I am sure, will increase their polling operations, though it is difficult to see how the Pat Caddells and Bob Teeters can do quantitatively more polling or more sophisticated polling than they did this time around. There hardly seems an orifice of the body politic that has not had a thermometer stuck in it to take yet another reading. In 1976, we endured exit polling, focus groups, and pretests of commercials. At the Harvard meeting there was talk of borrowing techniques from the television entertainment researchers. Prospective voters already have been wired to "choice" levers so that researchers can plot their minute-by-minute physical reactions to political materials—speeches, debates, candidates' commercials— against the unfolding content of the material: today the

galvanic skin response to *Charlie's Angels* at the Preview
Theater on Hollywood's Sunset Boulevard, tomorrow the rise
and fall of visceral emotion during a fireside chat by President Jimmy Carter.

Now that the campaign technocrats have spoken, the academic researchers will eventually come in with their weighty
assessments of the role that the press played in the elections.
For the News Study Group, enough returns are in for some
judgments. The group's vote is hardly a landslide of approval
for the press. It considers the press's performance, like that
of Carter and Ford in the campaign, generally uninspired.
The one reflected the other.

On one level the national political campaigns came across
to the general public as media campaigns. How else can the
candidate reach 80 million voters, except through news conferences, staged appearances, and other media events designed for television and the news cameras? In the Ford-
Carter race, the role of the press had been magnified by the
new campaign finance law. The relatively limited financial
resources available to Ford and to Carter meant that their
campaign strategists had to concentrate on a two-phase effort. First, they had to make the most of their use of free
media—the news coverage of campaign events by radio, television, and print reporters; second, they had to make the
most of their use of paid media—advertising, including spot
commercials, five-minute minidocumentaries, and half-hour
biographies on radio and television.

From the start Carter campaigned furiously. His schedulers
booked him on "three-market days," the now-standard jet
trips for national candidates that take them daily into three
different cities, and three different television markets, in time
to make the early evening local news in each. The Carter

people spent about $10 million on media advertising, with
most of their television time spots spread more or less evenly
throughout the campaign. In contrast, the Ford camp used
the "Rose Garden" strategy, keeping the president off the
stump and in the controlled confines of the White House.
The idea was for Ford to look "presidential." The White
House, as Theodore Roosevelt long ago observed, is a "bully
pulpit." The early Rose Garden campaign was complemented
by a final media blitz in the last two weeks of October when
the Ford camp spent upward of $8 million.

Little of this media strategy, in either camp, left much
room for serious political dialogue. There was, it is true,
plenty of apparent movement in the campaign; technically
the free media scheduling and the paid media television commercials were well done (some of us still can sing the Ford
jingle, "I'm Feelin' Good About America"). But they contributed very little substance to the campaign, and the press
coverage reflected this spiritlessness.

In the absence of an issue-oriented campaign—a campaign,
for example, like the past four presidential elections—the
press stirred itself mainly for cheap thrills:

•What the public opinion polls showed each day became the
single longest-running story of the campaign.
•The Carter interview in *Playboy* magazine, a nonstory,
dominated front pages for a full week (much to the dismay
of the Carter staff).
•Earl Butz's racist taste in "humor," as repeated in *New Times*
magazine, was a bad joke that ran for four or five days in the
press and, in a demonstration of Gresham's law, finally drove
the *Playboy* story off the front pages.

In the end, however, both the candidates and the press
were saved from their generally petty ways by a third force.
Taking advantage of a little-noticed change in the federal

rules governing political campaign coverage on television, the League of Women Voters staged three presidential debates and one vice-presidential debate. Freed from their issue-empty strategies, Gerald Ford and Jimmy Carter were at last permitted to speak for themselves, not through their carefully sculpted media images. The real candidates stood up.

The debates *were* the campaign, the major events and turning points in the race. George Gallup later observed that the second meeting in particular stopped Carter's downward plunge, greased by the *Playboy* interview (Gallup thus confirmed what Pat Caddell's polls were telling Carter). Carter himself told reporters a few days after the election that he won because of the favorable exposure he had received in the debates, especially since Ford's Rose Garden strategy was working and only Carter seemed to be making mistakes.

The league's role in the campaign puts in perspective the press's role by showing that the press, especially television, does not set national political agendas. Certainly it has less power than the politicians so dependent on good ink and prime air time. In the primaries we saw it was the campaign dynamics, and not the press, that made Pennsylvania the critical primary for the Democrats, and it was Mayor Daley who arbitrarily declared that Jimmy Carter had won the Democratic nomination after he had won the Ohio primary (even though Carter was still short of a majority of delegates).

The press—and television—is not unimportant in electoral politics. It would be foolish to argue that the media in general and television in particular have no effect on the selection of political candidates, their styles of political campaigning, and the outcome of elections—as foolish as saying that the television debates elected Carter. The daily serving of political speeches, jet trips and events like the Ford-Carter debates are the staff of life for journalists, campaign technocrats, and political activists. For the majority of citizens who don't get involved in the presidential political process until the last few weeks, they are distant events unfolding on a television set with its sound turned down, in a room crowded with children, spouses, and everyday things. Jody Powell is Carter's totally politicized press secretary. Most voters, says Powell, get interested in national politics "once every four years for about fifteen minutes." Even allowing for exaggeration, it is probably a good summary of the Carter campaign view.

Quite clearly the big media can inflate an unknown's recognition factor. The big media may also have long-term, cumulative effects on voting decisions; some political advertising may strengthen the resolve of the already committed voter. Other appeals may influence the undecideds. Also, once politicians stake out the ground—making one state, like Ohio, "crucial"—and once politicians frame the issues, then the press can spotlight that story. Television can bring Ford-Carter to 90 million viewers. But even then the press's role has been confirming rather than affirming.

Would anyone—journalist, candidate, or voter—want another kind of press playing a different role in the political process? Should news organizations take a more activist part in judging candidates? Should television news aggressively thrust issues before the electorate—"serious" matters such as the Humphrey-Hawkins bill—rather than going along with the candidates' sideshows, such as the Panama Canal or busing? Should the press try to exert real power rather than be satisfied with the appearance of power?

In order to begin to answer these questions, I would make some distinctions between what might be called the "mainstream" and the "opinion" press. The mainstream press includes the three major networks, the wire services, the news magazines, and the authoritative newspapers like the *New York Times*, the *Washington Post*, and the *Los Angeles Times*. The opinion press includes nonestablished, intellectual, and/or politicized publications like *Rolling Stone, Harper's, Washington Monthly, The New Republic, New Times,* and *National Review.* Mainstream outlets are respectful; they are generally gentle giants, unlikely to use their power in partisan politics. Whatever the faults of mainstream political reporters, partisanship is not one of them. The men and women who cover campaigns for the networks, the news magazines, and the authoritative newspapers do not slant copy to favor the "best man," or the candidate who talks sense to the American people, or even the man most reporters might prefer. Frank Mankiewicz, who helped run the McGovern campaign in 1972, has said that McGovern was subjected to the toughest grilling by reporters who were probably most sympathetic to his candidacy. For national journalists, to give any pronounced tilt goes against the tradition of objectivity (a tradition, by the way, less than a hundred years old and uniquely American).

The objective press seldom raises its voice. Ideally it is the voice of record, to be buried in time capsules. The opinion press doesn't fret about objectivity too much; it is more yeasty, less conscious of image and history, more inclined to be shrill or outrageous. Their front covers cry out, "Look me over! Pick me up!" They may be more likely to cock a snoot at authority. *Harper's,* for example, ran Steven Brill's unblinking article on Jimmy Carter. *Rolling Stone* gave us "political" reportage by Timothy Crouse and "Doctor" Hunter Thompson in 1972 and, in 1976, John Dean III. Marshall Frady in *New Times,* Garry Wills in the *New York Review of Books,*

Richard Reeves and Ken Auletta in *New York*, Jack New-
field, Alexander Cockburn, and James Ridgeway in the *Village Voice* offered counterpoint during the campaign to the
mandarins of Georgetown. We need, I suggest, both kinds of
press; campaign politics would be dull without the occasional
"unobjective" outrages of a Norman Mailer or a Jimmy Breslin. It would be fragmentary without the steady coverage of
the old reliable *New York Times*. There is room for both.

Those who have worked in the ranks of news organizations
don't expect more from political journalism. As political
writer Richard Reeves wisely points out, the press is ill suited
for a real power role. It is, he writes, "a child, essentially an
immature institution. It's a lovable little thing, distracted by
bits of color and light, eager and irresponsible, honest in its
simple way. And it has trouble concentrating on more than
one thing at a time. . . . It is not an institution consciously
and consistently dedicated to accumulating the exercise of
control over other institutions or other people's lives."

In its immaturity, it invites manipulation by the candidates.
"If you want to give a traditional speech," says Gary Hart,
"they'll ask you if it is worth turning the cameras on." When
Hart planned to make policy statements about water pollu-
tion or the need for housing during his Colorado Senate race,
he knew he would get very little attention if he invited the
reporters in to talk to him in his office. So like other candidates everywhere, he walked the banks of the local river and
visited a housing construction site to make his points. Similarly when candidate Jimmy Carter issued a twenty-page
position paper on the family, it was worth fifteen seconds on
the evening news or six paragraphs in the newspaper. For real
attention, the candidate learned to sleep in private homes and
make his own bed.

Many journalists, and academics who study "press-
candidate interactions," often can't understand why so many

citizens aren't as excited about the political process as we are.[2] It is fun and jobs for us. For them it may be that what Ford and Carter have to say does not seem to touch them directly. We know they are wrong, but to them what happens at the office or plant or the zoning board does touch them daily. It has yet to be demonstrated to many of them that the quadrennial struggles between those little figures on the television screen have anything very much to do with them. When ordinary citizens tell the public opinion samplers that "politicians are all the same" or "it doesn't make any difference who gets in," they are making a judgment on the political process—and the press process—that is more damning than any critic could render.

NEWS AS ENTERTAINMENT, ENTERTAINMENT AS NEWS

PART II

"AGENDA SETTING" AND OTHER MYTHS OF MEDIA POWER

CHAPTER 7

Everywhere, it seems, television's influence is being felt in American society. Gerald Ford and Jimmy Carter spent on television time over half of the $21.3 million allotted to them under the federal campaign laws. The hair styles of a television personality like Farrah Fawcett-Majors can be seen blossoming on thousands of heads on city streets from New York to San Francisco, just as the jokes of a television host such as Johnny Carson are retold from East Coast to West Coast the next day. Law officers and psychiatrists—and committees of the Congress—endlessly debate the alleged pervasive influence of television on young minds and disturbed minds: do sex and violence in popular entertainment programming encourage antisocial behavior? Do terrorists and other criminals take their cues from television, seizing hostages because they know these actions will guarantee exposure—for themselves or their causes—in the media?

I tend to be in the minority in these matters. The dominant

view is that television has reshaped American politics, American society, and American manners.[1] The critics tend to be impressed by the reach of American television. A few years ago, the MIT News Study Group examined the viewing habits of Americans and concluded that very few people are very far from a television set in the United States. By the mid-1970s, some 97 percent of all American households—some 75 million homes—had at least one television set; about one in every three households had two or more sets. Television watching in the mid-1970s has become the most frequent activity of Americans after work and sleep. This reach helps explain why someone with something to sell—for example, a consumer product manufacturer or a political candidate—has such high regard for this far-reaching medium. Pervasiveness is one thing, however, persuasion quite another.

The News Study Group's findings, reported in an earlier book, *The Tin Kazoo: Television, Politics, and the News,* concluded that although Americans were watching television more and more, they put less and less credibility in its importance. Television, I argued, was reflective of American styles rather than a major shaping force of these styles. In fact, as a mass medium television may be the last to know about and describe important events. My opinions ran counter to the prevalent critical view of television as a pacesetter and catalyst in American life. After all, is it not television where we hear and see the news, first and foremost? The answer is "yes" if we are talking about the headline news of the day. But most of the time, television by its nature cannot do a thorough job for anything that goes beyond the skeletal facts and statistics of the news. The three commercial networks—ABC, CBS, and NBC—spend millions of dollars every four years to bring the two major national political conventions to the home audience. This coverage is the showcase for

the networks' talents and energies, and they spend considerable thought and skill on it. But at the 1976 Democratic
national convention in New York City, the network anchormen and reporters kept assuring their listeners that it was a
"dull," "predictable," "foreordained," "suspenseless" convention—a "media event" for the benefit of the cameras,
since the Democratic candidate Jimmy Carter already had
captured the nomination. The televised proceedings were
predictable and dull, reflecting this lack of suspense. However,
the political writer Richard Reeves, assisted by a small group
of young reporters, brought the convention to life mar-
velously by exploring the people and the movement off the
floor—in the hotel suites, the caucuses, the corridors, and the
bars. Reeves's book *Convention* is one measure of just how
much the commercial networks—and their audience—missed
of the high excitement and low comedy in New York during
that July week.

I mention this example not to demonstrate the obvious—
that print often can bring the audience information better
than television can. More important is my argument that the
viewing publics have intuitively recognized that television is a
severely limited channel for the movement of information
with more content than headline news. It is, of course, an
unsurpassed medium for the communication of drama, involving, as it does, our senses of sight and sound in ways that
neither print nor radio can.

In *The Tin Kazoo* I argued that the viewing public has
grown increasingly skeptical about its television viewing.
The audience was not an inert mass to be worked over by the
camera. It approached television in a playful mood—for its
own purposes. It was becoming more selective.[2] No one
would deny the admirable journalistic professionalism of the
network news organizations or the care and time expended

by the writers and producers of such good entertainment
programs as "All in the Family" or "The Mary Tyler Moore
Show." But the key to understanding the real effects of television in American life is not to know the producers' purposes but to know the consumers' expectations. After trying
to formulate this idea in *The Tin Kazoo* (and not quite suc-
ceeding), I came across the work of a psychologist, James
Stephenson, an Englishman now on the faculty of the University of Missouri. In his study, *The Play Theory of Mass Communications*, Stephenson creates the intellectual framework
that can help us explain what the consumer of television is
experiencing and what I have been attempting to describe.
Stephenson's idea is simple—as many great ideas are. The
media consumer's life is divided into work and play. Work is
what people do at offices and factories; play happens in
people's leisure hours, including the play of watching television and reading newspapers, magazines, and books. For
many journalists, critics, and academics, of course, the con-
sumption of media is part of their work and not their play—
which is one reason why many intellectuals find it difficult to
understand the particular way the average man or woman
views television.

Because television watching is part of the average viewer's
play life, it is not something to be taken too seriously. Television is for relaxation, for entertainment, for fun. But it is
not mindless, it requires a great deal of concentration because
the form—spoken words and moving images on a small
screen—is ephemeral and demanding. Newspaper and magazine reading are also leisure-time activities, but they can have
serious purposes, and the attention demands are different.
Certainly different expectations may be brought to newspaper reading. Newspapers often serve workaday purposes—
for example, to find a job or a place to live in the classified

advertising pages; to learn if friends or neighbors have died in the obituary pages; to see the price of groceries and other necessities in the food ads.

Television producers and programmers have intuitively grasped that the various viewing publics approach their efforts as part of the play world. The need to engage viewers, to hold their attention—even a bemused or wandering attention—is the prime requirement of all television presentation. This task is made extraordinarily difficult by the ephemeral nature of those moving pictures—images that cannot be stored, underlined, or reexamined in the way print can. But the play expectations in the minds of the viewers also limit the kinds of messages received, just as surely as the information-poor channel that transmits these messages.

Television producers and users have set for themselves some serious goals. Advertisers want to sell their goods and services, candidates want the voters' ballot on election day and, once in office, the voters' continued support in the public opinion polls; broadcast journalists want to convey the important news of the day. But inevitably advertiser, politician, and news producer alike must package their messages in an appropriate form to get past the twin barriers of play expectation and data-poor channel to the viewer. When the journalist T.S. Matthews sought to describe the popular British newspapers of two decades ago, he titled his book *The Sugar-Coated Pill*; the news had to be tricked out with bright artwork, seductive headlines, and attractive photographs. With print, at least, the reading public has been prepared over decades to take its medicine of information with a surface wrapping of graphics. With the neophyte television audience, the coating has to be extra strength—as a television commercial might put it—because no one has ever trained the audience to ingest serious information from television. Once we begin to see television from the point of view of the audience, and once the idea of television-as-play has been grasped, a number of the seemingly contradictory current developments I mentioned at the beginning of this chapter fall into place.

Candidates for office in the United States today increasingly use television to convey auras to the voters rather than policies. The Ford-Carter campaign illustrates this point quite clearly. The candidates' strategists came to the conclusion early in their campaign that in 1976 the voter's presidential choice would turn on perceptions of character. No major substantive issues—as civil rights or the war in Vietnam had in the 1960s—divided the candidates. The question posed to the voters in 1976 was, in effect, who is best able to restore confidence in government and faith in the American way after the terrible events of Watergate, the excesses of the CIA and the FBI, Vietnam, and civil disorder. What more appropriate way to convey aura and a personality than to use the television medium, where performers constantly project images and emotions? Not surprisingly, both Ford and Carter eagerly accepted the offer of the League of Women Voters for a series of presidential debates on television to demonstrate this ability. Television did not make the 1976 elections an all but issueless campaign. The candidates themselves did, based on their reading of the electorate's yearnings. Campaign '76 turned on the stylistic issue of character, and television was used to project that character. When there was a need by the two candidates to offer some minimum requirement of issue-oriented politics, both Ford and Carter turned to other media, such as smaller weekly newspapers or ethnic radio stations. In these *narrow*casting efforts—as opposed to the *broad*casting techniques of television—the candidates were able to send specific information messages to specific target groups.

Anyone who doubts this analysis ought to listen to the radio materials the Carter campaign used in the last week before the election. There were two sets of campaign spots—one set for soul stations (black radio) in the South, and one set for country and western stations (white radio) in the South. These were high-content materials; on the soul stations, the Carter campaign spoke in a black preacher's voice about more jobs, more housing, better health care; on the country and western stations, the Carter spots used a white voice to talk about welfare reform, lower taxes, and fiscal responsibility in government. Toward the end of the campaign, the white commercials played on the themes of Deep South pride and the need to send a southerner to the White House to end the hundred-year exile of the region from national politics. "The spots just about waved the bloody shirt of the Civil War," a Carter man told me with a slightly embarrassed laugh. For a national political candidate, then, television campaigning may be a necessary—but not a sufficient—medium.

When television is watched from the consumer's perspective rather than the critic's, it is possible to see the relative political importance of nonpolitical programming such as daytime television. Daytime television is usually dismissed as "soap opera," so-called because the major sponsors are detergent makers who aim their laundry products at the predominantly female audience. The attention of this group is captured by dramatic serials of family life, which have multicharacter plots typically revolving around a woman or group of women facing such family problems as adultery, impotence, alcoholism, runaway children, pregnancy, abortion, or divorce. This is highly politicized material because these are the kinds of everyday issues most people face in our society. SALT II, South Africa, and the Lebanese civil war may occupy the attention of the evening newscasts, but most people find it difficult to pay too much attention to these global concerns unless they are directly affected (American Jews by developments in Israel or coffee drinkers by drought in Brazil, for example). And even then these events may be felt indirectly, abstractly. The dictator Joseph Stalin once observed, "Ten million deaths are a statistic; one death is a tragedy." Daytime television dramas have meaning to viewers precisely because they deal with "one life" or "one death" rather than with the statistics of tragedy. And, of course, the soaps treat this material in dramatic form.

One criticism of soap operas among intellectuals who go slumming infrequently on the daytime dial is that they are "boring." They do move with a snail's pace through the trauma of the moment—John's vasectomy or Mary's lesbian feelings. But there is a good reason for that. Larry Fraiberg, the president of Metromedia Television, is the man who gambled (and won) by bringing "Mary Hartman, Mary Hartman" to New York. In his view the soaps, including "Mary Hartman, Mary Hartman," are the one place where television treats issues slowly and continuously. "To change individual attitudes—even to exchange information—about drugs, sex, abortion, divorce, and child-raising may have to take a very long time," Fraiberg says, as earnest and handsome as a kindly doctor on "Days of Our Lives." "And it may have to be done in a humorous way."

The notion that television play is serious news during the day and that serious news is television play during the evening news is a somewhat perverse formulation. But the current place to find the validation of these ideas is in the nighttime television schedule. Prime-time television—the evening hours when 80 to 100 million Americans are grouped around their television sets—is unabashedly entertainment time. But when the careful viewer takes a closer look at certain entertainment programs, the same trends we have been talking about are evident. Two of the most intelligent and popular nighttime series of the past decade have been "All in the Family" and "The Mary Tyler Moore Show." "Family," for all its canned laugh lines, was built on bed-rock matters: husband-wife conflict and generational differences between parents and children. These bitter pills were sugar-coated with comic situations. Mary Tyler Moore's character, Mary Richards, was an unmarried woman in her early thirties who was dealing with the very real problems of identity and intimacy. These are emotional challenges every adult must face. Maturity, Freud suggested, means learning how to love and how to work, but it is not the kind of story that gets on the evening news, at least not yet.

If I were to make any predictions about the shape of television in the 1980s in America, I would guess that the lines separating "entertainment" and the "news" will become more and more blurred. Already we can see the development of a kind of news-as-entertainment and entertainment-as-news in the latest prime-time programming. The Israeli raid on Entebbe was quickly made into a dramatic documentary for television (in fact, there were two made-for-television versions). The story of the Hanafi hostages in Washington and the life of Lee Harvey Oswald received similar treatment. Perhaps the best example of this new television form was the serialization of Alex Haley's book *Roots*. The book itself, an account of one black American's efforts to trace his ancestry to its African genesis, may have taken certain dramatic liberties with history. The television version recast the narrative into further dramatic forms (including scenes of sex and violence and the use of well-known actors and actresses). As seen on television, "Roots" became symbolic history, much like the Ford-Carter debates were symbolic politics. It was not history but drama, and it succeeded as no other program had ever succeeded before; the largest audience in the history of television watched the program, discussed it, thought about it, and were moved by it.

Some cultural historians might be unhappy at these developments. It was bad enough to believe the theory that television was turning Americans into a nation of uncritical, video-tranquilized sheep. That idea has been exploded now by events over the past five years; the consumer movement and buyers' resistance to inferior products signify that Americans now examine advertising claims critically. (And Watergate showed no amount of flag waving and television talk by Richard Nixon could save him.) But in its place a more dismal notion may take hold: the idea that America is becoming a nation of cynics, who believe that everything has been staged, or restaged, for their immediate entertainment.

I doubt this. Television consumers are still involved with the world through their screens. The more they watch critically—and read, converse, and think—the more they are engaged in life and politics and society. The evening news may be journalistically superficial; the television series "Roots" may be historical fiction. But they are both connections to the present and to the past. As long as people in a democracy stay tuned in, even to such imperfect information, there is reason for hope.

THE SEDUCTION OF THE AUDIENCE

CHAPTER 8

If entertainment is serious on television and the news is entertaining—among other characteristics—then the attitude of serious critics of television becomes clearer. They should take entertainment time a little more seriously and news time a little less seriously. As soon as they adopt this stance, the level of nonsense being written and spoken about television will drop rapidly. At any rate, the News Study Group approached three recent examples of television news trends with this attitude in mind.

"The anchorman is the front page of TV news," Mel Bernstein, a veteran news director, told television critic Jeff Greenfield. To Greenfield, Bernstein's words stood McLuhanism on its head: instead of the medium being the message, the messenger becomes the medium, with news made understandable by the "persona" through which it is disseminated—"Uncle" Walter Cronkite, "Professor" John

Chancellor, and Barbara Walters, the $5 Million Woman. I respect both Bernstein and Greenfield, but I told them they were wrong and put my own views about anchormen into an article for *New York* magazine ("The Twilight of the Anchorman"), which appeared in 1974. For a time it looked as if I would be proved wrong by what seemed to be the dawning of a new era of messengers. But only for a time.

In the summer of 1975, the people at ABC News tried to put together a new television-news act. WABC-TV in New York City began to feature three anchormen to lead its "Eyewitness News" team. It was an experiment unusual even for the station that made stars out of Melba Tolliver, who had been working as an ABC secretary until a union strike pushed her into the newsroom, and Rose Ann Scamardella, an employee of the New York State Human Rights Commission until she was hired by WABC after a five-minute interview. For its new anchors WABC brought in Tom Ellis from Boston and Bill Bonds from Detroit. Ellis and Bonds joined Roger Grimsby as costars, or cocaptains, of the 6 P.M. and 11 P.M. news teams. Ellis, who worked for Mel Bernstein in Boston, was lured away by a salary offer of nearly $200,000 a year. Bonds got about the same offer. When added to Grimsby's $200,000-plus salary, ABC's new troika cost some $600,000 a year.

These particular moves caused some bemusement at other television news departments around the country. "The salary escalation is sheer idiocy," said Lee Hanna, an NBC News vice-president. One network's madness, of course, is another's good business practice; NBC news paid Tom Snyder some $425,000 a year to host the "Tomorrow" show and to anchor the "NewsCenter 4" program on WNBC in New York.

It's not that large salaries are new. A small constellation of news superstars, the Walter Cronkites and the Barbara

Walterses, have for years commanded long-term, multimil-
lion-dollar contracts. Beginning in the early 1970s, a kind of
double-digit salary inflation extended not only from network
stars to weather and sports personalities on local stations but
even to some street reporters.

Television news departments can afford to pay these rates.
Network profits after taxes in the past few years have rivaled
those of the oil companies. Television news departments
more than carry their own weight, especially at the network-
owned stations. In New York, for example, WNBC's two-
hour-long "NewsCenter 4" has twenty-four commercial
minutes to sell each night, at an average of $3,000 a minute.
But the cost of maintaining news leadership is now threatening to get out of hand—indeed out of sight. In a textbook
case of economic law, the demand has outstripped the
system's ability to supply television-news talent. Because so
much advertising sales money is involved in news leadership
in television markets—tens of millions in the New York market alone—there are enormous pressures to find and hire the
right people—or more precisely, to find and hire the right
on-camera people. Few news organizations are bidding up the
prices of writers or film editors.

Usually new faces come from one of the many small stations around the country that have become the farm teams
for the networks and the major metropolitan markets. "We
are always looking for qualified people," one network news
president told me, "and there aren't that many around." So
the networks, he explained, raid each other and the network-
owned-and-operated stations in New York, Los Angeles, and
the other remaining markets. The "O-and-O's" in turn steal
from the Top Ten stations in Washington or Boston; and the
Top Ten, in their turn, reach down to Minneapolis or Hous-
ton for new faces. Bill Beutel, for example, went from
WABC's "Eyewitness News" to ABC's "AM America" (and

from $125,000 a year to $250,000); his move pulled Ellis
and Bonds to New York. Tony Pepper, one of Ellis's replace-
ments, came from Denver, where his salary was $30,000 a
year. His salary in Boston more than doubled that. Demand-
pull inflation benefits individual performers enormously. In
1974, Chuck Scarborough was brought in from Boston for
"NewsCenter 4." Scarborough made $1.85 an hour when he
began a decade ago in Biloxi, Mississippi; in Boston in 1973,
he made $65,000. In New York he made over $150,000
in 1976.

The total pool of talent for television news isn't that big to
begin with—perhaps 500 stations with news departments
averaging three or four people at most. At many of these
smaller stations, training tends to be superficial. It is still the
"stick-the-microphone-in-the-police-chief's-face" school of
tape-recorder reporting. Talent then had time to sharpen
skills and get seasoning at newspapers or wire services; when
the ratings stakes were relatively low, news directors could
afford to experiment. The executive producer of the
"Today" show could try out any number of women on
camera—without losing his job—before finding Barbara
Walters.

The new talent, characteristically, rarely has time to learn
how to interview or to report. They move, like the tape
recorders they use, at fast-forward speed, right from journalism school (or beauty contests) and a year or two of what
passes for reporting to on-camera jobs. In Chicago, the
nation's third most important market, the NBC station hired
Jane Pauley, who had put in eighteen months at an Indiana-
polis television station after graduating from Indiana University. In a year Pauley moved on to NBC's "Today" show, as
a co-host. On the West Coast Sandy Hill got into television in
1969 with no journalism experience or training; she was Miss

Washington State while in college. In 1975, Hill became co-anchor of the evening news for CBS in Los Angeles, the second most important market. Bonds and Ellis are, let it be said, both veterans. Ellis spent seven years at a San Antonio television station as a reporter, producer, and anchorman before going to Boston in 1968. Bonds served at the ABC station in Detroit for seven years. But the qualities that make them desirable properties in WABC's eyes have little, if anything, to do with the fact that they paid their dues in every phase of the news business.

The second characteristic of the new talent is that they must be not journalists but "communicators." Ellis, a tall Texan with purposely tousled hair, got the ABC job, according to the running joke at WBZ, his old station, after a nationwide search determined that he was "the only man in America who could strut while sitting down." ABC's rivals play the same games. The career of blond, blue-eyed Chuck Scarborough at NBC has been helped along by NBC News research surveys showing that women viewers "respond" to him. When ABC brought in Ellis and Bonds, the New York CBS station went after Larry Kane from Philadelphia's high-rated "Action News" program on WPVI-TV. All three New York network stations tried to hire him in 1974 and 1975. I asked a news director why Kane, who is in his mid-thirties, was sought after. He replied, "He's bright, fast talking, and looks like he has a . . . nine miles long."

The anchor people who are so much in demand in New York exude a certain kind of appeal. Currently the key to audience success on the evening news is thought to be "18-49 female demographics," younger women viewers who are at home in relatively great numbers in the early-evening hours. According to one time-buyer's formula, these women combine high disposable income with high susceptibility to advertising. Advertisers have long coveted this buying group, but the strategies to lure them to the evening news have been changing in the past few years—and have intensified the demand for new talent.

Until a few years ago older, male authority figures were in demand. Nationally Chet Huntley—and more recently Walter Cronkite—brought a quality of style to this role. Local stations, too, had news figures who absolutely dominated the Nielsen ratings (for example, Jerry Dunphy of the CBS station in Los Angeles and Floyd Kalber of NBC in Chicago). In New York no single figure clearly emerged, though Jim Jensen on the CBS station has ranked highest. In each city, however, these top-rated programs began to slip in the ratings, usually because of inroads made by the "Eyewitness News" approach on the ABC stations in town. The orthodoxy of success switched to a belief in the team format. The father figure became passé; "communicators" were in demand. News directors now speak vaguely about "warmth," "communication," and—a good post-Watergate quality—"credibility." These attributes may be more the field of the mystic than of the journalist; they defy analysis, except that the faithful recognize quality when they see it. Al Primo, who developed "Eyewitness News" at ABC in New York, hired Geraldo Rivera after talking to him for ten minutes. With Rose Ann Scamardella, Primo needed five minutes to decide she could communicate.

In the search for warmer communicators and hotter ratings, Los Angeles's Jerry Dunphy—who had been on the air for CBS longer than Walter Cronkite—was replaced in 1975 by ex-New Yorker Joseph Benti. Dunphy was fifty-four years old; Benti was forty-two. Jim Topping, then the news director of KNXT, the CBS station, declared: "If someone says we made the change because Dunphy is old, they'd be wrong. He is not an old man. . . . Jerry and Joe both happen to have prematurely gray hair." But, Topping added, "It's how you're perceived. Benti is perceived as a more contemporary figure."

In the New York news war of the mid-1970s, Jim Jensen and the CBS 6 P.M. news were slightly ahead of WABC in the early-evening hours, with WNBC slowly coming up. "Jensen is old—but not that old," a rival news director said (Jensen was born in 1928). "It would be a real mistake to get rid of Jensen," one rival executive claimed. But another said Jensen needed "help."

In fact no one really knows what ingredients, singly or in combination, pull viewers to the news. Was NBC's 11 P.M. success the result of Chuck Scarborough's young blue eyes or the good lead-in effect of NBC's nightly entertainment schedule in 1976? Was ABC's early-evening news program faltering because Bill Beutel left and because Grimsby was growing older and more tired, almost on camera? Or was it because CBS and NBC had more camera crews and reporters on the street filming stories? Perhaps the TV audience doesn't notice anything but the communicators. Kenneth MacQueen, vice-president and general manager of WABC-TV, told the *New York Times* that anchormen were "the overriding compelling reason" why viewers select one newscast over another.

Ratings books can be read in such a way as to prove any of the above arguments, and MacQueen's views dominated for a time—hence the frenzied star wars. This faith in personalities represents a kind of backsliding from the professional news attitudes that have been struggling to survive on television in recent years. Television news directors have always understood that their programs were part show business and part journalism. To the extent that they could put their efforts and money into the journalism side—into more film crews, salaries for knowledgeable reporters and writers—rather than into high-priced personalities, the news on television became visibly better.

But television is a trendy business, and many managements began playing it safe again, relying on the stars rather than the vehicle, and, of course, paying heavily for the new communicators (all the while singing the salary blues). As long as the cost of the Bill Bondses and Tom Snyders comes out of special sales accounts—the accountants have magical ways of writing off extraordinary expenses, especially for network-owned stations—rather than news budgets, the quality of coverage need not suffer too much. When management pays heavily for stars, however, it begins looking around for ways to economize on journalism. It is not unusual for a desk editor to call off a film crew on assignment in order to save some loose change for fifteen minutes of overtime—while management is negotiating a four-year, half-million-dollar contract with a new weather reader.

The real winners, then, are not the viewers but those in the talent pool. The television-news business is like a tight little village; everyone knows everyone else's affairs. Videotape cassettes of performers and news programs are exchanged like baseball trading cards. Outside consulting firms hired by management also spread word about this "friendly" weatherman or that "believable" woman reporter.

In a way the new television talent has become the contemporary version of the old journeyman printer-newspaperman, going from town to town wherever work is available. In 1976, the early-evening anchormen on New York's three network stations all came from out of town; the same was true of most of the line-up in Los Angeles. Does it matter if these television journeymen know next to nothing about the

city they happen to be in? As Bonds said, he's there to read
the news, not to cover stories. But how believable can he be
even doing that? In her farewell to Tom Ellis, *Boston Globe*
columnist Diane White advised him on New York: "If you
get lost, remember, all the streets are numbered consecu-
tively. It's your kind of town." ABC, after all, had Rose Ann
Scamardella to call on when it needed someone who knew
that the Bronx is up and the Battery down.

This is the proper place to whisper a few words about the
question of sex on television. The popular impression is that
the entertainment schedule is saturated with sexual activities
or innuendo, while the news time is rather prim and proper.
Again, however, there is something of a reversal of roles.
Three researchers from the State University of New York at
Stony Brook analyzed the conduct of the characters on six-
ty-one prime-time entertainment programs shown during the
week of October 11, 1975. Though they set up categories for
no fewer than thirteen different kinds of "overt and verbal
sexual behaviors," the researchers still concluded, "Unlike
TV violence, direct research evidence on the influence of
sexual content is scanty and inconclusive."[1] Other investigators, looking for offense, find little to report. On an
"adult" program like "M*A*S*H," *TV Guide* found only
"an occasional collegiate bout of necking, genre early
1950s." Producer Norman Lear's string of successes ("All in
the Family," "The Jeffersons," "Sanford and Son," "Mary
Hartman, Mary Hartman") make him the Henry Ford of the
Hollywood dream factories and the most independent-
minded producer in television. A few seasons ago Lear
battled the CBS network over some material he wanted in
"One Day at a Time," his series with an "emerging woman"
theme. A male character was to pinch the rear of a female

character and she was to pinch him back; a teen-aged character was to tell how her boyfriend tried to sneak his hand up
her sweater. CBS wanted this material out. Lear righteously
called it "repression."

The news offers a contrast to the puritanical ethic in entertainment. Leo Seligsohn of *Newsday* took an unscientific
sampling of news and public affairs programming during
selected weeks during April and May 1977. He found that

on May 7, NBC's late-night magazine-style program "Weekend" devoted its entire 90 minutes to a study of the problem
of incest. On May 15, CBS' prime-time "60 Minutes" depart-
ed from its usual format by devoting half its show to the
subject of child pornography. A few weeks earlier, in a more
traditional vein, ABC News Closeup had presented a half
hour on prostitution called "Sex for Sale: the Urban Battle-
ground."
  ABC's "Good Morning, America" ran a two-part minidocumentary April 13 and 14 on child pornography. In the
New York area, WCBS-TV aired a two-part mini-documen-
tary on child pornography May 24 and 25.
  On May 25, the Public Broadcasting Service delivered its
initial telecast of "The People vs. Inez Garcia," a drama based
on the celebrated 1974 murder trial of a rape victim who
later killed the rapist's accomplice. On May 26, WABC-TV
presented a special called "The Rape Victims."

The SUNY researchers picked the middle of the television
season for their study. Seligsohn made a much shrewder
choice; his period included the weeks when Nielsen and Arbitron, the audience measurers, take their readings across the
nation, and he found that all the sexual activity was a way to
boost the ratings. According to Seligsohn, "The ABC network's April 22 special, 'Sex for Sale,' is a good example of
what sex can do for ratings. An ABC spokesman said the
show, which aired from 10 to 11 P.M. on a Friday, became
the network's highest-rated news documentary ever, scoring a

20.2 Nielsen rating (percent of total number of sets in the country) and winning its time period with a 37 percent share of the audience (percent of sets tuned in). 'News Closeup' usually does not do this well, the spokesman said."[2]

Sex has also been appearing where the researchers and critics have not been looking, including the evening news-casts, where it is symbolic rather than contextual, suggested rather than suggestive. A John Chancellor would never be caught using the language of a Norman Lear. Nor would he, or any of the minor league anchor people around the country, do anything blatant. Instead the news programs provide fantasy figures for some of the audience, along with news, weather, stocks, and sports. It is no accident that anchor-people from Maine to California are sought for their contemporary look and their believability. What are we supposed to believe about them? They have gotten noticeably younger and hairier in recent years. CBS's Charles Kuralt, whose "On the Road" series has taken him throughout the country for almost a decade, recently complained about all the time he spent watching television news in motel rooms: "My over-whelming impression of all those hours in all those years is of hair, . . . hair carefully styled and sprayed, hair neatly parted, hair abundant, and every hair in place . . . but I can't remember much that came out from beneath all that hair."

The reason we know that the audience is aware of the hair is market research, the most visible thing to happen to television styles since the perfection of a magnified TelePrompTer allowed certain distinguished anchormen to read the news without wearing glasses. Audience analysts know from their computer printouts that almost every viewer can recall the name and physiognomy of his or her anchor person, but who can distinguish Randolph Mantooth ("Emergency") from Kent McCord (("Adam 12") from Bruce Fairbarn ("The Rookies")?

Marketing sex on the six o'clock news is a delicate business.
The management of WBZ-TV, the Westinghouse station in
Boston, knew it had a hot property on hand in the person of
Tom Ellis. When the station's Nielsen's began to droop a bit,
its ad agency hit upon a promotional television spot of Tom
Ellis playing handball with his co-anchorman, Tony Pepper.
The ad revealed Ellis's legs and his tattoo.

No one should be surprised that sex made its appearance on
the six o'clock news cloaked in the long white coat of scientific research. Until a few years ago television news executives, worried about audience reaction, stayed far away from
any hint of sexuality in their choice of on-air talent. There
were the occasional "weather girls" with Ipana smiles, and
developing fronts, on the local news and an occasional strik-
ing-looking woman on the networks. By and large, however,
television reversed the familiar motion picture scenario (recall
"The Big Sleep" in which Dorothy Malone is wearing glasses
and has her hair in a bun and Humphrey Bogart comes along
and she removes the glasses, loosens a few bobby pins, and
the hair tumbles down to her shoulders and *she's beautiful*!).
On the television news until very recently, they put on the
glasses and tucked in the hair.

In the 1960s newsmen were supposed to represent old,
reliable authority figures; no one in the audience of a decade
ago was supposed to think about sex when listening to Father
Chet or Uncle Walter. The orthodoxy of success was clear;
we came as communicants to the Church of the News to
listen reverently as the high priests of the networks spoke. All
over the country, authority figures such as Huntley and
Cronkite, Floyd Kalber in Chicago, and Jerry Dunphy in Los
Angeles dominated the news. Not coincidentally older, more
rural, more blue-collar—and more traditional—viewers dominated the audience for television news. Beginning a few years

ago, however, the advertisers began shifting their interests
from the worship of raw numbers to the pursuit of good
demographics. As long as the television news audience was
older and male and blue collar, the authority figures presided.
"Older men don't particularly like the 'competition' of
younger men," says Tom Battista, the vice-president of station services for CBS. Nor did older men want women—
young or old—in authority positions. With the shift in power
in the marketplace to younger women, the older anchor
types began to be cast adrift.

The new tide of the 1970s swept in anchormen like Tom
Ellis, Larry Kane, and Tom Snyder. Snyder had the right
character for contemporary television, according to Tom
Battista, "not attractive in the good looking sense but because of the 'balls' he has" [that is, "balls" as in forcefulness
and honesty]. Pat Harper, a fortyish newswoman who works
for a competing channel in New York, thinks that "a great
deal of Snyder's success is in his eyes." "He's an actor with
sixteen years of news experience," she explains, "and he
uses it all."

Market research into the tastes of the desirable viewer also
brought changes in the kind of women who appear on the
news. According to Harvey Gersin, director of research for
ABC News in New York, younger men and younger women
will accept a woman who is "professional looking" and
"feminine looking." The older audience, on the other hand,
doesn't find a good-looking twenty-seven- or twenty-eight-
year-old woman credible. Says Pat Harper: "Beautiful females aren't supposed to be able to think."

Because older men and women are still watching the news
in significant numbers along with younger housewives
(younger working men and women tend not to be home
when the early evening news is on), there is a certain amount

of confusion of purpose in the minds of the television programmers. The goal is to please as many viewers as possible without offending anyone. One compromise is to try to keep both the older and the newer audiences happy by teaming a younger woman with an older man. No one expects the reverse: a young man with an older woman. "You just won't see Barbara Walters on the air when she gets as old as Cronkite or Chancellor," Pat Harper says. The general public won't be ready for that fantasy for perhaps a decade.

Another programming technique is to offer contrasting female styles on the air. In New York WABC for a time employed reporters Rose Ann Scamardella, a "nice Italian girl, married," and Kristi Witker, a former political worker for McGovern and a sophisticate (she wrote *How to Lose Everything in Politics Except Massachusetts*). John Mariani, a writer who went out with Scamardella on assignment, reports that the technicians tried to pinch Witker's rear but they patted Scamardella's cheek. In Washington, WTOP-TV, the Post-Newsweek station, has two highly competent and attractive black anchorwomen. J. C. Hayward is dark, warm, and southern; she has soul. The other, Maureen Bunyan, is light, cool, and midwestern; she has a master's from Harvard. Viewers have their choice of different fantasies. (Jeannette Smyth of the *Washington Post* wrote that Bunyan seems to regard "the television camera as a kind of roguish but resistible seducer.") Network news executives have tried to hire both women.

Achieving the perfect on-air chemistry is still a highly experimental art. The CBS Morning News thought it could cast reporter Sally Quinn as both a competent newswoman and the blonde sex bombshell a few seasons ago. Quinn got a big preshow publicity build-up but no preshow professional coaching. She developed acne and a cold right before air time; the audience found her neither very blonde, nor very sexy, nor very explosive. According to Quinn's own account, one CBS executive chided another executive who brought her into the network: "You promised us Deep Throat and we got Sore Throat."

When CBS tried to make Quinn a star, at least it recruited a newspaper editor with talent and experience. Many television news people resent the charges, made by television's critics, that they lack news experience. The real criticism is more damning. The drive, sustained by market research, to present contemporary and believable figures demands that otherwise competent newsmen and women become performers in a kind of simulated sex show. Bill Bonds once complained to a critic that "you have to forget all the writing, reporting, and editing talents that got you to the top when you get to the top. Instead, wink, smile, toss your curls, show the teeth."[3]

Today's received wisdom is tomorrow's quaint anachronism. The new era of sexy anchor people was a false dawn. By mid-1977, Ellis and Bonds were gone from ABC, Tom Snyder was off the news and back in Los Angeles. Barbara Walters did less and less studio news reading and more and more street reporting (and her program improved). And Walter Cronkite, like the Mississippi River, just kept rolling along, buoyed by his professionalism and CBS's hard news image.

TABLOID TELEVISION— AND AFTER

CHAPTER 9

The constant, feverish search for the right formula for television news often leads to the reinvention of television's past mistakes, or worse—the reinvention of the past mistakes of others.[1] There was a period, for example, when local television stations, though never the three national networks, experimented with "tabloid television," the video version of the mass newspapers of the 1920-1960 period like the *New York Mirror* and *New York Daily News.* On television the tabloid style emphasized action film and short items (what the trade calls *tonnage*).

When the definitive history of television is written, it will note that Ted Kavanau, a veteran New York news director, was the father of tabloid television. As practiced by Kavanau on channels 5 (WNEW), 11 (WPIX), and 7 (WABC), tabloid television was heavy on fires, crimes, human interest, and "pocketbook" (consumer) stories. Kavanau also gave the world the right-wing commentator Martin Abend, the scourge of liberalthink. The formula was an overnight success when Kavanau and his boss, John Corporon, first tried it on receptive New Yorkers in 1968, with channel 5's "Ten O'Clock News." Back then, at ABC, CBS, and NBC the news people were striving for the respectability of print journalism. Kavanau and Corporon went the other way and avoided head-to-head competition with the network stations by putting their news on at 10 P.M. in an attempt to win over working people who couldn't or didn't want to stay up until 11 P.M. for the late news.

Tabloid television worked so well that channel 5 achieved a nightly audience of over one million and profits of $3 million or $4 million a year. But in the summer of 1975, Kavanau resigned after a shouting match with channel 5 management over a particularly harsh Dr. Abend commentary on black immigration to New York. Kavanau was quickly hired again by Corporon, who had taken over as vice-president of channel 11. Kavanau created another scourge-of-the-liberals, Bob Grant, a radio disc jockey with strong conservative views. Also, perhaps for the first time in any city with a population of over 15,000, Kavanau fielded a sixteen-year-old street reporter—a Montclair, New Jersey, high school student named John Miller, who came in after school and on weekends and pushed his WPIX mike into the faces of newsmakers alongside the other stars of the media.

During his tenure at channel 11, Kavanau was reading some materials put out by the "antismut" forces involved in a West Virginia textbook fight. He found a "New York angle" to the story. One of the books, a guide to sex for seventh- and eighth-grade girls, was written by Wardell Pomeroy, a New York resident and a former associate of Dr. Alfred Kinsey. The Pomeroy book had been reviewed and recommended by *The School and Library Journal*, which, Kavanau found, was published in New York. Going through the Pomeroy guide himself, Kavanau marked passages on "heavy petting" and oral-genital contact; he had his anchorman, Joe Harper, read the passages over the air. "If 10- and 11-year-old girls have to read this stuff in school," Kavanau said, "why can't we read it over the air and let parents know what goes on in these textbooks?" Kavanau didn't stay long at channel 11; like a Johnny Appleseed, he moved on with his fertile ideas in 1976 to ABC and, soon after, to an Oakland, California, station.[2]

While some news directors careened down the snappy road of tabloid television, others have headed in opposite directions. Channel 5, under the leadership of its general manager, Lawrence Fraiberg, kept some of the better ingredients of the Kavanau period (including the gadfly Dr. Abend) and added some intelligent news people such as the arts critic, Stewart Klein. Channel 5 reporters, like Gabe Pressman and Steve Bauman, can be aggressive; in the typical Steve Bauman interview, when an interview victim is down on the ground, Bauman stands on his throat and asks why he doesn't speak up more. But, as Fraiberg said, "They aren't beautiful people in blazers. They're sweaty and they're real. We want to reflect the city—to be New York."

Chicago's NBC station, WMAQ, ruled its market in the 1960s when the Huntley-Brinkley news show at NBC was the national leader. For most of the 1970s, the station fell in ratings and esteem; then instead of the usual tabloid remedies for poor circulation—better pace, more items, fresh on-camera personalities—NBC decided to make the news itself the star of its broadcast schedule. What happened did not surprise those of us who are doubters of the conventional news wisdom. In a medium where style is supposed to be more important than substance and where people are supposed to prefer any kind of entertainment to information, the news became a ratings success.

Long-form news programs—programs that run 90 to 120 minutes each night—are now well established in Chicago and a half-dozen other cities. Preemptions for news and instant specials made possible with new electronic cameras have also achieved high ratings. News for news' sake has worked so well that it is possible to see the promise—some might call it threat—of something like all-news television developing in the next few years.

Long-form news was first tried out in New York City by the NBC station.[3] It received its biggest test at NBC's channel 5 in Chicago. Channel 5 now offers ninety minutes of news beginning at 4:30 P.M., and station management also pre-empts non-news programming for various stories. When Chicago Mayor Richard J. Daley died of a heart attack in December 1976, NBC went on the air at 4:18 P.M., cancelled all its commercials, and presented nothing but the Daley story through the entire newscast. A few months later when an elevated train went off the tracks on a major intersection, killing eleven passengers, NBC covered the story for almost two hours. The NBC network news, with John Chancellor, was preempted entirely, and so was the next half-hour entertainment show. After a riot in a Hispanic neighborhood, NBC also expanded its coverage. When Chicago shivered through the cold wave in the winter of 1976-77, the NBC station did a late-night news special. In each case the preemptions paid off in high ratings; the weather special attracted almost half the audience watching television (and an audience more than twice the size that normally tunes in for Johnny Carson's "Tonight Show").

This aggressive news judgment also paid off in the more insubstantial, but real, quality known as "image"; while NBC pieced together its moving obituary of Daley, other stations were doing news as usual (one weather reader was heard intoning, "In a day of chilling news, the weather forecast is for chill weather"). People noticed, including the critics.

"Major news breaks take precedence over anything else," explained Lee Hanna, the general manager of the NBC station in Chicago. Not every news day can bring the death of a Richard J. Daley or a train accident. One day a major news break at NBC in Chicago turned out to be a robbery in progress at a currency exchange in the city's black ghetto. The police surrounded the store, and the robbers asked that Russ Ewing, a black NBC reporter, serve as a negotiator to free hostages that had been taken. NBC wired Ewing for sound and carried his parley with the robbers live on television for two hours. It was good television—ratings shot up—but rather shaky law enforcement. "Chicago journalists live on the balls of their feet," Hanna said by way of parrying any questions about whether reporters ought to play such roles. "In this city, 'The Front Page' really lives."

The men who run NBC, however, did not hit upon the idea of long-form news solely out of 1920s instincts. The local station had fallen so far behind its ABC and CBS competition that it had dragged the national news ratings down with it. On the theory that "you can't fall *out* of the basement"— that is, nothing worse could happen to the ratings—NBC management refocused on the basics, a concern for the content of the news. ("With their bad entertainment ratings, I'd emphasize the news, too," a CBS man told me.) Beginning in New York in 1974, NBC management set out to build a new kind of news program. They had a new studio built and hired new anchor people (the usual sets-and-studs formula). They also brought in more writers, researchers, and reporters and put them under the direction of Earl Ubell, a former newspaperman with a lively sense of television's possibilities. Ubell and Hanna started a system that was frankly imitative of the news magazines; there were departments called "Health," "People," "Beat the System," and "Topic A" ("our daily cover story"). The anchor person's style was subordinated to program content. "NewsCenter 4," as the program is called, gradually built its New York audience and closed the ratings gap, separating it from CBS and ABC.

In the summer of 1976, NBC sent Hanna to Chicago, where its station was in deeper trouble than even the New York station had been. Hanna brought in New York talent, including his news director, Shelley Hoffman, and a reporter, Norma Quarles. They built a replica of the New York set and called the program "NewsCenter 5." The station's two anchors, Floyd Kalber and Jane Pauley, went off to new assignments with the network's "Today" show. Hanna also won a news budget of over $10 million a year, almost double the previous budget. He increased the news staff from 100 to 200 and put more camera crews on the streets. He also hired top reporters away from the Chicago newspapers to work the various beats, just as he had done in New York. One acquisition was Ron Powers, the former *Chicago Sun-Times* television critic and a Pulitzer Prize winner; he is now "NewsCenter 5" critic-at-large.

In New York, "NewsCenter 4," had attracted attention when a bomb went off in the TWA baggage area at La Guardia Airport, and NBC was the first station to get a live television signal back from the explosion site. As New Yorkers came home that night, television sets went on—and viewers tuned to NBC. Some of them decided to stay with the station in subsequent weeks. "NewsCenter 5" has been trying to replicate that experience in Chicago. The news, particularly the disaster news, has cooperated. The 1977 Nielsen figures showed that the station was running first or second in its early evening news competition.

The successes that "NewsCenter 5" has achieved tell us something about the audience for television and about the future of the news on television. Television *can* be a mirror to see ourselves. The established programming doctrine has been that Chicago is a blue-collar town. "Advanced" ideas might work back in the effete East (and a preference for content over personality is one mark of television progress), but not in the heartland. The warm "people-relating-to-other-people" form of television news known as "happy talk" originated at ABC's Chicago station. ABC has commanded the largest share of the Chicago audience during the early and mid-1970s, with its mix of soft reporting and anchor banter about the weather reader's taste in ties. This light approach apparently satisfies the younger, blue-collar audience from day to day, but when heavy-duty news happens, "happy talk" rings hollow. On the day Mayor Daley died, ABC programmed news and entertainment as usual; it suffered in the ratings.

When "NewsCenter 5" premiered in September 1976, it was heralded by an elaborate newspaper advertising campaign. The program cut into its rivals' share of the audience at a faster rate than the original New York version. In part the city of Chicago may explain the "NewsCenter 5" success. Chicago is still boisterously competitive. Saul Bellow, the Chicagoan and Nobel laureate, once called his home town a "white knuckle" kind of city—tough, gritty, and brawling. Everything does seem bolder in Chicago: the architecture, the symphony, the graft, and the journalism (Hecht and Mac-Arthur's "The Front Page" is replayed daily in the city's newspapers). Geographically the city can be challenging; the Chicago television market, about as large in areas as the tristate New York market, has one-third the people and the traffic. Camera crews can easily move around to cover breaking stories. According to Hanna even the technicians' unions are easier to deal with than, say, in New York or Washington, where the NBC station operates at the pay scales of the network contracts.

Long-form news is not the single answer to television news' troubles. The idea, or at least a poorly executed version of it, has made no gains at all at NBC's Cleveland station or at NBC in Washington, where the dominant competition, the Post-Newsweek station, WTOP-TV, is strong in both hard and feature news.[4] In Chicago some of the department features seem to drag on, but that may be because "happy talk" has conditioned us all to thirty- and forty-five second news items. The fault with perceived "draggy" five-minute news segments may lie not in the material but in ourselves, or in those producers of the moving-right-along-now-folks style of television. Also it may be relatively easy to preempt programming for a big story because new electronic news-gathering equipment is making live broadcasting from remote sites a staple of the news. But human skills have not kept pace with technology. On-scene reporters may have very little to say about a developing news event, except to say it breathlessly. There the fault lies not in the equipment but in how management selects and trains its reporters to use the new technology.

Some critics might wonder if there is enough news to fill ninety minutes a day in Chicago and two hours a day in New York. Most news directors will say that they can find ninety minutes of news every day in Pottstown, Pennsylvania. But then what counts is the definition of news. The departmental beats of the long-form idea are actually informational journalism rather than strict "this just in" news. The same general trend is evident in hard news newspapers—the *Chicago Tribune*, the *New York Times*—as they move toward specialized feature sections. There is enough information available to sustain the news. The same can be said about the "big

story" approach to news. Not every preemption need be for
death or destruction; there are other big stories. The same
technology that brings disaster events into living rooms can
also bring in city council hearings and news conferences.
Commentaries, consumer news, going-out guides, and other
features could help fill out the schedule, as with all-news
radio.

The idea of more news, especially more television news,
upsets many communications experts. The nerve endings of
the American media consumer may already be jangling from
too much stimulation about too many subjects. Because
viewers believe that they can do very little about the natural
gas shortage, or a train crash, it may be easier to dial out on
public events completely. Some studies suggest that heavy
viewers of crime shows (Kojak, S.W.A.T.) are more para-
noidal about the amount of real-life crime than light viewers
are.[5] But the idea of informational television appears less
threatening. Material like "Beat the System" and other service
stories puts the news on the side of the audience. Information about what is actually going on may be an antidote to
fantasy. There may in fact be a positive hunger for information as opposed to news.

THE MARK OF THE Q

CHAPTER 10

Each spring, as predictably as April showers and income tax returns, a plastic-ringed report about the size of the Manhattan telephone book arrives on the desks of the network programming executives who put together the fall's new television schedules. The report is called "The Performer Popularity Poll," and it is just that—the latest rankings of some 550 performers and personalities—from Alda, Alan, to Zimbalist, Efrem Jr.—on the basis of their "likability." The 1975 report, for example, showed that John Wayne was the most likable male star in the whole entertainment cosmos and Jean Stapleton the most beloved female (though more people knew Lucille Ball than any other woman performer on or off the air). The report also showed that at the very back of the performer popularity bus sat the talented Broadway actress Jane Alexander and the no-talent host Ralph Story (all the news isn't bad).

Traditionally the cover jackets of the studies run to pastel colors. In 1974 it was lime; in 1973 it was lemon. To many television people, this constitutes deceptive packaging. "The reports are blacklists," says writer-producer David Dortort. "It is a subtler, more vicious form than the McCarthy-era blacklists. A producer tells a network he wants this writer or that actor to do such and such a program," Dortort says, "but he keeps hearing that the people or the ideas are 'unacceptable' . . . they've consulted their data, and that ends it."

Dortort served as chairman of the Caucus for Producers, Writers and Directors, a Los Angeles-based group whose officers have included Norman Lear (producer of "All in the Family" and "Maude") and James Komack ("Chico and the Man"). The caucus, organized in 1973 specifically to fight the use of such ratings research by the networks, now claims 150 members. The concerns of the caucus seem genuine enough. Gradually control over television programming has been slipping away from those who see themselves as the creative forces of the industry and toward the network schedulers, armed with audience surveys and test data. In past seasons it was possible for a few shows of originality to make it through the prime-time blending machinery. In the last few seasons, however, the increasing competition among the three networks has placed greater importance than ever before on the decisions of the schedulers. More and more they can be expected to rely on their computer printouts to tell which performers and what programs will play in Peoria and at what optimum times. The rise of the schedulers may or may not signal that research finally has replaced art—what was left of it, anyway—on television; but each new season now bears the mark of the "Q," a widely feared but little-known rating system.

Herb Altman, the man behind the Q, doesn't see himself infringing on artistic integrity or destroying quality programming. Altman, in his late forties and a City College of New York graduate, once served as vice-president of Marketing Evaluations, the company that publishes the likability reports from offices in Port Washington, New York. "If anything," says Altman, "we publish a white list. Many creative people have been helped rather than hurt in their careers by this service." Nevertheless Marketing Evaluation guards its studies closely.[1] The only material Altman would share with a visitor was the reprint of a short article about Marketing Evaluations that appeared in *TV Guide* in 1974. His secretiveness is understandable; his clients—a closely guarded list that includes ABC, NBC, Paramount, MGM, Young & Rubicam, and Doyle, Dane, Bernbach—pay several thousand dollars for the reports each year. Marketing Evaluations issues eight reports during the television season.

The May report annually ranks performer Q; the seven other periodic reports rank television-program Q (TVQ). Unlike the Nielsen or Arbitron services, which are intended to tell only how many people are watching their television sets at a given time, the Q ratings supposedly tell the audience's "awareness" of a particular program or of a particular performer plus the "degree of enthusiasm" for the program or the performer. The typical report gives two scores for a program or performer—the percentage of public familiarity (FAM score) and the percentage of likability (Q score). The Q number is found by dividing the percentage of people saying the program or performer is "one of my favorites" by the percentage familiar with the program or performer.

These scores are broken down into several demographic categories based on audience age, sex, education, family income, hours of viewing, and geographic region. At the same time, there are multiple performer and program "typologies." Television performers may be put into any one of fifteen

categories, including male/female, comedy/dramatic, hosts/
reporters/sportscasters, and star/supporting. Some 350 programs rated in the TVQ books fall into similar categories. The
performer Q ratings include people who aren't television
regulars—and even some who have been dead for some time.
The results in 1975 showed that, in the noncurrent category,
the time-worn John Wayne has the highest FAM (89) and Q
scores (55), followed by the late Spencer Tracy (79 FAM,
50Q) and the late Will Rogers (75 FAM, 46 Q). In the com-
plementary typology, "female performers not currently in
TV series," there was more ancestor worship, with Katharine
Hepburn (78 FAM, 40Q) and Myrna Loy (56 FAM, 25Q) at
the top of the list. The book on the dead, according to one Q
document, can be used "to estimate the strength of a movie
for TV showing."

The more frequent use of the reports, however, is to determine performer and program Q both absolutely and in rela-
tion to other performers and programs of the same type.
They also help compare, as one Q paper points out, "whether
a star is carrying his vehicle, or vice versa."

The Q scores, then, become an intricate game of combina-
tions all ad agencies can play. CBS can pluck a supporting
actress like Betty White, with a high Q playing in a high FAM
series ("The Mary Tyler Moore Show"), carefully nurture
her own FAM through spot guest appearances, and then
move the new star into her own show. Casting was done
entirely by the FAM yardstick for at least one of ABC's
made-for-television movies. The two featured players in the
movie had to score a combined FAM of 80 before they were
given the parts. An established Hollywood actress and a new-
comer from the East finally added up to the correct FAM.
Similarly, if a performer has a high Q, it can mean the chance
for good roles even when the casting may be inappropriate.

Black actress Cicely Tyson had such a solid Q (23) that the producers wanted her to play the white Gail Sheehy character in the ABC movie-of-the-week "Hustling."

A good part of the secret Q and FAM reports confirms commonsense expectations. For example, in 1975, Bob Hope led all "comedians, comediennes and comedy teams, televised and non-televised," with an FAM of 93 and a Q of 48; Carol Burnett was second, with a high FAM (96) but a lower Q (38). On the other hand Joey Bishop had a high FAM of 84 but a very low Q of 11; almost everyone knew him but relatively few liked him (9 percent of the sample listed Bishop in their favorite category, while 35 percent rated him fair to poor). "New York" humorists like Woody Allen, with an 81 FAM, 10 Q, and Godfrey Cambridge (60 FAM, 12 Q) also did badly; but in metropolitan areas in the East, Allen not unexpectedly went up to a 15 Q. At the bottom of the comedy list was Dick Shawn, with a 45 FAM and a 7 Q. As a group, the funny men and women had a collective 23 Q score—below "actors in current and recent dramatic series" (26 Q) and just ahead of "newscasters and reporters" (20 Q).

Among "newscasters and reporters," Walter Cronkite topped everyone in 1975 and 1976 with a 92 FAM and a 33 Q nationally. His nearest competitor was Harry Reasoner, with an 82 FAM and a 29 Q. Newscaster scores in individual markets may vary; in Kansas City, for example, Cronkite, Reasoner, Howard K. Smith, and John Chancellor all had about the same FAM scores—in the mid-80s—but Cronkite earned a 47 Q to Smith-Reasoner's 31 Q and Chancellor's 19 Q (Chancellor may take some comfort in the fact that Howard Cosell had an even lower Q).

Programs play differently for different demographic groups as well. The finish for the top network series of the 1974-1975 season (high FAM and high Q) went like this:

1. "M*A*S*H"
2. "Good Times"
3. "Happy Days"
4. "Little House on the Prairie"
5. "All in the Family"
6. "The Waltons"

Among teenagers "M*A*S*H" was third, after "The Waltons" and "Little House on the Prairie." And in the six- to
eleven-year group, "M*A*S*H" fell to thirteenth place.

Altman maintains that the performer Q and TVQ scores are
much more valuable than the Nielsens or Arbitrons because
the Qs measure audience "involvement, enthusiasm, and
attentiveness." This last quality is a matter of some importance to sponsors. The Nielsen researchers normally install
tiny meters to register the channel a set is tuned to, while
Arbitron asks families to keep diaries of their viewing habits.
The Q service uses consumer mail panel "cells." Nielsen and
Arbitron make token payments to their people. Altman does
too, in a somewhat different fashion: the cells are a "scientific cross-section" of about 1,000 people (similar to Nielsen's and Arbitron's), but the Q people are picked from a
pool of some 90,000 families around the country who have
been lined up by a company called Home Testing Institute.
HTI is Marketing Evaluations' sister company, and it is in the
product-testing business. If everyone over six years old in a
designated Q family fills out the Q questionnaires properly,
then the family gets to keep a product HTI has given it to
test (the television Q studies, it seems, ride piggyback on HTI
tests for home-appliance companies). Altman won't indicate
what the test products are except to say, "They are substantial—that's the incentive to cooperate."[2]

In his comments Altman tends to alternate between a becoming modesty about his role in programming ("we're just

one more source of information for the networks") and a salesman's conviction that the Q may hold the key to the scheduler's success. The ratings' appeal of any given program, he explains, is based on two factors. One is the program's inherent value; the other is the position in the schedule— whether the program is benefiting from or losing from the lead-in (the show preceding it on the same channel), or the lead-out, or the nature of the opposition. If the program's value is inherent, then the Nielsen and the Q may agree. But if the rating is a result of the program's position, then the Q and the other services would be in disagreement.

ABC's "Kung Fu" is the example usually cited to illustrate "the classic TVQ story." When "Kung Fu" first came on the air, it took a bad beating in the standard Nielsen ratings; but the Q scores showed that those who knew of it liked it very much. It had inherent value. In a different time slot, "Kung Fu" did much better in the Nielsen ratings. A high Q can also boost the career of a performer with only a modest FAM score. In 1974, Rich Little ranked twenty-second among comedians in FAM (68) but third in Q (37). The NBC network brass gave Little more exposure as a guest host with Johnny Carson, a move that increased his FAM score and eventually meant Little got his own program. Altman sees a predictive value in a performer's score: "With some people, you don't ever get changes; Bob Hope's FAM and Q just stay up there . . . but you can see other people growing in aware-ness and preference."

Although Altman and his staff don't want to talk about their subscribers, some programming executives were a bit more forthcoming when the News Study Group interviewed them in 1975 and 1976. Among the networks, ABC's prime-time schedulers appear to make the most use of the Q and FAM scores. "The service is primarily used as a guide," reported Marvin Mord, ABC's vice-president in charge of audience analysis and primary research. "It gives an indication where the appeal of a particular person lies, who appeals to which segment of the population. It can also uncover a program's strengths and weaknesses, which don't show up in the Nielsens." But, added Mord, "the Q scores are less valid for people like Woody Allen, Howard Cosell, or Cher—people who get volatile reactions. Researchers have to be aware of that." ABC News also uses the Q. "Basically, we look for trends," Francine Karasik, a senior analyst in the ABC News research development department, told the group. "We want to see how the same newscasters score over a period of years."

NBC has been a long-time Q client. "It's like your bank statement," said Paul Klein, who headed NBC's audience measurement for ten years. "If you don't know how to read it, it's not helpful." According to Klein the researchers "can make a lot of mistakes. Johnny Carson had a low Q rating at first, and somebody had to stand up for him." William S. Rubens, NBC's vice-president for research and corporate planning, said that the Q service is "supplemental—we conduct our own custom surveys." Researchers at NBC believe that performer Q can't always be used for prediction: "Lorne Greene was great in 'Bonanza' but couldn't hold his own in a special." On the other hand an actor in a high-Q series can make a successful shift to a similar type of program, as Michael Landon did when he graduated from son in "Bonanza" to father in "Little House on the Prairie."

CBS says it doesn't subscribe to the Q service; "I think we buy something from them," said a CBS vice-president, Jay Eliasberg. "But it is not on any continuing or regular basis." According to several advertising-agency people, however, CBS uses a testing method of its own so closely resembling the Q testing that it doesn't have to subscribe. In any event three CBS shows have been among the biggest beneficiaries of favorable Q ratings. "All in the Family," "The Waltons," and "Good Times" initially all had high Q but low Nielsens, and when they were shifted to different times, all flourished. "The Q helps new performers," reported Mel Conner of Dancer-Fitzgerald-Sample in New York. "Who ever heard of the actors in 'The Waltons' before the series started?" Advertising agencies look for just such "hot buys"—high-Q but low-cost programs that will grow.

If the networks tend to play down their use of the Q when speaking for the record, the artists may tend to exaggerate the perceived threat. According to *TV Guide*, a poll of the membership of the Directors Guild and the Producers Guild revealed that half of the respondents believed that their casting decisions had been rejected by the networks because of performer Q scores. But a skeptical group is convinced that the "creative process" in Los Angeles still follows the old ways. "Some network guy sticks his head out of his office," says one writer, "and shouts to his secretary, 'What do you think of so-and-so?' and a star is born." The position of the Caucus for Producers, Writers and Directors, according to Dave Dortort, is that "the networks have a right to determine audience tastes." But, he adds, "decisions are being made by the wrong people for the wrong reasons."

Dortort and the other caucus members say that the Q service is only the most visible part of the Research monster. "An outfit called ASI Market Research runs the Preview House over on Sunset Boulevard," Dortort says. "The seats are equipped with voting levers. They bring in some casuals from the street—who knows what kind of people are walking around Sunset during the day?—and ask them to rate a pilot or a performer with the levers. The computer digests it all.

One mechanical error or one nutty lever operator and someone's career is over."

The caucus is fighting like any other pressure group—with
position papers and press interviews. But the tide seems to be
going against the artists. Each spring the networks delay their
decisions on the new season's programs as they poke, probe,
and poll the audience, consult "the numbers" and the Q, and
jockey among themselves for schedule position. In 1975, all
the back-and-forthing among the FCC, the broadcasters, and
the Congress about the "family viewing" hours delayed
scheduling. "We used to announce the schedules in February," acknowledged NBC president Herbert Schlosser. "Now
it's April or May." The later the decision, the shorter the
time for production and the greater the toll on artists' health
and program quality.

Altman remains cool in the face of such criticism. "The
creative guy is a breed unto himself," he says. "His gut feeling is important. But we all make mistakes. Millions of dollars
are involved in programming decisions, and the networks
want to be sure." Research is regarded as a key to certainty.
Altman told me of a service called "concept testing." Long
before a writer puts pencil to paper, Marketing Evaluations
will run a story idea up the polls and see who in the cells
might salute it. One morning as we were talking, Altman took
a call from a prospective client. As I tried alternately to listen
in and to decipher the "current projects" list on the bulletin
board behind his desk, I caught some of the concept he was
trying to sell: "Looking to the bicentennial . . . we were
thinking about testing some historical figures and events. . . .
What might be the level of public interest—Q score and FAM
score—for George Washington, Thomas Jefferson, Tom Paine,
and Valley Forge?"[3]

Rich Little could play all the parts.

BROADCASTING AND THE FIRST AMENDMENT

CHAPTER 11

The Q fun and the anchor games help give television its brassy, show-business image, just as the photo opportunities and the media events give political campaigns their stagy look. But campaigns have serious purposes and so does broadcasting. The founding fathers thought about the role of journalism in a democratic society and decided to make freedom of the press the first guarantee of the Bill of Rights. But too often, both politicians and press overlook this legacy.

In the spring of 1977, a bright young Washington television reporter I know received a thirteen-page questionnaire from his news director. The questionnaire, sent out to newsrooms around the country by Columbia University, was intended to find out just how much journalists knew about the law as it affects reporters' rights and responsibilities. The young reporter, along with the other people in his newsroom, answered the multiple choice questions willingly, although somewhat nervously. "I'm sure I didn't do well," the re-

porter, a graduate of a large eastern university, acknowledged. "Very few of us in this business know the law." Yet
we know that station managements annually have television
journalists sign documents stating that they understand the
FCC provisions about the fairness doctrine and equal time.
As another broadcast journalist friend of mine said, "We
mumble something, and sign, but I could never get the two
straight in my mind."[1]

The ignorance of many reporters about the law is understandable. Until a few years ago it was possible to be a very
good journalist in the big media without knowing—or caring
—very much about constitutional law or press rights. The
First Amendment was there for our protection, we thought,
enabling us to print or to broadcast what we wanted. Of
course in those years we were a relatively passive and tranquil
lot, at least in the establishment press; we didn't push our
rights too far, especially into areas of government policy. The
only real rule we thought to remember back then was not to
call in the company lawyers because they always say "no."

But a variety of factors have combined to bring that era of
legal innocence to an end with the sharpness of a stern
judge's gavel in a quiet courtroom. The press, shaped as much
by the Watergate years as by a permissive society, now aggressively pursues old sacred cows and new definitions of
"news." For its part the public—including government officials, private individuals, citizens' lobbies, business pressure
groups, and the big corporations—has become an equally
assertive claimant of its own First Amendment rights.
Hardly a week goes by without one or another claim being
put forward:

• Eric Sevareid, the dean of television commentators, tells
the National Association of Broadcasters, the leading industry group, that the time has come for broadcasters to use

their full First Amendment freedom. "I have never understood the reasoning of those critics who seem to be saying that broadcasting will enjoy full rights under the First Amendment, when it is worthy of them," Sevareid argued. "Constitutional rights do not have to be earned; we were all born with them."

• The Radio and Television News Directors Association asks the Congress to rewrite the communications law to give broadcasters the same First Amendment rights as the printed press. The news directors want "nonregulation"—or "deregulation"—of programming content: no more governmental rules telling broadcasters what to air or when to air it.

• In Los Angeles a group of writers, producers, and directors organizes to end "artificially imposed restraints" on what artists can create for television entertainment programs (one such restraint was the "family viewing" time concept of a few seasons ago, which moved adult themes to later in the evening).

• The National Parent-Teachers Association and the American Medical Association "mount a campaign," as the news reports put it, "to curtail violence on television." They join a cause that has long been led by the indomitable Peggy Charren of Action for Children's Television. The PTA and the AMA want enforcement of industry guidelines stating what can and cannot be included in entertainment programs. ACT worries about government censorship, but it also worries about so-called cultural violence—for example, stereotypes of ethnic groups—as well as physical violence.

• The cable television industry, fighting FCC regulations that, in effect, keep major motion pictures and sporting events off cable systems, takes its case to the U.S. Court of Appeals. The group argues that its members are being deprived of their constitutional rights of free speech by over-the-air broadcasters intent on suppressing competition.

• The Texaco Company, seeking to present a series of institutional advertisements about the oil business to the presumably influential audience in the Washington, D.C., area, brings its proposed ads to WTOP-TV, the top-rated television station in the area. The initial storyboards show the various stages of oil production as a jigsaw puzzle; the copy proclaims, "It all fits together." Station management believes the ad is "too blatant" and constitutes an unacceptable form of "editorial advertising" (because the neat fit of exploration, production, and sales seemed to be a pitch for keeping the oil companies intact—an issue of public and congressional concern). The ad is revised; a second version is accepted, and the spots go on the air. Energy Action, an environmental group, protests that the new spots advocate an antidivestiture viewpoint on "a controversial issue of public importance." It files a complaint with the FCC. The commission rules the fairness doctrine requires that WTOP give time to Energy Action to present ads favoring divestiture of oil company holdings. Without agreeing with the ruling, WTOP gives free time for reply to Energy Action.[2]

The resulting clash of interests is exhilarating to those First Amendment zealots, among journalists and other citizens, who go along with the Supreme Court in the *New York Times Co.* v. *Sullivan.* The majority in that landmark 1964 case spoke out for "uninhibited, robust, wide open" debate and extended the limits of what the press could say about public officials. But it is dismaying to those who fear, along with Chief Justice Warren Burger, that the United States is fast becoming a litigious society in which everyone is taking everyone else to court. Yet First Amendment issues can't be settled solely by the lawyers. For all of us in the television audience, the way these issues are settled will go a long way toward determining the kind of television we have in this country—from the presentation of news and public affairs programming to the content of popular entertainment shows. Broadcasting law is too important to be left to the lawyers.

Sevareid and the news directors want broadcasting free of government dictate; but the Congress and the courts generally want to ensure that many viewpoints are heard on issues. For example, Texaco deserves the right to be heard on the subject of oil divestiture. Is free speech available then mostly to those who can afford to buy the time? What about the less affluent environmentalists? Do we want a free press or a fair press? The Hollywood writers and producers want artistic freedom, but the parents of PTA and ACT don't want rapes and beatings depicted on television when their children may be watching. Free press or clean press? The over-the-air television industry wants deregulation of its business; but industry lobbyists work to keep the rival interests of the cable television business tied up in government regulations. Free press or favored press? In pursuit of what they consider more "positive" programming, activist groups urge boycotts of advertisers who buy commercial time on so-called objectionable programs. During the summer of 1977, various Catholic church groups, including a publication by the archdiocese of Los Angeles, urged parishioners to boycott products advertised on ABC's new sexually explicit comedy "Soap." Free press or pressured press?

These are serious questions that are difficult to reduce to simple multiple choice answers. When Fred Friendly, the former CBS News president and now a professor at Columbia University, decided to write a book about the fairness doctrine, he called it *The Good Guys, the Bad Guys and the First Amendment.*[3] In the confused and contradictory field of broadcasting law, it is truly hard for the audience to know which side to root for. The first step to intelligent public policy is understanding. The citizen must sort through the jungle of broadcasting law, now overgrown with fifty years of regulations.

The First Amendment seems to say that the press, which includes broadcasting, should be free of government regulation and censorship. However, the fairness doctrine, a rule of the federal communications law, says that broadcasters have to allocate a "reasonable amount of time to the discussion of controversial issues" in order to afford reasonable opportunities for the expression of opposing viewpoints. (The federal government got into broadcasting in the first place in the early days of radio in order to control the timing and power of the conflicting signals being sent out by individual stations; there are only so many wave lengths for transmissions and, as in an unruly classroom, when all the students are shouting at once, no one can be heard.) The First Amendment protection of the broadcasters is placed in conflict with the public's right to hear or see discussion about controversial issues. This doctrine has led the FCC to consider the "fairness" of all kinds of public affair broadcasts; for instance, was CBS's "Hunger in America" slanted to exaggerate the hunger problem? Was CBS's "Selling of the Pentagon" deliberately distorted? Did NBC's "Pensions: The Broken Promise" give adequate time to the more positive aspects of the pension picture?

The fairness doctrine ought not be confused with the so-called equal time provision of Section 315 of the Communications Act, even though both regulations contain some of the same language and both can apply in the same situation. The fairness doctrine applies generally to the broadcasters' regulatory obligation to be fair and balanced in their news coverage and their public affairs programming. The equal time provision applies specifically to the treatment of political candidates and to the broadcasters' obligations to make time available to all candidates so that his or her opponent, who may be rich and/or the incumbent, does not monopolize the broadcast time. The equal time requirement keeps communications lawyers busy with its many exceptions; one exception made the televised Ford-Carter presidential debates possible.

Although the fairness doctrine and the equal time rule are the two most notorious examples of government limits on broadcasters' First Amendment rights, there have been other incursions, including the family viewing time concept and the prime-time access rule (limiting the amount of network programming a station may carry). Moreover the government gets into broadcasting in the most intrusive way from the start, with its power to license stations in the first place and to revoke licenses and shut down stations in the last resort.

Most of these constitutional issues could have been avoided, and a wholly different system of truly free—that is, unregulated—broadcasting could have evolved in the United States if electronic technology had developed at a different rate. The camel's nose of government regulation came into the tent of American broadcasting not because of the laws of man. Rather it was a law of physics—the limited spectrum of over-the-air radio broadcasting frequencies back in the 1920s.

In the early days of radio, signals wandered all over the spectrum: a police call in Albany might interfere with a musical interlude from Pittsburgh, and vice versa. The radio spectrum was limited, and there were many claimants for space. One federal authority was needed to assign broadcast frequencies from among competing claims . . . and so the regulation of aerial speech began.

But radio—and later, television with its limited spectrum—might have developed another way. The technology of multiplexing enables many signals to be carried along one relatively inexpensive bundle of wires. Multiplexing makes possible cable television, which in cities like New York brings in not only the established networks and independent stations but also a dozen new channels. Suppose, however, that multiplexing had been fully developed in the 1920s when radio began coming into American homes, or even in the 1940s, with the arrival of commercial television. "If the right technology had been around, there would have been no scarcity," a well-versed lawyer and head of a leading broadcasting chain once mused to me. "Then who would have needed government in broadcasting?" The Congress can say that the airways belong "to the people"—which seemed to be a good idea at the time —but cable lines go under the ground.

It is usually in the name of "the people" that government has sought to limit free speech in broadcasting. Once the Congress determined that the Federal Communications Commission could act as a kind of traffic cop to keep stations from interfering with each other, the way was open for new duties for government. Speaking for the majority of the Supreme Court in 1943, Justice Felix Frankfurter declared that the Congress had not merely restricted the commission to supervision of radio traffic. Instead, he said, "it puts upon the commission the burden of *determining the composition of that traffic*" [italics added]. Further, the Court held that it was not a denial of free speech when the government chose the few stations that would be allowed to broadcast.

Between Frankfurter in 1943 and today's Court, a series of judicial decisions have shuffled broadcasters' free speech rights backward and forward. The Red Lion case (1969) got its name from the town in Pennsylvania where radio station WGCB (the World for God, Christ, and the Bible) was located. On WGCB the Reverend Billy James Hargis attacked

journalist Fred L. Cook for being a "defender" of Alger Hiss
and a writer for a "communist-affiliated" publication. Cook
requested the right to reply to this "personal attack." The
station refused; the Supreme Court forced a reply, ruling that
because of limitations on the number of available frequencies, Congress and the FCC may impose "fiduciary" duties on
the licensee "with obligations to present those views and
voices which are representative of his community and which
would otherwise, by necessity, be barred from the air-
waves . . . It is the right of the viewers and listeners, not the
right of the broadcasters, which is paramount."

In *CBS* v. *Democratic National Committee* (1973) the
Democrats argued that they had First Amendment rights to
purchase air time from broadcasters to deliver a message on
the Vietnam War; but the Court refused to order the FCC to
approve the sale of time (interestingly the ruling left open the
question of whether the Court would have upheld the FCC if
the commission had approved the sale of "editorial advertising"). Finally in the Tornillo case (1973) the Court ruled
favorably for newspapers' First Amendment rights in a situation that appears applicable to broadcasters' rights. The state
of Florida had a right-of-reply law not unlike the FCC's fairness doctrine. Tornillo, a teachers' group official, demanded
the right to reply to editorial material in the *Miami Herald*.[4]
The paper refused, and the case made its way to the Supreme
Court, where the Burger majority held the reply unconstitutional.

The choice of material to go into a newspaper, and the decisions made as to limitations on the size and content of the
papers, and treatment of public issues and public officials—
whether fair or unfair—constitute the exercise of editorial
control and judgment. It has yet to be demonstrated how
governmental regulation of this crucial process can be exer-
cised consistent with . . . First Amendment guarantees.

Or, as Chief Justice Burger noted, "Editing is what editors are for." But if the Florida reply law was unconstitutional, then why is the fairness doctrine, as well as other limits on broadcasters' rights, still on the books? The fact is, as Eric Sevareid suggests, broadcast journalists are treated as second-class journalists; newspapers have free speech rights that television stations lack, even though a reporter from the *New York Times* and a reporter from NBC News stand toe to toe at the same news conferences, asking the same questions, reporting the same events, analyzing the same news.

This inequality exists, at least in part, because of the persistence of certain myths. In no particular order of importance, these are:

• *The show business myth. Broadcasting is, primarily, an entertainment medium and therefore only a qualified form of the press.* But surely newspapers and magazines seek to entertain as well as to educate or to sell ads.

• *The myth of television's persuasive powers. Television watching is intellectually passive—they can sell you anything. Reading requires more critical skills, and therefore little can be put over on the reader.* Pure bunkum. Viewers are not idiots; neither does all of television speak with one voice on every issue.

• *The myth that newspapers are private business enterprises but broadcast stations are public utilities.* This is known as a circular argument: if the government got out of broadcasting, then broadcasting would also be a private enterprise.

• *The myth that broadcasters operate a monopoly business while newspapers are highly competitive.* More nonsense. The latest figures show that there are some 10,000 broadcast outlets in the United States (8,240 AM and FM radio stations; 984 VHF and UHF TV stations). By contrast there are some 1,720 daily newspapers in the country. Of all localities with

daily newspapers, nine out of every ten have only one newspaper, a good definition of monopoly.
• *The myth of spectrum scarcity. Because the number of
wavelengths is limited, the government has to ration its
uses to ensure that everyone is heard.* Newspapers also have
limited resources—newsprint, delivery trucks, distribution
points—but the private market, such as it is, is allowed to
operate without government control.
• *The myth that, without government regulation, only the
monied interests would be heard.* Who's kidding whom? The
richest people in town—the bankers, insurance company
owners, real estate operators, what Kansas editor William
White called the "country club set"—own both newspapers
and broadcast stations now. It is foolish to lump together, as
Professor Jerome A. Barron of George Washington University
Law School has pointed out, "the fighting colonial printer-
editor John Peter Zenger and the modern media conglomerates."
• *The myth that government rules ensure diversity of ideas,
the airing of controversy, and the chance for both sides to be
heard on television.* If only this were true. In practice too
many broadcasters worry about broadcasting anything that
might interfere with the nice sounds of their ringing cash
registers. Towers of jello already, many station managements
try to avoid any kind of programming that might conceivably
stir any controversy. Also, where is it written that all issues
have two sides, and two sides only? There may be more than
two sides; often there may be just one side to an issue, when
it properly can be argued "on the only hand."

Very few people who have thought about it will disagree
that the present broadcasting system in the United States is
confusing and contradictory. It is a legal hybrid, a private
enterprise licensed by the state, with some of the First

Amendment protections of the Constitution, except when it comes to "controversy," political campaigns, ideological ads, and a half-dozen other exceptions. Some prefer this jerry-built structure, with the FCC or the courts mediating the clashing interests of various pressure groups—the broadcast journalists who want their full First Amendment rights; the Hollywood artists who want creative freedom; the parents and teachers who exercise their free speech, demanding an end to violence on television; Texaco clamors to be heard, and so do the environmentalists, political parties, and presidential candidates. That's one form of democracy; the "squeaky wheel" theory where the loudest or most powerful claimants get the attention.

Suppose we take as desirable a broadcast system embracing everyone's goals, no matter how conflicting: a press that is free and fair, open and ideological, private and public, creative and clean. I think it's possible. How do we get there from here?

An intelligent first step is recommended in Fred Friendly's study of the fairness doctrine. Friendly would keep the FCC, he would keep the fairness doctrine, and he would keep the private character of station ownership. The proprietors would still have to come before the commission when their broadcast licenses were up for renewal. Private citizens and public interest groups—from the antisex-and-violence forces to the prodivestiture lobby—would still be encouraged to bring their complaints about content and bias to the FCC. But instead of hearing and judging complaints individually on a case-by-case basis, the FCC's role would be limited to judging complaints in the context of the station's total performance at license renewal time. As Friendly writes,

With this approach, a licensee that broadcast a substantial number of programs on controversial issues and therefore had received a large number of complaints would not be punished (for devoting a reasonable amount of time to discussion of controversial issues); indeed, the station would be encouraged to continue to broadcast controversial programs, and at the renewal hearing it would be considered an affirmative indication that the licensee was living up to its obligations as a public trustee.

Another sensible legislative step has been proposed by Senator William Proxmire of Wisconsin. His First Amendment clarification bill of 1977 would have the Congress go on record as telling the FCC and its commissioners and staff they have no role, direct or indirect, in deciding program content. Proxmire says he hopes to stop the "raised eyebrow effect" that FCC actions or pronouncements may have on already timid broadcasters. If the government gets its censorious nose out of day-to-day broadcasting decisions, there will still be the question of possibly biased broadcasters. As Professor Barron observes, "The myth says that if the press is kept 'free,' liberty of discussion is assured. But in how few hands is left the exercise of 'freedom.' " As a check, Friendly proposes a system of voluntary public access on a regular basis, a form of "letters to the editor" column for television and radio.

We would still have the question of clashing tastes and program content: one person's "action-adventure" series may be another's poisonous pornography. ABC's sex-saturated series "Soap" was a hotly argued program during the 1977-78 season. The "Soap" writer's freedom to speak sexually clashes with the home viewer's freedom not to hear, especially if choices are limited. Here, I think, cable television technology will soon overtake the argument and settle it. Cable television is, face it, pay television. The watcher pays, monthly or hourly, for the programs delivered. But the present offerings of "free television" are also a form of pay television; all consumers, regular viewers or not, pay an invisible tax on the products advertised on television (and, to be fair, advertised in print as well). With pay cable television, large, undifferentiated audiences can be broken down into smaller, more homogeneous, more targeted demographic groups as the number of channels multiplies. There can be, as there is on the cable dial in New York City right now, channel room for Hispanic programming (and Japanese-, French-, and Italian-language programming), for religious programming, for gay programming, for soccer, for local politics, for neighborhood news, for minority tastes for all kinds. "Star Trek" and the "Lawrence Welk Show," to take just two examples, were dropped from national television because they drew audiences in the low millions—too small by network standards. On cable pay television, however, seven to eight million people, at one dollar a household, is a box office winner.

But then won't the poor, who watch a bit more television on the average than the middle and upper classes, suffer disproportionately by having to pay for their major form of entertainment? The columnist Nicholas von Hoffman, half seriously, suggests that the poor be given entertainment stamps just as they are given food stamps. If watching television is deemed a necessity by our society, then the Department of Health, Education and Welfare can see to it that people get their minimum daily requirement.

It is an outrageous idea, of course, but consider it for a moment. Is it any more outrageous than the present situation in broadcasting? Entertainment stamps aren't unconstitutional. That statement cannot be made with certainty about the antics of the FCC, the Congress, and the courts, as they go about the dubious task of regulating broadcasting in the United States.

"WE'RE NUMBER ONE!"

CHAPTER 12

A network executive, distinguished and rich in honors,
recently lay convalescent in a hospital bed, while an associate
outlined a plan to make his network the leader in news.
"Number One! Number One!" the captain of industry
shouted, jumping out of bed and waggling his index finger
over his head, "Number One!"

The arrival of Roone Arledge to run ABC News in time for
the 1977-78 season represents one network's drive toward
being first in audience size, in advertising dollars, and in that
bubble known as reputation, whose pursuit causes grown
men to act like college cheerleaders. Arledge is a remarkable
choreographer of television, the creator of prima personalities
and dazzling on-camera routines. Although news gathering
and production is a collective enterprise, if any one man can
put his mark on television news, it would be someone very
much like Arledge, at a moment in the development of television news very much like the present. The question is, What

will he do to become supreme, and is it what television—and its audience—needs right now?

Since 1960, Arledge has labored for ABC Sports (since 1968, as its president). During the 1960s, he changed the presentation of sports on television by bringing some of the reality of the games into our living rooms. Directional microphones enabled ABC to pick up the sounds of the kickoff and the clatter of the linemen as the ball was snapped. Arledge put the bite back into sports announcing by promoting Howard Cosell and backing him, through a blizzard of hate mail, until Cosell became—as Cosell himself modestly puts it—"a legend in my own time." Arledge also created "Wide World of Sports," "The American Sportsman," and the "Superstars," all of them featuring a numbing blur of made-for-television sports events for the weekend viewer. And on the Eighth Day, he made "Monday Night Football," the top-rated sports series in the whole universe. But Roone Arledge also changed the reality of sports along the way. He used the latest technology and packaging devices to make the event on television more entertaining than the actual event on the field. His major innovations—slow-motion and stop-motion videotape, instant replays and isolated-action cameras, blimp cameras and hand-held cameras, split screens and "honey" shots of good-looking females in the stands—were designed to fill television "dead time" (intrinsic but static elements of the game like huddles and time-outs). If to the contemporary mind most sports are really twenty minutes of action crammed into three hours, Arledge made sure that there would be something happening on the screen often enough to keep the audience from drifting away from the set, and from sponsors' messages.

Arledge's chief choreography, however, occurred not with the traditional American sports, which had their own audiences, but with the Olympic games. He took events that were drawn out or obscure (to American eyes) and made tens of millions watch, and care about, luge racing, Greco-Roman wrestling, and parallel bars competition. He turned a fifteen-year-old Rumanian nymph named Nadia Comaneci into an instant American celebrity by recognizing that every television series should have at least one star.

It made for good television, as well as good profits for ABC. And those who tend to think that Arledge will produce a new and exciting era of television news tend, not surprisingly, to be people within the network. "Roone's the brightest guy I have met in broadcasting," says Cosell. "He has the strength not to be traditional." Cosell adds: "I think I belong in the news." "I've been hoping for this," says Barbara Walters, who moved to ABC from NBC in 1976: "We've needed Roone and his ideas for a long time." Even Arledge's rivals have a great deal of respect for him as a competitor. In early 1976, NBC tried to hire him away from ABC before he was offered the ABC News presidency. "There were some deals that would have made me a very rich man," Arledge acknowledges. (He is already rich, with earnings approaching one-half million dollars a year.)

According to CBS News president Richard Salant, when Arledge took over at ABC News early in the summer of 1974, Salant got calls from "across town"—meaning network and corporate executives, whose normal paranoia heightens as the new season approaches. "They wanted to know, 'What are your plans?' I told them, 'I have no plans,' " says Salant. "I'm being watchful." At NBC News, President Richard Wald also had a wary attitude. "Let's see if he puts Sybil the Soothsayer on the news." (Sybil was one of the outrageous gimmicks used to increase the news ratings at the pseudonymous United Broadcasting Company in Paddy Chayevsky's motion picture, "Network.") Arledge's detractors worry that his new job means the final triumph of show business values in a news form: a case of nature imitating art.

The corporate, personal, and journalistic stakes involved in the entry of Roone Arledge into the network news competition are extremely high. Arledge was brought in to increase the audience for ABC news programs, principally the network's evening news with Harry Reasoner and Barbara Walters. The ratings battle has grown more intense because the television audience has become increasingly selective about what it watches, swinging restlessly around the dial (thus confounding the established Newtonian Law of Programming that a dial at rest remains at rest unless acted upon by a strong outside force). Most people are not loyalists in their habits toward television the way they are toward newspapers. These past two seasons, 1975-1977, for example, the audience kept CBS in the lead for daytime and early evening news time but switched by the millions to ABC for prime-time entertainment. Late at night and early in the morning NBC leads with the "Tonight" and "Today" shows. ABC's stunning entertainment success, engineered by programming wunderkind Fred Silverman, directly raised ABC television's net profits 186 percent (to $83 million) in 1976.[1] Any significant growth in the Reasoner-Walters audience—say, one rating point, or one million television households—could translate into added tens of millions of dollars in net profits a year, a considerable expense to NBC and CBS.[2]

Preferences in the evening news help influence viewers when it comes to tuning in on other news programming— conventions, election nights, special reports, the morning news, documentaries, and panel shows—all with their own commercial minutes to be sold. The evening news, as a network centerpiece, can add profit all around the schedule.

The question of which network waggles its finger and proclaims that it is number one has some direct meaning for the
viewers and the kind of television journalism they will be
getting. Two current sets of prejudices exist about broadcast
journalism. The first, held by a diminishing band of tradition-
alists from print, dismisses television news as a kind of junk
journalism. On-air news people are regarded as actors who do
no more than "rip and read" from the AP or UPI wires. Part
of this prejudice is based on competitive feelings; part is
based on a vision that looks through a rear-view mirror at a
mythic landscape. The second prejudice is held by academics,
perhaps out of competitive feelings of another kind. The
communications researchers constantly talk about the supposed enormous power of the network news programs.
Polls are produced purporting to show that "the masses"
(though never "the intellectuals") get most of their national
and international news from television. As it happens, these
studies are often sponsored by the broadcast industry.

The "expert" perception is that the three mighty pulpits of
Cronkite, Chancellor, and Reasoner-Walters regularly instruct
Americans on the surpassing issues of the day. (According to
one recent pop-eyed analysis, television encouraged the civil
rights movement of the 1960s.) Politicians sometimes share
in these misapprehensions. The Nixon White House prepared
nightly analyses of each of the network news shows; in the
last campaign Jimmy Carter's advisers had their candidate
study videotapes of the evening news. Carter's exasperated
reaction was something to the effect that "I kill myself on
eighteen-hour days and they show forty-five seconds." In fact
the highly intelligent men and women who make television
news programs have few illusions about their power. They
know those forty-five seconds don't add up to very much,
politically or journalistically; that realization is responsible

for part of the media excitement surrounding the entry of
Arledge into the news competition.

The CBS Evening news, the NBC Nightly News, and the
ABC Evening News have existed in their present form since
the networks went to thirty-minute newscasts in 1963. There
has been little difference among them. In New York, Boston,
and Washington they go on the air at the same inconvenient
time, 7 P.M., when many adults are still getting home from
work, eating dinner, or doing errands. They run about
twenty-four minutes (ABC, NBC) to twenty-five minutes
(CBS), after commercials and station identification
"bumpers" are subtracted. The form is highly constricted,
overly stylized, low in information. The line-up is predictable: Washington (Carter Day, Congress Day), Foreign
(Middle East Negotiations, Africa), Heartland (Natural Disas-
ters, Unnatural Crimes), and Warm-Hearted Feature (The
Kicker). "It's boring and dull," Arledge says. "It comes out
like links of sausage," says Wald. With the form and content
of television news increasingly predictable, the prevalent
belief among television producers has been that only the
anchor persons make any difference in viewers' choices. His
or her personality and authority was said to be the only iden-
tifying or differentiating feature of the product. This is, in
effect, a more sophisticated version of the old newspaperman's prejudice.

Like some prejudices, it has an element of truth. Walter
Cronkite became the most trusted journalist in America because he was a calm, reliable, authoritative communicator at
the scene of national traumas. He helped get the astronauts
safely back from orbit; he anchored our emotions during
assassinations and riots. Producers like to cast both Cronkite
and John Chancellor as demigods. Although both insist that
this is not their role, they nevertheless appear as God's

messengers—Paracletes. The belief in the need for differenti-
ation (buy my soap, it's rounder) led ABC News executives
to try an experiment the year before Arledge was brought in.
They hired Barbara Walters, who had served as a co-host and
skilled interviewer on the "Today" show. ABC told Walters
the evening news show would be lengthened to forty-five
minutes, which would broaden the news coverage and give
scope to her talents as an interviewer. That increase, plus the
notoriety—unsought—Walters had received as America's first
important anchorwoman, would boost ABC toward parity
with CBS and NBC.

For a variety of reasons, having to do with government
regulations and affiliate contracts, the only place ABC could
get the extra fifteen minutes was from the news programs of
its affiliates. Not too long after Walters joined ABC, the affiliates' board voted nine to one against giving the network the
time, putting their own profits from the commercial minutes
they would have to carve out of their local newscasts above
the principle of an expanded network newscast. The practical
result at ABC was that Walters was confined to reading news
from a TelePrompter, a routine she does without special
distinction. For her co-anchor, Harry Reasoner, the arrival of
Walters meant three minutes or so of nightly air time rather
than the five or six minutes he was accustomed to as solo
anchor. Moreover he was getting about $6 per spoken word
compared with Walters's $9.50. Reasoner made no secret of
his displeasure at sharing the camera with Walters and about
their salary differences (since adjusted).

Viewers saw, or thought they saw, bad feelings between the
two on the air. What Reasoner was saying about Walters, or
what Walters was thinking about Reasoner, became a bigger
story than anything they were reporting on the air. "When
people turned on the program," Arledge recalled, "it was like

coming into a married couple's home after there had been a big fight." Walters's arrival and the attendant publicity had helped the ABC program pick up about a million samplers in the first weeks of October and November after her debut. But by February 1977, the ratings were back down again. "We had lost direction, we had no point of view and no strong hand," Walters remembered. "We were treading water."

Enter Roone Arledge, pink and curly as a lifeguard, carrying an unlit Monte Cristo in his hand, safari jacket cuffs turned up to reveal the hair on his forearms, down as golden as an Olympic medal. A friendly-cool smile, aviator glasses, and a dry-look hair style complete the image of the news czar. In early 1977, as the ABC Evening News foundered, Arledge, Walters, and Fred Pierce, ABC-TV president, had a long dinner at one of the better French restaurants in New York. Arledge explained what could be done to fix the program. If he succeeds, he is a hero. If he fails, the verdict could be that ABC News can't be helped. And Arledge will still keep his job as head of ABC Sports. It is an executive's dream assignment.

Roone Arledge had spent his entire adult life working in network television. Interestingly there were no stops at local stations or at newspapers or wire services, the usual route taken to television news' top ranks (Wald, for example, worked at the old *New York Herald Tribune*; Cronkite labored long ago for UPI; Chancellor first attracted attention as a Chicago newspaper reporter; Richard Salant, an exception to this tradition, was a lawyer before taking over at CBS). A native New Yorker, Arledge graduated from Columbia in 1952—where he was, he says, a "lousy wrestler" —and went to work for the Dumont television network as a production assistant. After serving in the army, he joined

NBC in 1954 and served in various production jobs: stage manager, unit manager, director and producer of a children's program called "Hi, Mom," with Shari Lewis and her puppets.

At ABC Sports in the early 1960s, Arledge had the freedom to develop some of the techniques that won him so much praise later. ABC telecast the early American Football League games; since nobody was watching anyway, Arledge says, he "fooled around" on air and hit upon the isolated camera idea to focus in on one player's movements as the action unfolded. His first hit show, "Wide World of Sports," filled the Saturday void created by major league baseball's blackout rule (no games televised in the home market). Arledge dug up demolition derbies, boxing spectaculars, and other "media" sports events. Along the way he made his reputation as a skilled producer, as well as a difficult executive to work with. "He didn't know how to delegate," says a fellow ABC executive. Columnist Robert Lipsyte worked for Arledge briefly in 1976 as a writer when Arledge produced "Saturday Night Live" with Howard Cosell. "Saturday Night Live" was a short-lived disaster in entertainment programming that represents Arledge's first major venture outside sports. When the program foundered, Lipsyte waited for Arledge to provide the leadership for an innovative program. Instead, he said, Arledge told the staff that television was like politics—you can't be a statesman until you get elected. Lipstye took that to mean no quality until the ratings go up. Arledge has a different memory; when the ratings fell after two weeks of the show, he "panicked along with everyone else."

In his new job Arledge won't have the opportunity to fiddle around with no one watching. The critics are waiting for any sign of news tailored for ratings. His first moves, for the most part, were journalistically sound. He bought back Av

Westin, a knowledgeable producer, to run the evening news; he hired the veteran Sander Vanocur to head a Washington investigative and political reporting unit, and he signed on Cassie Mackin of NBC and Sylvia Chase of CBS. But there remained the immediate glaring blemish on ABC's face to the world: the sour union of Reasoner and Walters.

Arledge's next efforts were therefore mostly cosmetic. If the audience felt an uncomfortable chill in the presence of Walters and Reasoner, then technology can make sure that they won't be seen together. The evening news no longer uses the wide "two shot" of its anchors between program segments and commercial segments. And if the communicants in the audience persist in their belief that there is only one true anchorman in America and his name is Cronkite, then why feature any anchors at all? Rather, differentiate in the other direction, away from the single venerable voice of authority. Howard K. Smith and other ABC correspondents around the country are being built up as "subanchors" while Walters and Reasoner are being used as "on-scene reporters," casting them further adrift from their anchor duties. Walters has gone to Washington to cover the debate over federal assistance for abortion and to the Middle East to interview Arafat. Reasoner prepared a report card on Jimmy Carter and a special report on South Africa. The sought-after quality called "pace" is achieved with shorter items, snappier items, and fast "whip-arounds"—field correspondents who each add an element to the story. The sausage links are varied. The night David Berkowitz, the suspected "Son of Sam" killer, was taken into custody, the ABC Evening News devoted fully twenty minutes to the story (CBS did 8:40 and NBC 8:56).

Beneath these cosmetics of the news, however, are some enduring Arledge hallmarks. Arledge believes in "personalities," as reporters and subjects. On "Monday Night Football," he played off the "New York Jew" Cosell against the "down home cowboy" Don Meredith. Cosell wore the black hat, the nonathlete who dared to criticize a player's perform-ance, while Meredith, the ex-football quarterback, was in the white hat. When the friends of an affiliate station owner down at the country club complained about the wise guy, Arledge had the ratings to back his judgment. On "Wide World of Sports" and in the Olympics coverage, ABC didn't just show competitors like Comaneci competing; Arledge built film stories around them. The idea was to get the viewer to know the athlete personally.

ABC News is now beginning to personalize its team of correspondents. Some of these journalists are competent specialists like Dan Cordtz (economics) and Jules Bergman (science). Arledge promises more specialists. But others among his team—Geraldo Rivera springs out from the set— seem to specialize in their own celebrity. Of Rivera, Arledge says, "I sat him down and had a long talk with him about his future in the news . . . he has a rapport with the street." During the "Son of Sam" story, Arledge had Rivera do some major pieces. In jeans and tee shirt, the thirty-four-year-old reporter walked the streets near the murder scene and deliv-ered an overwrought "analysis." Among other things, Rivera referred to Berkowitz as a "fiend." A week after the Rivera broadcast, members of the ABC Washington bureau wrote a confidential letter to Arledge complaining about the "exces-sive" coverage of the story.

The new ABC news regime clearly intends to punch up stories by aggressively employing technology, by spending money, and by self-promotion. ABC chartered Lear jets to cover a supper club fire in Kentucky and dispatched camera crews to the homes of the families of a U.S. helicopter crew shot down inside North Korea in a border incident in mid-

July 1977. The network built a substudio (for its subanchors) in London just like the home studio; Arledge envisions whiparounds from London—and from Johannesburg and Moscow. If the right opportunity arises, Arledge says, he will pay certain newsmakers for the rights to the news, just as he paid for football or the Olympics. He wanted ABC to outbid David Frost for the Richard Nixon interviews and has thought about how he would have produced the show.

Aggressive news gathering has to be harnessed to experienced news judgment. ABC News interrupted regular programming no fewer than ten times with bulletins about the downed helicopter in North Korea. Later that week Arledge ordered the news staff to prepare specials on the New York City blackout as well as on the helicopter incident—and asked the network to clear prime time. The Korean story proved to be, in hindsight, a two-day wonder rather than the beginning of World War III; but a lot of people, hearing all those bulletins, must have felt some adrenalin flowing. The Korean special report was abandoned. Still, says Arledge, he had established the news presence at his own network and "tested the motivation of ABC management." The New York blackout special was aired in prime time, preempting the entertainment show "Fish."

The similarities between sports and news, of course, don't go very far. Before games, the producer arrives days in advance and plots camera positions. News doesn't start at 2:35. "The news is a big bear," says a television news director with twenty-five years experience. "How can you control it?" A broadcast group president, while expecting great things from Arledge, is still cautious: "Arledge needs someone to say no to him," he says. Though ABC researchers claimed to detect some audience response to the new ABC news, the early tremors don't count. There are three audiences that Arledge must win over.

The first audience is, obviously, the viewers. Arledge offers
up all the correct high-minded goals in his interviews—the
need for credibility in the news, the need for more investigative reporting, the belief that ratings follow excellence. Real-
istically the ABC prime-time audience is skewed toward
younger (eighteen to forty-nine) women, a demographic
group highly prized by advertisers. This group likes ABC's
brand of entertainment—hard-line action, youthful leads
(such as Starsky and Hutch), personalities over plausibility.
They are Arledge's target. "Older people tend to watch the
news more than younger people," he says, "and our first task
is to get the ones who aren't watching to watch."

The second audience is the news peer group. Executives
fret, like the rest of us, about what coworkers, friends, competitors—and, yes, the critics—are saying about them. When
Walters did a special report on Castro and Cuba, she recalls,
"Everybody in my world saw it, but it got a 20 share" (20
percent of all television sets that were on were watching
ABC). When she did an interview with the comic Bob Hope,
"nobody" she knew saw it, but it got a 36 share.

"I want peer acceptance," Arledge says. But an editor
friend of his, one of the luminaries of the newspaper business, told him, "Forget about what those bastards say about
you; follow your own instincts." Arledge knows there are
ways he can raise the ratings, but they would be wrong. He
wouldn't, he says, do the kinds of stories that the *National
Enquirer* or Rupert Murdoch favors. Arledge wouldn't put
Rona Barrett, ABC's version of Sybil, on the evening news.
Howard Cosell is another matter. Arledge used Cosell for an
evocative piece on Jackie Robinson timed to the all-star baseball game; he says he will use Cosell again whenever the casting is right. Arledge's team at work seems reasonably content.
Walters sounds convincing when she argues that all Arledge
has done really is "trim the anchor fat and make room for

more reporting." Bureau reporters remain somewhat skeptical, however, and not just of Geraldo Rivera. Shortly before Arledge took over, he summoned selected correspondents to meet at the Montauk Yacht Club on the eastern end of Long Island. One Washington correspondent admired Arledge's style—people arrived by chartered sea plane—but says that, after listening to him, "I'm not sure what he said."

The third audience, in many ways the most important, is composed of the affiliated stations of a network. The number of affiliates a network has, and the quality of their signals, directly influences ratings. For years ABC was the also-ran network, in part because it has fewer affiliate outlets around the country. As the network offered more competitive programming, more stations wanted to affiliate, trading their megaphones for ABC's message. In 1970, 123 stations broadcast the ABC evening news; in 1977, the figure is 193, compared with 208 for NBC and 199 for CBS. With ABC now as large as its rivals, the present competition centers on trading up each outlet. While the gossip columns were full of Harry-and-Barbara-and-Walter-and-John tales, the important news was happening in places like North Carolina and Kentucky. In Charlotte a resurgent ABC shuffled off a UHF station whose signal reached 10,000 households and signed on the former NBC affiliate, with an audience of 88,000 households. (NBC thought the defection was important enough to realign its top executive ranks to create one vice-president directly responsible for keeping affiliates happy.) In Louisville ABC thought it had won over the strong CBS affiliate, but the station decided to stay with CBS because of the Cronkite news—or so a CBS News executive says. The same executive also reports that at least one CBS affiliate in a top-ten market wanted to change affiliation to get ABC's prime-time schedule but was waiting to see what Arledge did. "Affiliates normally have five-year contracts with a network," another network official explains, "and loyalty lasts as long as the contract, and the amount of money it makes for you. Everyone wants to be with the leader." If the affiliate audience is won over, a significant part of the viewer audience may follow, no matter what the peer audience is saying.

This is one reason why Arledge's arrival has stirred up CBS and NBC. According to NBC's Dick Wald, "You can only take chances in this business when you are a commanding number one or a dismal number three." Since NBC News is a reasonably close second, Wald saw no need to gamble. The new NBC Nightly News format, introduced in mid-September 1977, represents a fine tuning rather than any radically new development. Wald called it a "catching up" with the best trends from around the country. More time is given to the lead section of the program, the top story of the day. The second section is "news around the world," told in a "fast-paced, quick moving style." The third is an eight- to ten-minute minidocumentary, something like the longer pieces done on local NBC news programs, such as "NewsCenter 4" in New York. The final section is a headline summary of the day and a closing feature. The new electronic cameras (minicams) are being used for more live reports from the field.[3]

CBS has the commanding lead. Though its prime-time audience plummeted in 1976, the number of Cronkite viewers increased a bit (the reverse of the ABC pattern). Salant scoffs at the idea of two people—or three or four—anchoring the evening news. "There's no earthly reason for it," he says, "If one person can't handle six minutes of reading, then that person doesn't belong on the air." As the news leader, Salant takes an appropriately conservative attitude toward the minicam technology. He rejects the idea of "going live for the sake of going live. . . . I want my reporters to have time to think, and my editors time to edit . . . I don't want the new technology to wag my dog." CBS has stopped "supering" (superimposing electronically) the words *via satellite* on its reports, because "viewers don't give a damn how the picture get there, as long as it's there."

Nevertheless the Cronkite news visibly changed in the 1977-78 season. Eric Sevareid, whose lapidary commentaries appeared four times a week on the evening news, retired. (John Chancellor discussed Sevareid's job briefly with CBS before signing his new NBC contract.) Charles Kuralt's "On the Road" now appears on the evening news. Actually this is a reversion rather than a response, since Kuralt appeared on Cronkite before going over to CBS's ill-starred "Who's Who." By coincidence or not, the homey Americana of Kuralt tends to balance the people-oriented features that Arledge and his company are talking about.

By concentrating on the personalities and excitement of the battle for the evening news audiences, critics and students of television are acting somewhat star-struck themselves, and they lose sight of the bigger picture of television. There may be a morphology of news working itself out behind all the set changes and surface transformations. It is something like this.

In the 1950s, there was no television news at all. The after-glow of television's alleged "golden age" hazes over the reality that 1950s television had appropriated the techniques of the motion picture documentary for its celebrated reports and the techniques of the movie theater newsreel for its fif-teen-minute newscasts (John Cameron Swayze "hop-scotch-ing the world for headlines"). In the 1960s and early 1970s, network television news had a different model: the "objec-tive" presentation of information and events in the style of print journalism. The print model was one reason why so many television journalists of that era came from newspapers.

Over the past few years, the model has shifted from newspapers toward news magazines. This is why television producers talk of their life-style features and their "back of the
book" departments. While television news is in transition
now, the network news of the late 1970s and early 1980s will
probably have television itself for a model. NBC and CBS
(the former more than the latter) will probably look like the
local news productions of good stations like WNBC-TV in
New York and the Washington Post's WTOP-TV in Washington. In the late 1980s and 1990s—to finish this leap of imagination—the model for television may be 1970s-style radio, as
cable television systems, direct satellite broadcasts, and video
disks inevitably fragment the mass audience into twenty or
thirty or forty special interest audiences, each with a channel
of its own.

Roone Arledge and ABC News—now the dreadful third in
the news competition—have the least to lose in this current
transitional stage. ABC will become less print oriented and
more videolike, and at a faster pace than the others.
Arledge, Walters, and their colleagues are a television-bred
generation and, on the whole, younger than their counterparts at CBS and NBC. (Cosell says, "I'm part of the television generation, too. . . . I'm . . . 58 . . . going on . . .
30. . . . Don't . . . you . . . forget.") ABC may be in a better
position to produce a more visual, more technologically dazzling, more exciting news service with, in Fred Pierce's phrase,
a "new frame of reference."

The "new frame of reference" won't be a rip-and-read
production, as the television haters persist in believing. It
probably won't have a Paraclete anchoring the news (though
Arledge believes in the star system and might push forward
some young correspondent in the right circumstances). It
certainly won't be a towering platform for ideology, as the

communications experts fear and as Paddy Chayevsky fanta-
sized. Nature does sometimes imitate art, but the critics who
looked for Arledge in "Network" had the wrong script.
Arledge is better cast as the Frank Mallory character in the
Dan Jenkins-Edwin Shrake novel *Limo*: the energetic Captain
Success, who is sufficiently intelligent to prepare a speech
denouncing television's money-grubbing streak and sufficiently ambitious not to deliver it.

A "Captain Success" news operation might very well look
like ABC Sports productions in some ways. The news
might be recast into more entertaining packages, and at no
harm to the news. The celebrification of the news—personalities interviewing personalities—might contribute, somehow, to
public understanding. Less traditional news doesn't necessarily mean less thoughtful news. More lively analysis and
dramatic curbside interpretation may build up a strong, informed public opinion on complex issues rather than a sense
of despair and the reinforcement of prejudices. Perhaps ABC
can pursue its goal of being the top-rated network and still
deliver that "steady supply of trustworthy and relevant
news" that Walter Lippmann thought was necessary to a
democracy. I suspect, however, that the real hero of television news will be the leader who takes the risks of not only
lengthening the network evening news program, but also
moving it to prime time. No innovations in technology or
pacing can make up for the opportunities opened up by those
extra minutes at a time more congenial to thoroughness and
thoughtfulness.

SUSPENDED SENTENCES

PART III

THE CELEBRIFICATION OF THE NEWS

CHAPTER 13

More than a decade ago, the historian Daniel Boorstin worried that Americans had gone from the celebration of heroes —people who had actually achieved something—to the celebration of celebrities—people well known simply for being well known. It was a keen insight, but it has had hardly any slowing effect on the ways of the press. We seem to celebrate celebrity even more these days, for the flimsiest of reasons and for ever shorter spans of attention. Margaux Hemingway, Ernest's granddaughter, streaks on the scene; she is this year's Lauren Hutton, who was last year's Jean Shrimpton. Did you miss Margaux? Wait a microsecond; here's her sister Muffin—for a flash. Cher's navel simultaneously dimples a thousand newsstands across the country and then vanishes like the first crocuses of spring.

Not so long ago, the following appeared in the *New York Daily News*'s "Gossip Column":

Word is that California bachelor Governor Jerry Brown has a girl friend tucked away someplace. Reporters think that the reason Brown is reluctant to give many interviews is that he doesn't want to be grilled about his private life. In fact, his press secretary, in responding to requests for interviews, warns writers that Brown will not discuss personal matters. Listen, Governor, it's spring and we're all for a little romance.

This item ought to tell us that something has been happening to our heroes, or at least to those men and women of genuine power or accomplishment who are in the public eye: they get the same trivializing celebrity treatment. What kind of star is Governor Brown? the gossip column seems to ask. Why hasn't he been entertaining us as much as he should? The secretary of state or the head of the Federal Reserve Board—as much as the model of the moment—now exists principally as personalities. Almost every media consumer could name the "girls" from Henry Kissinger's salad days, but his views on nuclear-weapons policy, first enunciated in the 1950s, still are not widely appreciated.

There is an apparently insatiable desire for "items" about the "beautiful people" and public figures alike. According to the winter 1977 issue of *The Journal of Communication*, an analysis of all syndicated gossip columns appearing in the three major Philadelphia dailies during the 1950s, 1960s, and 1970s shows that politicians are five times more likely to be covered today than they were twenty years ago (entertainers still dominate the columns, accounting for half of all 1975 items).[1] Serving up politicians or entertainers, the gossip machinery of the press works around the clock to feed the appetite, often suspending the normal rules of journalism. In a sense, that is what the word *gossip* implies: the story doesn't have to be true. The law of libel, from *Sullivan* v. *New York Times* on, implies as much; the press can say just about anything it wants about public persons as long as what it says isn't recklessly untrue or malicious. It can be a half-truth—a factoid, to use Norman Mailer's term. A certain plausibility is all that is necessary as long as an item is readable. No news retailer is above churning out these items; a speculative story that Aristotle Onassis had cut his widow out of her inheritance earned page-one space in the *New York Times* not too long ago.

Such a situation ought to be impossible. In the old Hobbesian days, a glimpse of royalty served to lift us commoners out of our nasty, brutish, and short lives. With the growing affluence and sophistication of the media's audience, however, the need for vicarious living should have subsided a bit. But in a perverse, populist way, the national mood after the Watergate scandals may have helped to stimulate a taste for revealing items. As a young magazine editor explained to me recently, "The people have a right to know what their leaders are doing *all* the time; that's what Watergate was about." She added, "We want to see them squirming a bit too." The right to know now has a corollary: the right to entertainment at the expense of public figures. These figures, it seems, exist for both the gossip press and its audience to use. Around newsrooms, you hear a blunt phrase for this expropriation: *star-fucking.*

In our post industrial society, then, we no longer need public figures to revere or to emulate. Instead they are there, as temporarily interesting equals, to entertain us, preferably by doing something sensational. It is the boredom of leisure times, rather than the boredom of the assembly line or the farm, that must be assuaged.

Newspapers, magazines, television, and books in their various ways have all been responding to—and helping to create —this new celebration of celebrity. Walter Winchell, Hedda Hopper, and Ed Sullivan are dead and the old-style Broadway column may be buried with them, but the journalistic gossip form still lives. Now it has moved from Broadway and Holly-wood to the real centers of power. *New York* magazine has its "Intelligencer" page; the *New York Times* offers "Notes on People." *Women's Wear Daily*'s "Eye" gossip column proved so popular that *WWD* now runs "Eye II." And the *Washington Star* has its "Ear" column to prattle on the powerful of Georgetown: Kissinger-and-tell journalism.[2]

At least one new magazine, *People*, has been created to meet the growing hunger in the larger cities and suburbs for "more sophisticated" gossip in the form of personality stor-ies. *People* is the first successful national weekly magazine started since 1954. Its real importance lies in what it tells us about ourselves. Time Inc., its parent, has a magazine-devel-opment group that for the past several years has been doing meticulous research into possible new ventures. The group has weighed, among other projects, magazines about tele-vision, about photography, and about health; *Money* magazine was its first child. The idea for *People*, it is said, came from Marion Heiskell, the wife of the chairman of the board of Time Inc. According to one Time Inc. editor, Mrs. Heiskell reasoned that most people are interested in other people. After *Money* and before *Health* comes people. In just one year, *People*'s circulation had reached some 1.25 million. By the end of its second year of existence, its success was caus-ing envy at other media conglomerates, and in early 1977 the New York Times Company started a *People* look-alike called *Us*.

People magazine is a weekly celebration of the new enter-tainers of our postindustrial society. It is a magazine for people who don't want to read too much about the stars; *People* readers don't get "into" the Jackie story the way the less urbane readers in the heartland do. In the cities there is less time for true celebrity worship. *People* makes fewer

demands; it can be dealt with like television. *People* subjects
are "profiled" in a few hundred words. Some of *People*'s
people, as the writer Nora Ephron recently pointed out, can
be handled in a caption—"Here the name Telly Savalas
springs instantly to mind." If Boorstin was concerned that
the media celebrity had replaced the genuine American hero,
then what would he make of the rise of the four-hundred-
word "personality" in *People*? The magazine has surpassed
Andy Warhol's prediction that "in the future, everyone
would be famous for fifteen minutes." The personalities of
People live only until the page is turned.

People works. It has a low overhead and a small, dedicated
staff that labors long hours; it uses only black-and-white
photography and is sold chiefly at newsstands. With its growing circulation, it is the magazine success of the 1970s.
The urban, educated, high-income consumer—the "upscale"
audience sought by advertisers—wouldn't be caught dead
with the *National Enquirer* or *Modern Screen* magazine.
People is respectable enough to buy or scan. It is the perfect
reading material for the dentist's or doctor's waiting room—
not too long and not too tacky. In the *National Star* we read
the detailed predictions of "top psychics" who say Jackie
will soon remarry; in *People* we drop in on Betty Friedan
teaching at Queens College.

When *Commonweal* magazine asked me to review two
newly published books about CBS, I had an opportunity to learn how the gossip form works. Robert Metz, a
New York Times reporter, wrote a long and intermittently
interesting history of CBS dating back to the decision of a
wealthy young Philadelphian named William S. Paley to in-
vest some of his family's cigar-business money in a limping
venture called radio broadcasting (*CBS: Reflections in a
Bloodshot Eye*). Sally Quinn, a *Washington Post* feature

writer, had a much more limited story to tell: her four months as an anchorwoman on the CBS Morning News in the fall and winter of 1973 (*We're Going to Make You a Star*). Metz is thorough, giving names, dates, facts, and anecdotes about every phase of CBS's corporate, news, and entertainment operations. He has interviewed scores of people and read every word written on the subject. It is a workmanlike job. Quinn, on the other hand, did no research. She gives a personal account of her wretched television career. CBS hired her to "knock off" NBC's Barbara Walters and the "Today" show in the Holy Nielsen ratings. But she has no broadcast experience and Vassar lockjaw speech. Nobody tells her what to wear, how to do her hair, how to write or speak for television, or even where to look when the camera is on (she claims not to have known that the red light means the camera is working). Worse, she was promoted as a "sex bomb." The first day one thing was clear: she was a disaster on camera.

Quinn comes through in her own pages as egotistical. Yet we devour every word of it. And ultimately we learn more about CBS from Quinn's account than from Metz's or any number of other "objective" narratives. One reason is that Quinn is not working objectively. She is in another literary tradition. She succeeds in giving us the feel of the real CBS because she was there—and simply and uninhibitedly put down everything that happened. We grow to like her and take her side. No amount of research, even by a professional like Metz, can recreate the sensation of being inside the CBS corporate whale. And so we lap up Quinn's story because we are made to realize "that's the way it is"—and not the way Walter Cronkite might tell it—behind scenes at CBS. Quinn offers not large insights about the media but "zingy" little items. In an earlier day of the Winchells and Hoppers, this was known as "gents' room journalism" (with a small research grant, someone might be able to trace the form back to Addison and Steele). Quinn is as good as any at the form.

The success of the gossip form, in *People* and elsewhere, has not gone unnoticed at the established magazines. Each week the reader can sense *Time* and *Newsweek* straining their traditional forms in order to pack more "personalities" into the pages. They want to become "easy readers" too. The irony is that *People* is the logical extension of the weekly news magazine idea into the personality-hungry 1970s. *Time* and *Newsweek*, since their inceptions, have covered both heroes and celebrities, political leaders and pop-culture figures, as well as serious artists. It is all part of the passing parade, which is, as news-magazine editors will tell you, "the franchise"—the weekly summary of the world's events for the hurried.

In the normal run of events, the newsweekly cultural departments produce a cover story every two months or so. After a series of gloom or doom covers, *Time* and *Newsweek* managing editors are seized by a powerful editorial urge: "Let's get off the reader's back." Successive stories on energy, the economy, and the Middle East are enough to bring on this feeling. This means it is time to run a features cover. The back of the book is regarded as visual relief for readers bowed over with the cares of the world. It is not art for art's sake (as it should be) but art for the reader's sake. One week after "The Agony of Cambodia" on the cover of *Newsweek* and "The American Jews and Israel" on *Time*'s cover, actress Liv Ullmann appeared on the front of *Newsweek* and singer Cher on *Time*. It could easily have happened the other way around; a few cycles ago on the celebrity circuit, *Time* had Ullmann on its cover and *Newsweek* had Shirley MacLaine. *Time*'s timing was the appearance of Ullmann in the American-made film "Lost Horizon"; *News-*

week's was her New York opening in Ibsen's *A Doll's House*. Although the "news peg" is not really required in the 1970s-style *People* magazine, the traditional news magazines still find it necessary to justify their personality stories. Usually the reason, found no more than two or three paragraphs down in the story, explains to the busy reader why nonpublic affairs material is must reading that week and not some other week. Thus *Newsweek*: "[Ullmann is] at the moment possibly the most charismatic actress in the world." And *Time*: "Cher proves that at least one American dream lives; she gives evidence that show business can still reach out among the adolescent millions and—with a little luck and a lot of hype—transform a mildly talented woman into a hot, multi-million dollar property." Few editors are above this sort of thing (including the editors of the straight, serious *Columbia Journalism Review*; when I wrote about the rise of the personality story for them, they thought it offered a rare opportunity to put Liv Ullmann on the cover of their magazine).

The daily newspapers are also deeply in the gossip business. Many newspapers, to their credit, have cut back drastically on the Hedda-from-Hollywood column fixtures, just as many newspapers have finally abandoned the old "women's pages" rubric and the columns of "club" news. Sections are now called "Family" or "Living" or "Tempo" or "Style" or "Accent." These changes have visibly raised the quality of newspapers across the country, most notably in New York, Washington, Chicago, Boston, and Los Angeles. But no one should be fooled by the new graphics and titles. Newspaper gossip has been repackaged in a form somewhere between the *National Star* and *People*. Perhaps the two most striking examples of the new newspaper pages are the *Washington Post*'s "Style" section and the *Washington Star*'s "Portfolio." Both sections are well read, according to the readership surveys conducted by the papers. Both sections are well written; one *Post* editor told me that the "Style" section was "the only place in our paper with any bright passages." Both sections go in heavily for personality stories, and both sometimes look alike; the *Star* and the *Post* had almost identical oversize close-up photos of Cybill Shepherd in their feature pages when she was in Washington promoting a new motion picture.

Television has its own versions of the newspaper "Style" sections and the magazine personality pieces. Shows such as NBC's "Today," ABC's "Good Morning America," and "Dinah!" are like newspaper feature pages or newsmagazine cultural departments; they are the television "back of the book" to the "serious" front of the book of the Cronkite or Chancellor or Walters-Reasoner evening news.[3] These shows are more voracious consumers of star personalities than the newspapers. Even local shows in major markets have producers who are nothing more than full-time bookers of celebrity talent. Dianne Ellis, a former associate producer of "Dinah!," recalls a hard-and-fast rule: "With five shows a week, in four of them we must have a name." Some personalities became known mostly for being on the talk shows (Orson Bean and Totie Fields, for example). Others are names who are usually interested in appearing to plug something; everyone scratches each other's back. To break up the appearance of too-obvious promotion for the guest's new film, book, or record album, the producers of "Dinah!" hit upon an "on-your-feet-demo" format. Guests would be asked to demonstrate a hobby or a cooking skill—and then segue into the "sit-down talk segment," where the talent could work in the plug.

Ellis coordinated the talent for "Take It from Here," a mid-morning program on WRC in Washington, D.C., where everyone's gossip antennas continually quiver and the personality form has taken over the mid-morning television dial. In Washington programs like WJLA's "AM Washington," WTOP's "Morning Break," and WTTG's "Panorama"—as well as the dozens of other television talk-and-hawk shows across the country—receive almost no attention from communications scholars or social critics. But they should be seen for what they are: electronic reflections of *People* magazine, which in turn is modeled on a television style of brevity. Judith Martin of the *Washington Post*, a sharp-eyed "Style" writer who used to be known as a "society reporter," has developed an intriguing theory to explain why so many people like to listen to the small talk of star personalities. She believes that the talk shows are substitutes for traditional social discourse. If you invite people into your home, you have to make real conversation with them, which requires real thought. But if you invite television company, you don't need to cook, keep your shoes on, or make "even one civil comment." So every day and night, Martin says, "for hours and hours, a small group of actors and their friends relax on sofas placed in front of cameras and have mild, polite, social conversations." Sammy Davis, Jr., tells Dinah Shore that she is looking just great—that, in fact, she is the greatest! Dinah Shore smiles and says, Sammy *you* are the greatest. Remember the time you were on my show and we had such fun? And Sammy Davis says, Yes, that's why I'm so happy to have you here on my show. And then they and the others talk shop talk. The viewer can "have" these people without moving from bed or board. It is the mass media's realization of the comment made by one of the young homosexuals in Mart Crowley's play *The Boys in the Band*: "One nice thing about masturbation is that you don't have to dress for it."

Most serious journalists have paid little professional attention to the celebrity explosion. The gossip style is generally perceived as harmless stuff. "It's almost not worth getting upset about," Nora Ephron observed, writing about the success of *People* magazine. Anything that can be disposed of in less than fifteen minutes should perhaps be treated like Kleenex. But the cult of personalities has steadily infiltrated the "front of the book" in magazines, newspapers, and television.

This kind of empty entertainment uses not only show-business types (who gladly seek it out as perhaps their only way to make a living by building a career of ephemeral media appearances). The voracious appetite for personalities, the growing demand for *People*'s kind of respectable middle-class gossip, has made the celebrity circuit lucrative and tempting for artists, writers, musicians, and politicians, who also gladly, naively, or fearfully allow themselves to be offered up as sacrifices to the people's right to a constant diet of undemanding entertainment. When artists, scientists, or politicians are turned for a brief time into celebrities, they are presented to the public emptied of complexity, inevitably trivialized by the show-business imperatives of the thousand-word feature article, the ten-minute talk show appearance. Like the candidates in the primary races, they are labeled. Erica Jong? Sexy poet and novelist. Leonard Bernstein? Sexy conductor, knows Jackie Onassis. Henry Kissinger? Used to date a lot, now married to Nancy, who is very tall.[4] What about literature, music, foreign policy? To use the media's own deadly phrase, they are turn-offs, boring. They make people switch channels, read the sports section, read *People*. So: *Get off the reader's back.*

But when editors who pride themselves on their seriousness are confronted with one of these accomplished celebrities—as opposed to Boorstin's celebrity, who is well known only for being well known—they tend to be wary of serious content. *Newsweek* posed Erica Jong for a cover picture, and *Time* had a Matina Horner story in preparation for almost a year. Jong was a poet before she became a celebrity. She may not be the best woman poet writing today, but she is fast becoming famous as the best looking. Horner also had achieved professional status before she became president of Radcliffe College and therefore a celebrity. But while the Ullmann and Cher stories zipped right through the newsweekly editorial blenders, the Jong and Horner stories got stuck week after week. Jong eventually appeared inside the magazine the week the Saigon regime collapsed. The personality profile format can't always carry the serious ideas of feminism or women's education. For the traditional news magazine, it is often easier to handle personalities in the bite-size format of the "Newsmakers" and "People" sections of the book—which are the best-read pages in any case.

The newest accomplished people to be transformed into celebrities are journalists themselves. Mike and Lorraine Wallace and Tom and Pam Wicker have been couples featured in *People.* The April 1975 cover of *The Washingtonian* magazine featured a story, "The New Society" ("Power and Media Are In/Money and Manners Are Out"). The cover was a photograph of a blonde reporter coyly identified as Sally Starr of the *Washington Post.* For someone from out of town who doesn't immediately get the reference, the story makes it all clear: the media have become our newest aristocracy; they are more important than the people they cover. One day Gerald Ford or Jimmy Carter will show up at the Sans Souci and get turned away at the door; the media stars—from Buchwald to Quinn to Woodstein—have all the reserved tables.

The idea of a media aristocracy looks less ridiculous every day. While *The Washingtonian* article was still on the news-

stands, the *Post* "Style" section devoted a long, multiple
by-line article to the making of the film *All the President's
Men*—based on the bestseller written by *Post* reporters Bob
Woodward and Carl Bernstein—and to the production's effect
on the reporters and their editors and associates. The resulting corridor-of-mirrors effect—editors editing copy about
themselves—was so mind-bending that Alexander Cockburn
was led to complain in the *Village Voice:*

> The piece ends up on some sort of mad further shore of jour-
> nalism where [*Post* executive editor Benjamin C.] Bradlee
> portentously allows himself to be quoted as saying "The
> press has a profound effect on life in America. If we are going
> to support the people's right to know then we're going to
> have to support the people's right to know about us."
>   Evidently Bradlee feels "the people" are right to demand
> their right, and wants to spend as much time as possible ad-
> justing his tie and combing his hair in the mirror of his own
> newspaper.

But viewed logically, the *Post* looking at Hollywood looking at the *Post* looking at Watergate in the name of reader
interest is the inevitable result of 1970s journalism. Bradlee
was right. As a *Post* writer explained to me, "We made the
old society with our attention, and now they turn on us
when we direct the publicity spotlight somewhere else." And,
anyway, the *Post* writer added, "Press people are more interesting than a lot of other people."

In real life as well, public figures have learned to play their
roles as news-making, accessible entertainers. Presidential
candidates arrive at airports and throw their arms around
local politicians they have never seen before—just like the
show business folk do at the Tony Awards. Academics
develop *shtick*. John Kenneth Galbraith is tall and dour;
Milton Friedman is bald and deflating; Eliot Janeway is rude
(Johnny Carson actually does a Janeway imitation). Jimmy

Carter wears jeans and Hamilton Jordan doesn't wear a tie.[5]
Dr. Rae Goodell of MIT has discovered and explained for us
the "visible scientists," experts who are expert on using the
media and thus get their names in the papers and their faces
on television all the time. The Margaret Meads, Linus Paul-
ings, and Barry Commoners know how to make news on
public policy issues: "Visible scientists" are issue oriented,
controversial, articulate, colorful, and credible; consequently
they are usually called upon for issue-oriented, controversial,
articulate, etc., etc., comment by reporters who have come to
expect headline-grabbing quotes and colorful copy.

As complex problems are reduced to personality stories,
world events and the news itself become trivialized. A *Newsweek* cover cartoon once depicted Henry Kissinger as Gulliver
being swarmed over by Lilliputian figures representing the
fighting in Indochina, Greek-Turkish tensions, the Ninety-
Fourth Congress, and the collapse of Arab-Israeli negotiations. Caricature is an old art; but in *Newsweek* the Kissinger
personality replaced the traditional Uncle Sam figure and
literally dwarfed the biggest issues of the day. It was a kind
of cartoon justice (but poor politics) when one public
response to the fall of Saigon in 1975 was to demand the
resignation of the star rather than to call into question the
underlying assumptions of American policy in Indochina
and around the world.

The demand for Kissinger's resignation subsided quickly
enough, and the spectacle of the most decisive military defeat
in American history and the wreckage of twenty-five years of
foreign policy soon sank with hardly a trace in the big media.
A few months later Kissinger was helping provide new entertainment again, albeit unwittingly this time. An enterprising
reporter had gone through Henry's and Nancy's garbage cans
on a Georgetown street and dutifully described his findings in

the *National Enquirer.* After the first public shock had worn off, the act that the Kissingers called "disgusting" could be seen for what it was: the logical, final extension of the media search for "items" (in fact, rock writer A.J. Weberman did the same garbage rifling on Bob Dylan years ago). The free press had become garbage scavengers. It was not what the founding fathers—or even the editors of *People* magazine— had in mind.

THE MID-LIFE CRISIS OF THE NEWS MAGAZINES

CHAPTER 14

Magazines, like people, have life cycles. *Time* and *Newsweek* are in their middle years now. Outwardly their vital signs seem healthy: circulation is good; advertising has improved after the recession of 1974-1975; the editorial matter reads smoothly; the news-gathering operations of the two magazines remain second in size only to the *New York Times* among the retailers of the news. Underneath the flush of prosperity, however, there seems to be a sense of uncertainty. One set of editors arrives; another departs.[1] Book excerpts appear. Outside writers contribute cover stories, unthinkable in earlier days. These changes are all symptoms of deeper apprehensions about the magazine itself. *Time* and *Newsweek*, in their mid-life passage, are having an identity crisis.

In separate interviews, Edward Kosner, the editor of *Newsweek*, and Henry A. Grunwald, his counterpart at *Time*, both used almost identical language to reaffirm their faith in the original newsweekly ideal. *Time* began in 1923, *Newsweek*

ten years later. Both were children of the same Henry Luce-
Briton Hadden insight that they could make millions by
sitting busy people down once a week and having them read
what has been rewritten for them about what happened the
week before. The department approach to the news—with
rubrics from art to world politics—may well be the single
most ingenious idea for organizing information since the
encyclopedias of the French Enlightenment.

But newsweeklies change. Their staffs, though perhaps not
readers, have grown increasingly tired of repackaged news.
Grunwald and Kosner used almost the same language to describe how they were trying to strike a balance between the
old "rewrite-sheet" form and a newer ideal of original reporting and writing. *Newsweek*'s purchase of the book rights to
The Final Days, for instance, grew out of discussions at a
retreat for editors in Mount Kisco, New York. (In palmier
days, these periodic soul searchings were held in places like
Dorado Beach, Puerto Rico.) "We thought about ways to
make the product better," one participant, Peter Goldman, a
senior editor, remembers. The Mount Kisco retreat concluded
that some of the most distinguished reporting around was
appearing in books and in other magazines, but not in the
newsweeklies. Grunwald also went outside his staff to commission essays from academics and writers who worked on
other Time Inc. publications. A *Time* cover story on the
1976 baseball season, a predictable rite of spring, carried a
surprise for *Time* people: it was done by a *Sports Illustrated*
writer. Grunwald has also mused about moving the magazine
out of New York City in order to give it a fresher perspective;
a few years ago, he recalled, he actually took *Time*'s
national-affairs staff to Washington to do their work there for
two weeks as an experiment to get away from "insularity."

The anxieties are institutional. *Time* and *Newsweek* feel the

challenge of competitors who have borrowed their formula.
There is a sense that their influence may be declining, and
there is a feeling of exhaustion about the form itself.[1]

In the past the news magazines alone enjoyed, in Grunwald's words, "the essential luxury of having a few days more
to gather, organize, and put the news together." Now newspapers and the wire services are staffed to offer, almost routinely, such luxury items, often done by former news magazine people. Ten years ago, *Time* and *Newsweek* reporting
and writing jobs typically paid $5,000 to $10,000 more than
similar newspaper work. Now a dozen papers can afford to
pay salaries in the $25,000 to $30,000 range offered by news
magazines. Newspapers, and television to some extent, have
also taken over the styles of contemporary newsweekly
journalism—"People" and "Newsmaker" columns, trend
stories, roundups with bureau contributions, news organized
in rubrics.

On major stories *Newsweek* and *Time* may not be able to
top what readers can get from the supplementary press services and special-interest magazines that have grown up in the
past decade. When Patty Hearst was captured, both *Time* and
Newsweek gave the story extensive cover treatment, yet all
the pictures, and most of the words, could have been found
in newspapers the weekend before the newsmagazines came
out. The weeklies can still add some *frissons. Time,* for example, reported that Hearst didn't wear a bra in her court appearance; *Newsweek* wrote that she had been allowed to
change the panties she had wet when arrested. But the added
time at their editors' command does not guarantee authorita-
tiveness. *Time* also said Hearst had been captured because she
was too hot for the Weather underground to hide; *Newsweek*
suggested that she had remained at large so long because the
Weather underground perhaps had been hiding her.

Newsweek separates fact from opinion, the magazine's best-known promotion campaign used to claim. The slogan took aim at *Time*'s eastern orthodox Republicanism. Instances of *Time*'s slanting of politics during its obstreperous adolescence fills a book: W.A. Swanberg's *Luce and His Empire*. In the past, what *Time* said about a Dewey or a Taft or a MacArthur mattered. In 1952 *Time* "made" Adlai Stevenson, at the time an obscure governor of Illinois. Later *Time* turned on him and deified his opponent, Dwight Eisenhower.

Newsweek had its own pantheon of heroes during this period. Business leaders and chairmen of the Joint Chiefs of Staff peered from its covers. *Newsweek*'s romance with Detroit was so ardent that the magazine ran an annual new-car cover with one or another of the auto industry's executives of the year posed with the latest models. The office joke about *Newsweek*'s coverage of corporate America went, "We separate fact from opinion—and publish the opinion."

Almost all of this kind of coverage changed at *Time* when Hedley Donovan took over from Luce as editor in chief, and at *Newsweek* when Philip Graham's *Washington Post* bought the magazine from the estate of Vincent Astor in the early 1960s. Donovan made Grunwald the top editor at *Time*. Graham made Osborn Elliott the top editor at *Newsweek*. The pronounced Republican slant disappeared from *Time*. The dough-faced corporate leaders faded from *Newsweek*. More effort and resources went into the reporting and writing of the news at the two magazines. Editorial budgets increased; *Newsweek*'s has doubled to around $14 million a year, not far below the $16 million or so spent by *Time*. Both magazines became more serious, more self-conscious, more responsible. They stopped concocting fake letters to the editors (which had been used to make the letter pages livelier or to fill them out). When a story was picked up from the *Times* or the wire services, bureaus were asked to collect the same information again; if the news magazines were to remain rewrite sheets in some part, then the rewriting would be, at a minimum, of their own reporting.

The magazines also have become increasingly powerless. Today they almost always confirm, rather than announce, developments. They follow, not lead. The most influential piece on Carter, for example, appeared in the *New York Times* six months before the *Time* and *Newsweek* covers. R.W. Apple, Jr., reported that Carter—a southerner, unheralded, unknown (despite a 1971 *Time* cover)—would do very well in the Iowa caucuses. That story got Carter a call from CBS's "Face the Nation." Supposedly the news magazines spot trends and break them first. Martin Arnold, in a *New York Times* article, credited *Newsweek* with alertly picking up on the "new ignorance" among students ("Why Johnny Can't Write"). The Arnold piece raised a few bitter laughs among the *Newsweek* staff because the "trend story" had been reported, written, and edited months before.

Time and *Newsweek* editors implicitly acknowledge the evidence of declining influence. "It's a more polycentric world these days. Others—newspapers, television, magazines—have influence too," says Kosner. It is not just that there are more bodies tugging at public opinion, but also more authoritative bodies. Is the subject politics? Apple in the *Times*, Richard Reeves in *New York*, and David Broder in the *Washington Post* have authority. Financial news? *Business Week* articles or *Forbes* pieces make stocks move on Wall Street. Trend stories? *Wall Street Journal* articles create more chatter. Books, rock music, sports, movies, show business, or the other back-of-the-book departments? Twenty years ago there was no competition; now *Sports Illustrated, Rolling Stone*, and a half-dozen other new authorities exist.

Sophisticated readers have become less interested in what the *Time/Newsweek* collective says than in what individual writers write. Cosmetic changes in the format, such as occasional reports from the field, can't mask the inherent group nature of the product—news gathered by one set of journalists, written by a second set, edited by a third. If anything, *Time* under Grunwald and *Newsweek* under Kosner have been consciously moving away from influence. "We are less judgmental, less heavy-handed today," says Grunwald. *Time*'s more evenhanded approach makes for straighter, fairer stories. But if the rough edges are gone, so are some of the juices of youth. The journalistic development that has caused the most self-doubt at the news magazines in the last few years has been, not the triumph of investigative reporting at the Watergate but the rise of *People* magazine, which has stolen the news magazine's most consistently popular department and spread it over eight pages.

Anyone who has worked at *Time* or *Newsweek* can do a seer's routine and envision, for friends, the shape of next week's magazines. When Howard Hughes died on April 5, 1975, he made possible the perfect news magazine cover story—a developing but finite event that unfolds over the middle workdays of the week, involving several widely separated American cities and touching on politics, finance, show business, and people. It organizes, writes, and lays itself out. *Time*'s April 19 issue had a sketch of Hughes on the cover; so did *Newsweek*'s April 19 issue. Both stories began "on scene," at the Princess Hotel in Acapulco, and ran for eight pages. *Time* had a three-column chart of the Hughes empire; so did *Newsweek*. Both articles had the same photos of the early set of Hughes girlfriends and the last set of Hughes aides. Part of the price of this predictability is ennui.

When the news magazines were younger, they aimed for

urbanity and culture. Grunwald, Viennese born and an
adopted New Yorker, muted the "American century" politics
that Henry Luce imposed on *Time*, and he enlivened the
back-of-the-book departments and the popular arts. Osborn
Elliott and Kermit Lansner, editors of *Newsweek* for most of
the 1960s and early 1970s, were both native New Yorkers.
Elliott had started in the early 1950s at *Time* as a business
writer; Lansner had written short pieces for *Art News* and
was its managing editor before joining *Newsweek* as a book
reviewer. Like Grunwald they brought a Manhattan sensibility, much desired at the time, to editing (the hard-news men
at the magazine kidded Lansner as the "night city editor of
Art News"). "In the 1960s," Lansner says, "we got the form
to fly as high as it could." Elliott, restive after nearly twenty
years of newsweekly editing, took on business-side responsibilities and made Lansner the chief pilot. The high was over.
Lansner seemed dilatory; he was merely bored. Elliott came
back, as a transitional figure to the next generation of editors. The mirror-image situation at *Time* pictured Grunwald
as stale, though the magazine was better journalistically than
it had been under other editors. Ray Cave, the new editor,
came from *Sports Illustrated* with the reputation of closing
pages fast; he'll make *Time* run on time.[2]

When Elliott replaced Lansner at *Newsweek*, he started a
new feature called "My Turn" (more outside writers). Elliott
also expanded the "Newsmakers" section—*Time* has done the
same thing with its "People" section—and began using splash-
ier pictures there and throughout the magazine. When Kosner
took over, he made the pictures even bigger. *Time*'s press
section, preparing a story on the Elliott-Kosner shift, called
Lansner for comment. "Big pictures, little pictures," he told
the interviewer. "Little pictures, big pictures . . . it's still the
same magazine." *Time* never ran the quote or the story.

The magazines can afford, financially at least, a period of soul searching. The vital circulation and advertising signs are still good, thanks to a series of key decisions on the business side over the past ten years. *Time* and *Newsweek* together claim a total readership of some 38 million to 40 million, about 8 million of that "overlap" (people who read both magazines). This is just about a sweep of the up-scale, college-educated, upper-income audience. Their circulations— 4.25 million for *Time* and 2.9 million for *Newsweek*—have not grown significantly in the past few years. But that is a deceptive measure. Both magazines have chosen not to pursue bigger audiences, partly because of the increased paper and mailing costs, partly because of the examples of *Life* and other mass magazines.

Ten to fifteen years ago, the accepted formula for publishing success held that advertising revenues were all that mattered; it was unimportant how circulation was acquired. This was the give-away era of magazines. "The magazine industry spent years telling people all the great things they would get for nothing," Ralph Davidson, once the publisher of *Time*, recalls rather ruefully. Toward the end of *Life*'s life—the magazine folded in December 1972—it was selling at around fifteen cents a copy to many subscribers while costing twenty cents per copy to produce. "The expectation was that advertising dollars would make up the difference," says Robert Campbell, publisher of *Newsweek*. "But television came along and took that money away."

Davidson and Campbell believe their own magazines in the early 1970s were careening down the same fatal road as *Life* (though *Newsweek*, with its smaller circulation, was less vulnerable than *Time*). One obvious way to apply the brakes would have been to raise the price the buyer has to pay for a copy. But as late as 1972, the per-issue cost for a trial subscription to *Newsweek* or *Time* was fourteen cents. The price per copy was kept low, executives assured each other, because if trial-subscription prices were raised one or two pennies, the extra revenue taken in from the new subscribers would be just about given back in the cost of the direct-mail campaign needed to get them.

Richard Nixon and runaway inflation—everyone else's enemies—probably saved the news magazines. In April 1973, the price of a trial subscription to *Time* or *Newsweek* was sixteen cents. By the fall, when the Senate Watergate hearings had run their course, the *Newsweek* and *Time* trial-subscription price had reached twenty cents. A year later when the House Judiciary Committee began debating articles of impeachment, the trial-subscription price hit thirty cents and the newsstand price sixty cents. Cigarettes, candy bars, bread, all cost more—why not the news? While many general magazines raised their prices, the news magazines kept selling strongly week after week with each fresh Watergate revelation. "It was a seller's market for us," *Newsweek* circulation director Robert Riordan said at the time. "We decided to seize the day." By the end of the extraordinary year of 1974, *Newsweek* had reached a pricing structure of 37 1/2 cents per copy to subscribers and 75 cents on the newsstand without driving anyone away. (*Time* was close—35 and 75 cents, respectively). "We turned circulation into a profit center," Campbell now says. In 1975, despite a 17 percent drop in advertising pages, *Newsweek* made more money than in any other year in its history—$11.9 million on revenues of $128.5 million in 1974. *Time*, with an 11 percent drop in ad pages, still earned well over $10 million on revenues of $157 million.

The newsweeklies are still seeking to make the most of their momentum. With its issue of April 19, 1976, *Time*

raised its cover price to $1. *Newsweek* then followed on July
5. The only certainty about newsstand sales, it is often said,
is that price boosts don't help. The fact is, however, that it
hasn't hurt *Time*'s newsstand sales. The real point of the
boost may be to drive readers into the subscriber file. As the
cover price rises, trial-subscription offers can be made more
tempting. A saving of half a dollar per copy, on a 50 cents
for subscribers and $1 on the newsstands formula, has a nice
ring to it.

Serious business problems remain. According to Winston
Cox, a Time Inc. specialist in postal affairs, it costs four to
five cents per copy to deliver *Time* through the mail, and the
Postal Service has the right to raise the cost to eight cents a
copy by 1979. By then it could ask to charge even more—
some pessimists fear as much as twelve cents. With *Newsweek*
looking over its shoulder, *Time* has begun exploring alternative delivery systems, including using local newspaper carriers
to get magazine copies to subscribers.

The editorial side has to make some key decisions for the
future as well. Kosner talks about making *Newsweek* more
"competitive" across the board. *Time* writers hear talk of
their magazine becoming more politicized, taking up the
American century idea aggressively once again and opposing
Henry Kissinger's gloomy Spenglerian vision of declining U.S.
power. But neither *Time* nor *Newsweek*, this late in their
passages, seems likely to break out of the basic newsweekly
role they perform so competently. They have nowhere else to
go; 40 million Americans can't be wrong. Both must continue
to look substantially the way they do, perhaps imitating
People, the brassy kid brother.

Conceivably *Time* and *Newsweek* may choose to switch
places with each other. *Newsweek* traditionally has been the
more competitive of the two magazines; its editors, trying to

find out what would be on the cover of *Time* the next week,
used Donald Segretti-type dirty tricks (such as phoning
the *Time* library to see what folders had been checked out).
Time, in contrast, seldom deigned to look over its shoulder at
what *Newsweek* might be planning. *Time* imagined itself as
the settled champion, secure in its primacy. "*Newsweek*'s
sense of identity has never been as strong as ours," Grunwald
noted. "They never have been quite sure who they are and
what they want to be." But lately *Time* has been doing the
scrambling. Grunwald ordered up a Bruce Springsteen story
when he learned that *Newsweek* had a story on the rock star
in the works. Grunwald parried the *Newsweek* purchase of
The Final Days by running the most sensational material
from the book the week before, *Newsweek*, in its turn, may
be growing more like *Time* in important but less noticeable
ways. In the 1960s, *Newsweek* ran more or less collegially.
Editors endlessly tussled, tummeled, and shored up each
other's weaknesses. The top editors came to be called the
Flying Wallendas, after the trapeze act. Kosner has disbanded
the Wallendas. There are fewer balancing acts. Decision
making has narrowed. Kosner says he doesn't want the new
Newsweek to be "white shirt and highly structured" like
Time; yet his one-man rule has more in common with Grunwald's *Time* than with the old *Newsweek*.

For a while a few years ago, the two magazines actually
waged a battle—the Great Passalong War. *Newsweek*, with
fewer subscribers, claimed almost as high a circulation as
Time, based on studies showing it had more readers per copy.
The battle has been all but forgotten, and *Newsweek* is now
selling itself to advertisers as a "combination buy" with
Time. "The last thing we want anymore," Davidson said, "is
a circulation war with *Newsweek*. It could kill us both."

Indeed, however much they compete for stories, *Time* and

Newsweek need each other physically, financially, editorially. They share printing plants in Old Saybrook, Connecticut, Chicago, and Los Angeles. They share space on newsstands. They share—tacitly because of the antitrust laws—the same pricing structure (one month after *Time* went to $1, *Newsweek* announced it would do the same). And they may someday share a new home-delivery system independent of the U.S. Postal Service.

Most of all, *Time* and *Newsweek* share the same successful newsweekly "franchise." Why do they "always" have the same covers, readers and others ask, eyes narrowing suspiciously at the thought of media collusion. Because that's how the formula works. Elliott and Grunwald, or Kosner and Cave, don't have to phone each other to know that Jimmy Carter or Howard Hughes or the Olympics or convention preview will be next week's big story. *Time* and *Newsweek* in middle age resemble two television wrestlers, pros who know each other's moves.

There is one characteristic that could set the two lookalikes apart: the proprietors. Whatever his ideological slant, Harry Luce cared about his magazine's quality. Now a bottom-line psychology may be taking hold at Time Inc., especially with the growing influence of the "Eastex Mafia," the business-oriented executives who are playing a larger role in corporate affairs as a result of the merger between Time Inc.'s Eastex paper-products company and Temple Industries, a Texas-based building-materials firm. At *Newsweek*, meanwhile, the proprietorship is still firmly in family hands. Katharine Graham may not be the founding father of *Newsweek*, but she has begun to exert a Luce-like influence on her magazine.

The threats to *Time* and *Newsweek* won't come from their mutual grapplings; their rivalry is too friendly to do harm.

Even the competition from television, radio, newspapers, and other magazines hasn't been too damaging. Between 1957 and 1970—a period of rapid growth of television, of rapid development of a number of excellent national and regional newspapers, and the birth of new special-interest magazines— *Time* and *Newsweek* enjoyed some of the best years of their lives. The reason, I think, lies in the genius of the original idea. In the past, the news magazines provided needed protein for the information-poor countryside. Now, the figures show, the news magazines also pull in readers in cities where information exists in abundance. The sociologists of communications perhaps can explain why. Jacques Ellul, for example, believes that too much news may be bad for mental health. The "objective" presentation of information, by Chancellor or Cronkite or by newspapers, raises multiple problems each day without appearing to offer any satisfactory answers. The bigger the story, and the more air time and newspaper space it commands, the greater the likelihood of psychic overload. The hard-news retailers, like television, drive audiences to *Time* and *Newsweek* for relief. The news magazine machine sorts the news, packages it, holds it all back for a while, then administers it in the form of a smooth, weekly inoculation against too much news.

Information overload, so far at least, has worked for *Time* and *Newsweek*. The danger is that the audience, growing ever more educated and sophisticated, will begin to notice that the news magazines provide no real guidance through the news thickets either. If *Time* and *Newsweek* depart from the original summarizing formula, they will contribute to the information overload themselves, becoming part of the problem rather than a solution. If they depend on cleverness and packaging to conceal the fact that they have no real point of view, smarter readers will smell out that condescension too.

Their editors face an enormous task: they must innovate and change without losing their established positions among readers. The whole process is further complicated by the leverage factors in mass publishing. When trends start going against general magazines, the downward slide for a $100-million-a-year operation can be awesomely rapid. The bigger they are, the harder they fall. In late middle age, any rapid descent could be fatal.[3]

Will it happen to the news magazines? *Time* will tell—unless *Newsweek* does first.

THE FALL AND RISE OF THE OLDSPAPER

CHAPTER 15

Early 1974 for many Americans was a winter of discontent. Gas station lines grew long and tempers got short during the Arab oil boycott. Watergate revelations piled up, but Richard Nixon seemed determined to save his presidency even if he sank the rest of the country in the process. Into this climate the Australian publisher Rupert Murdoch sent Americans a new weekly tabloid, the *National Star*. A typical issue had forty-eight pages, big pictures, and no story longer than 800 words; the *Star* took care of the problem of what to do while waiting in the gas line after reading the morning paper. When the stern visages of H.R. Haldeman, John Erhlichman, and the rest of the White House people who were indicted for Watergate offenses stared out from the front pages of just about every other newspaper in the United States, the *Star* had its own page-one political scandal: a deep-cleavage account of how the actress Connie Stevens would fight with "everything I have" to get a studio ban lifted on a film she had made based on the life of Marilyn Monroe.

Rupert Murdoch himself is perhaps the biggest newspaper
story of the 1970s. He is wagering millions of dollars that a
substantial number of Americans really don't want news in
their newspapers, whether of Watergate or of other worldly
affairs. What the people really want, the *National Star* fairly
screams in its spray-paint headlines and subway-car graffiti
layout, is not the news but the "olds"—pretested and familiar
stories about movie-television-rock stars, the Kennedys,
crime, sports, witchcraft, ESP, and imminent disaster. In the
first issue of the *Star*, a ferocious swarm of man-killing bees
was reportedly buzzing its way north toward the United
States. At a time when more and more American newspapers
were talking in properly grave voices about the need for more
investigative reporting, more in-depth analysis, more consumer affairs coverage, and all the rest of the post-Watergate
murmur, the *National Star* was offering Tarzan posters (plus
a chance to win a tree house) and a life-size, stand-up, cut-
out of Tony De Franco (the lead singer, in case you were
wondering, of the De Francos, "the hottest new pop group
around ").[1]
Murdoch is the life-size, stand-up, cut-out of that dying
breed, "the press lord." He took over his father's small newspaper in 1953. In 1977, at the age of 45, he controlled eleven
magazines and some eighty newspapers in what was once
widely known as the British Commonwealth. His biggest
winner is England's rock 'em, sock 'em *News of the World*,
the largest selling (6.2 million copies) English-language newspaper in the world. Murdoch also pumped new life into the
London Sun, increasing its circulation from 800,000 to 3
million in less than five years with a formula of crime,
scandal, and sex. Quoting what he claims is an old Australian
expression, Murdoch says "it is better to be a titman than a
titmouse." In 1974, Murdoch bought three newspapers in the

southwestern United States, a kind of reconnaissance before
his full-scale assault in 1975 on the rest of the country. The
National Star also started out regionally; it was sold originally
in the Northeast and parts of the Midwest and didn't buzz its
ferocious way across the rest of the country until spring
1975. In 1976, Murdoch acquired the *New York Post* and in
early 1977 *New York* magazine, *New West* magazine, and the
Village Voice weekly.

The Murdoch assault plan turns on one major calculation.
At a New York City news conference heralding the birth of
the *National Star* in early February 1974, Murdoch maintained that "papers and magazines in this country are written
to please Madison Avenue and the friends of the publishers.
They have lost touch with the desires of the reading public."[2] More to the point, Murdoch believes that there is in the
United States an audience of young eighteen-to-forty-year-
old working-class families who have gotten out of the daily
newspaper habit. Instead they group around the television
set—hence the *National Star*'s heavy servings of television
personalities and, more important, its $1 million television
promotion campaign featuring commercials as insistent as a
sledgehammer. This reliance on television was no accident;
with its acknowledged dedication to "unabashed entertainment," the *National Star* may be closer in content and format to prime-time entertainment television than to other
newspapers, magazines, or television news programs.

Other publications—notably the *National Enquirer, Midnight*, and *Tattler*—have entered the entertainment field, but
the *National Star*'s advertising manager predicted that the
Star's appeal would be different from, say, the *Enquirer*,
because of the *Star*'s "concept of total family involvement." As he puts it, "You wouldn't be afraid to leave the
Star around the house for any member of the family to

read." In the first few issues the *Star*'s girlie pictures showed less skin than in its British counterparts; there has been as much beefcake—all fifteen men who have played Tarzan—as cheesecake. But Murdoch wasn't trying to tell Americans something about themselves. The *Star*'s main appeal is to the star-watching instinct rather than to sexual prurience. It may well be that Murdoch is right when he suggests that a less educated, less sophisticated audience has been left behind by America's mainstream newspapers and magazines as they have pulled themselves up from the sensationalism of the 1930s and pursued better "demographics." And it may well be that many people, bowed by the weight of national politics and international economics—Nixon and Exxon—were eager for thirty minutes of noncommunications under the hair dryer or on the subway. In the same month that Murdoch began his seduction of the blue-collar classes, Time Inc. brought forth *People.* Slicker, better written, more expensive (thirty-five cents to the *Star*'s twenty-five cents), more tastefully designed than the *Star*, Time Inc.'s *People* nevertheless took dead aim on the same supposed "lower class" taste for personalities. *People* also was launched with the help of an expensive television advertising campaign.

Murdoch went looking for the old newspaper readership in front of the home screen and tried to make it his new clientele. The *Star* did not, in its first two years, achieve the successes of its British counterparts. This did not surprise those of us who believe that American blue-collar readers stopped moving their lips while reading many years ago. I met Murdoch after he acquired the *New York Post* in late 1976. Clay Felker, a friend and associate of mine, and former *New York* publisher and editor, introduced us. We told Murdoch how great it was for New York City that he was acquiring the *Post.* I understood what kind of junk-food journalism he used to fill his pages. Still the *New York Post* by any standard had been a sorry newspaper: dull, colorless, lacking fire or any sign of real commitment to the basic concerns of the New York area. (Do-gooder editorials hardly warm a tenement day when the landlord isn't sending up the heat.) Murdoch planned to spend some money, hire a new staff, change the graphics, and attract younger readers—and the advertisers who want to reach them. Murdoch's *Post* would, of course, be an *oldspaper*—full of heartwarming features, superstar gossip, the tried and the untrue—rather than a newspaper. But along the way Murdoch might nail a venal judge or stop an oil spill.

At the least, Murdoch and his *Post*, I thought, were a new journalistic sensibility in town. The *New York Times* was finally coming out of its financial doldrums; the *New York Daily News* had been born again under the editorial leadership of Mike O'Neill; *Newsday* was lively and well on Long Island; the *Village Voice* was paying its writers and was readable again, and, most important of all, had found an effective antiestablishment voice. *New York* magazine had outgrown its trendy East-Side survival kit image and had become an energy center for new ideas. A Ford Foundation study tracing the development of new ideas in American found that *New York* magazine contributed an outsize share of these innovative ideas in politics, behavior, and communications. In all, the good news was that journalism was looking up in the New York area, and at just the time when the beleaguered city needed it.

Then we found out that Murdoch was moving to acquire the magazines Felker edited. I was a contributing editor at *New York* and joined with other writers and staff people to try to stop the Murdoch takeover. We failed. (For an insider's account of what went on, see Gail Sheehy's article in *Rolling Stone* magazine, July 14, 1977.) Observing our noisy but futile efforts, a friend of mine said to me, "What's all the fuss about? Hungry sharks take over corporations all the time. Do you think journalists are the exceptions in the real world?" Big fish are always swallowing little fish, whether it is the corner candy store, the biggest electronics dealer in town, or, in this case, *New York* magazine. The writer Alexander Cockburn observed, "That's life—or rather that's capitalism." But I want to make the argument that it *does* matter when a magazine or newspaper is taken over by a remote supercorporation and that the readers have a direct stake in these predatory capitalists' fights. It was not just a good table at Elaine's restaurant on Second Avenue that was at stake.

Murdoch buys newspapers and magazines the way other men and women buy newspapers and magazines, but he doesn't just put down twenty cents to pick up a copy. He peels off $20 million or leverages a bank loan and buys the company outright. The *New York Post* is one of New York City's three daily papers. The weekly *New York* magazine, the *Village Voice*, also a weekly, and *New West*, a weekly based in California, owe their current successes largely to the efforts of Felker, their editor and publisher. Did it matter that Murdoch bought three of the New York area's news outlets and that instead of more media voices, the city now has fewer? Publishers are all bottom-line business people anyway, aren't they? The *Washington Post* editors and reporters fastened on to the Watergate scandals without checking with publisher Katharine Graham. But Graham had hired a certain breed of editors in the first place, and these editors went out and hired a certain breed of reporters. Not all capitalists are the same.

No, Rupert Murdoch wasn't good for New York or for the media consumer. New York needed real journalism, not Burt Reynolds's sex life, killer bees, and other freak shows. Murdoch took the old *New York Post*, which had been merely mediocre, and produced a screamingly pernicious sheet that pandered, or tried to pander, to the fears and fantasies of a no-collar class.[3] It was 1920s *Daily News* tabloid journalism at a time when the *Daily News* itself had been steadily altering its bad old ways. The good *News*, in fact, can serve as a journalistic and commercial model of what can be done in the way of a 1970 mass-class newspaper.

During the 1950s and 1960s the *News*'s daily and Sunday circulation had been declining. In the days before television, the Sunday *News* had sold as many as 4.6 million papers. By 1960, Sunday circulation in the metropolitan area had dropped to 2,283,000; by 1970, it was 2,242,000. The daily circulation had traced a similar downward slide—2.4 million in 1948, 2.1 million in 1969. In the early 1970s, both the daily and Sunday papers stopped their plummet and began to pick up readers by the thousands again, many of them white-collar people who had abandoned the paper as they moved outward and upward from the city to the suburbs. The daily and Sunday papers registered remarkable gains in advertising in the face of the generally poor economic climate in New York.

For much of its first fifty years of existence, the *News* wasn't a newspaper at all, in the sense of conveying what was new in the world. International and national events were treated in wire service briefs; no real effort was made to cover the city. The "education writer," for example, sat at the board of education building at 110 Livingston Street and rarely ventured into a schoolhouse or classroom. The *News*'s specialties were murder trials, family shootouts, hospital dramas, spicy divorce court dockets, "human interest" stories—reliable, wheezy organs on which the paper's veteran rewriters could play the time-tested tunes. The straphangers and the luncheonette crowd consumed these stories, along with the comic strips and the sports and race results, during a twenty-minute subway ride or over a cup of coffee and then saved the paper for the ride home, polishing off the Broadway columns, the features, and the service pieces. (Cultural historians someday will get around to studying how many first- and second-generation New Yorkers were acculturated by reading "The Correct Thing.")

The *News* has more and more become a newspaper; it is carrying *new* news in the form of real information, background, and interpretation. It now covers the city in a serious, reasonably straight, and competent manner. The *News* had always been well connected to the police; when urban violence escalated from two-bit barroom fights to the level of institutionalized bombings and riots, this connection paid off. The paper has also broadened its coverage of other metropolitan beats, such as the environment and poverty/ welfare. In the opinion of at least one New York State environmentalist, "The *News* does the best consistent job of covering my field." The new *News* is a better paper compared with the old *News*, which didn't cover the city consistently. It is a better paper than the *Post*, which doesn't cover anything consistently. But to ask if the *News* covers the city better than the *New York Times* is a stacked question. The *Times*'s editors have set for themselves a near-impossible task—comprehensive Washington coverage, plus comprehensive national coverage, plus comprehensive metropolitan coverage. Like the well-intentioned, well-educated, high-income people who read it, the *Times* has developed more concerns in recent years. Unfortunately, though the paper is interested in more things, it has a relatively fixed space for news, some 200 standard columns. The *News*, with no unbreakable commitment to events beyond the metropolitan area, averages 155 tabloid columns plus sometimes as many as fifty columns in its special zone sections for the Bronx-Westchester, Queens-Nassau, Manhattan-Staten Island, and New Jersey.

The *News* also has some qualitative advantages in this competition with the *Times*. Its punchy heads and tightly written stories are celebrated. *News* stories get down to essentials faster. Much of the credit for the new *News* goes to editor Mike O'Neill. Under him the supervisory staff, which often resembled a geriatrics ward, has been rejuvenated; the editor who once told a reporter, "We've got our nigger story for today," no longer is at the paper. Major surgery removed the daily fiction installments, and the precious editorial space once wasted on serialized thrillers and pulpy stories was turned over to a feature page, facing the editorial page, written by younger staff people. There are now a few black and Puerto Rican faces in the city room. They help cover what one editor calls "the scene"—youth, the barrios, music. Columnists Jimmy Breslin, Pete Hamill, and Gerald Nachman have attracted new readers. College-trained specialists have been hired. "Reporters now have to be able to write and writers report," one reporter told me. "We had a guy who worked here for thirty-four years and used to boast that he never wrote a story in his life—just dictated the 'facts' over the phone." The women's pages had a facelift when Mary King Patterson, octogenarian widow of the *News*'s founder, Captain Joseph Patterson, finally stepped aside. The business and financial pages have been similarly brightened with better layouts and type treatment.

The *News* still tells us about "Your Stars Today," but Dorothy Rose no longer offers "Decorations and Ornaments Youngsters Can Make." There is still the drumbeat of stories promoting the Harvest Moon Ball and the Golden Gloves matches, but Dr. Theodore R. Van Dellen, who prescribed

for arthritis and other senior-citizen ailments, has been replaced by youthful Dr. Tim Johnson. The photograph accom-
panying "The Correct Thing" has been dropped—and that
may be one of the surest signs of progress. Every day the
photo would show the wife and children of one of the *News's*
editors doing the correct thing in their apartment.

There is no lack of plans for other major changes at the
News. O'Neill came up from the paper's Washington bureau
in 1966 and spent his first year working with a small task
force on a projected afternoon version of the *News*. It was a
clean, airy "daily magazine" not unlike *Newsday* in appearance. The project was stillborn, but it remains a model of
what an ideal *News* could look like. O'Neill says only that
"what you can do with a new paper and what you can do
with an old paper are different. The same is true about the
differences between a home-delivered paper and a paper
dependent on street sales" (newsstand sales account for 85
percent of the *News*'s circulation).

Almost everyone concerned wants to keep the *News*'s
breezy tabloid style and tight writing, but the paper's knee-
jerk conservative cartoons and editorials are another matter.
"It's hard for me to imagine the *News* moving far enough
from its right-wing editorial approach to attract younger,
brighter readers," one *News*man said. But suppose for the
moment that middle-class readers themselves have been
moving to the right. The middle Americans of New York are
visibly uncomfortable with the *Times* and the *Post*, just as
they were uncomfortable with Senator Jacob Javits and former Mayor John Lindsay. "Isn't it time *we* had a senator?"
the James Buckley campaign slogan asked. Now the old *Herald Tribune* reader from Manhasset and the old *Journal-
American* reader from Staten Island may be discovering that
"we" have a paper.[4]

The *News* still has the major share of the black and Puerto Rican newspaper readership. "We're not read much in Harlem or Bedford-Stuyvesant," acknowledges a *Times* metropolitan editor, "but we do reach the leaders." Charlayne Hunter-Gault of the *Times* tells a familiar story: "We 'gentlemen and ladies' from the *Times* think we're the important ones; but people in Harlem won't start a news conference until the *News* gets there."

Some see in the *News* the true American version of the British "people's paper." But these mass-circulation dailies are moderately left in outlook, and it is unlikely that the *News* will ever be a people's paper in that sense. Yet there is a vital people's function beyond ideology that the paper can perform. New York urgently needed a populist voice, a newspaper that will regularly take on the hidden villains who are killing the city—the bankers, an insensitive Washington administration, incompetent officials (including the police), venal unionists, and cheating landlords. This is the role the *News* has approached in the 1970s and gained its audience, even as Murdoch's *Post* was making a giant leap backward to the 1920s, where very few New Yorkers still live.

BUSING COMES TO BOSTON: A MEDIA DRAMA IN TWO ACTS

CHAPTER 16

How do we know what we know? Epistemological questions are a proper study for consumers and critics of the press. News events and news images are refracted differently by the various news organizations, for understandable reasons. Sometimes they are not refracted at all; that is also understandable but not necessarily excusable.

On a sunny, brisk, late November day in 1974, the corridors of South Boston High School are quiet; black and white students pass uneventfully in the shabby old building. Four state-police troopers are lounging just inside the front door where metal detectors have been set up to intercept students carrying weapons. Outside in Dorchester Heights surrounding the school, all is peaceful too. Whites and young blacks crowd onto the Red Line subway at Andrews Square without incident. Yet a "Southie" business-education teacher is worried. "There is a feeling of tension here," she says, as she stands next to the school's huge glass trophy case. "You know something is going to happen."

In early December the incidents of violence between white and black students at Southie do, in fact, build. First there are fistfights and taunts; then a hammer-swinging fight between two students in machine shop; then a restroom battle involving fifty or sixty girls; finally a corridor clash on December 11, ending with the near-fatal stabbing of a white student.

Which was the true picture of South Boston during that school term: the apparently deceptive quiet of November or the seeming jungle world of December? If you lived outside the city and depended on the national media for information, the answer was clear. The place is "going to hell," NBC news correspondent Robert Hager was quoted as saying in *Time* magazine (September 30, 1974). As a part-time resident of Boston, I frequently wondered what city the national news outlets were describing; my knowledge came from different information. Epistemologically I probably was reacting the same way white southerners must have reacted a decade ago when the northern press came to cover the racial stories there.

Anyone who has been to war or seen urban riots realizes that there are always large zones of seeming tranquility during the height of battle: "pockets of combat" is the more correct metaphor than "pockets of quiet." The "media's Boston"—more precisely, the national media's Boston—was only a tiny piece of the real Boston. When school began, the city as a whole was not in "turmoil," as *U.S. News and World Report* said in its October 21, 1974, issue, nor was it "edging toward hysteria," as Paul Cowan, usually a sensitive and careful observer, wrote in the *Village Voice.* Rather a good part of the school year was a depressing replay of past years in the city's neglected schools where education had deteriorated without any special notice from the media.

How did Boston become the busing story of the 1974-1975 academic year, rather than, say, Destrehan, Louisiana, where a student was shot to death in a schoolyard in October 1974, months before the stabbing in Boston. Why Boston rather than New York City, where black and white students engaged in lunchroom clashes and after-school incidents similar to Boston's all through the fall semester, but only received attention in the metropolitan pages of the *New York Times*, back in the second section, and attracted not a word on the national evening news?

Part of the reason we heard about Boston was because of the unique image of Boston and its best-known political celebrities, the Kennedy family. The Boston busing story entered the national news consciousness on September 9, 1974, when Senator Edward Kennedy was chased by a crowd of whites as he tried to address a rally of Bostonians protesting the federal court order to begin busing (to correct racial imbalance in the city's schools). The photographs of Kennedy and the angry parents—who were mainly Irish, Catholic, blue-collar people—clashed with the conventional picture of liberal, Kennedyphile Boston: *those were his people jeering at him.* Actually as the Boston writer and critic Alan Lupo has said, "Those were *not* Kennedy's people. He lives on Beacon Hill, when he's in Boston. Those were Louise Day Hick's people."[1] There was a serious confusion of realms; the image of Boston as the northern capital of tolerance does a disservice to reality. Liberal Boston is a state of mind—found in parts of the city itself, like upper-class Beacon Hill, the student haunts around Boston University, and in such politically separate towns as Cambridge, Newton, and Brookline. The real Boston is a series of distinct enclaves. Louise Day Hicks, the champion of the neighborhood school, has her people; Elaine Noble, the lesbian who won a seat in the state legislature, has her people; and John Kenneth Galbraith and Congressman Robert Drinan have their people.

The national news coverage of the Boston busing story never got much beyond the basic drama of that first Kennedy scene. The players' roles had been assigned. There were "leaders" who no longer led; the angry white parents, the "ethnics," who, once again, were being asked to bear the consequences of social panaceas; and, of course, the "liberal" judiciary, represented in Boston by Federal District Court Judge W. Arthur Garrity, Jr., who had ordered busing.

Although the Kennedy and Cambridge connections helped put the busing story on the evening news and on page one in New York, Washington, and points west and south, even a good cast needs fast action to stay in the national news flow. Episodes of mob violence, the real kind, helped make Boston good copy for the first few weeks of school. But even then Boston was hardly the besieged city of the national news leads. By the most generous estimates, about 125 arrests were made during the first four weeks of the school year. School buses were stoned, blacks beaten by whites (and vice versa), scores of faces bloodied and knees skinned—surely a disgraceful spectacle. None of these facts are in dispute. But by way of contrast, the number of arrests made in one month of Boston's "busing riots" was still less than one night's arrests in Dallas on the weekend of the annual Texas-Oklahoma football game. The football riot isn't "news"; it happens every year.

Busing received the usual breathless handling. One wire service editor recalled the "spot news orientation" of his bureau:

In the first four weeks, we were writing one lead every hour, and we got to the point where we'd lead with fights involving five or six people with no injuries. The problem was that some of the stuff wasn't worth reporting. Everybody—New York, the subscribers—was keyed up about "the Boston school situation," and so you've got to come up with a story, even though there wasn't a story there.

A radio wire reporter added: "The tendency was for several weeks to play up the violence. . . . For example, a rifle shot was fired at a Boston high school, through a door where an hour earlier a policeman had been sitting. The story came back from the desk as 'gunfire erupted today in Boston high schools.' "

If a story went out of Boston with "classes were generally peaceful" in the lead paragraph, a wire-service reporter recalled, New York would ask the bureau to move up the violence from the fifth or sixth paragraph. Reporters soon got the message.

There was another development in the Boston busing story at this same time, one that was wholly different from the usual media process. The word got out that Boston's news organizations were deliberately censoring the news in order to play down the city's racial problems. The Boston press, it was said, was not reporting the negative news about busing (usually black violence against whites) while it was accenting the positive news (attendance figures, pro-integration sentiment). This charge probably originated in the ranks of the antibusing forces. It was repeated by both demonstrators and national reporters. The preparations for coverage by the Boston news organizations should have earned the respect and approval of thoughtful professionals, if not blind partisans. The Boston media, in trying to perform the way that the press is always being told that it is supposed to perform in crises, came under attack in the Boston busing story. Their credibility suffered unnecessarily.

Before the opening of school, executives of news organiza-

tions in the Boston area, some people from Boston's black
and white neighborhoods, and members of the city administration had met a number of times to consider what might
happen when the buses began transporting black children to
previously white schools (and white children to previously
black schools). The meetings grew out of some genuine fears,
and an intuitive sense of epistemology.

For ten years neighborhood leaders like Mrs. Hicks and
John Kerrigan, the chairman in 1974 of the Boston School
Committee (the elected group that runs the city's public
schools), had been telling their constituents that cross-neigh-
borhood busing would never come, that the Massachusetts
racial-imbalance law, which in effect prohibits schools with
more than 50 percent black enrollment, was unenforceable.
Hack politicians built whole careers on this impossible promise. Worse, the school committee, as Judge Garrity ruled in
June 1974 on a suit brought by the NAACP, had actively
maintained a racially segregated dual school system—by measures such as districting, the location of new school buildings,
and busing black children out of a school district. Judge
Garrity's ruling called for cross-busing in two phases. The
first was to involve some 18,000 of the city's 93,000 public-
school students. The order meant that after ten years of false
promises, Boston would have less than three months to prepare for peaceful compliance. Among other neighborhoods,
South Boston, where many of the poorest of the city's whites
lived, and Roxbury, where the black poor lived, would be
part of phase one. There were predictions that the buses and
the schools would burn and that Boston would become "another Belfast."

During the summer of these forecasts, most of the Massachusetts political leadership, with the exception of the antibusing school committee members, found themselves other-

wise engaged. The Republican governor, Francis Sargent, was
in serious trouble in his reelection race with Democrat
Michael Dukakis (Sargent lost). The state's congressional
delegations waffled badly. Congressman Joseph Moakley
issued a brief statement in which he tiptoed around the issue.
(President Gerald Ford offered similar "support" for the law
during the worst of the disturbances a few weeks later.) All
this crabwise movement left Boston Mayor Kevin White,
himself up for reelection in 1975, alone and exposed. "There
was a vacuum of leadership," recalls John F. Crohan, general
manager of Boston radio station WCOP.

The Boston Community Media Council, which grew out of
earlier racial troubles in the city during the 1960s, attempted
to provide some leadership. All the council representatives
came from the management side of the media; they cooperated on a "children's safety" campaign. Some 50,000 bumper
stickers were printed bearing the legend, "Take It Easy, for
the Kids' Sake." For students being transferred to new districts, special "know your schools" brochures were prepared
(complete with school slogans and descriptive materials). A
series of more than thirty radio and television public-service
spots was produced by Intercom, an independent arm of the
Boston Advertising Club, with the general theme, "It's not
going to be easy, but that never stopped Boston." Boston's
top professional athletes—Jim Plunkett, Bobby Orr, and
Satch Sanders, among others—delivered the line; Kevin White
and Senators Kennedy and Brooke also made spot announce-
ments. Finally, on Sunday, August 25, a "Boston media
statement" was issued, repeating the safety theme: "In Boston, it is our children who are important. . . . Their safety
and education must be assured above all else. We need all
Bostonians to help make school opening this September safe
and quiet." The statement was signed by representatives of

the twenty council members, including the general managers
of Boston's radio and television stations and the publishers of
the two major Boston dailies, the *Globe* and the *Herald
American.*

During this period newsmen attending summer meetings
discussed ways of covering any antibusing demonstrations
and violence that might occur. There was never any secret
about the meetings, contrary to later allegations. "We had
one very large press briefing, with as many as 150 people
present, editors and reporters, and two special sessions—one
for disc jockeys and one for reporters and cameramen from
the national networks," explained George Regan, the mayor's
assistant press secretary. The briefings at times emphasized
the obvious: the importance of checking out rumors and tips,
the need to be inconspicuous and to stand back from any
outbreaks to avoid the appearance of encouraging them. The
television people weighed the use of filmed reports, which
could be edited to provide a sense of perspective, over the use
of live remotes; the newspaper people stressed the importance of avoiding code words of inflammatory descriptions
such as "cruel," "savage," or "brutal" in their copy. A thir-
teen-point "Memo to All Hands on the Boston School Opening," written by Thomas Winship, the editor of the *Boston
Globe*, set down some of these basic rules.

The participation of the *Herald American* and its executive
editor, Sam Bornstein, at the meetings had special significance. The liberal *Globe* had editorially supported desegregation efforts. The Hearst-owned *Herald American* aimed at a
conservative audience. A year before phase one in Boston, a
young white woman died after, it was said, she was set on fire
by a group of black youths. The *Herald American* gave the
"torch murder" the full 1930s-style treatment—and received
plenty of criticism in return. "They made it sound like a race

war was imminent," remembered *Globe* columnist Ellen
Goodman. (The torch murder case was still unsolved four
years later, though police have hinted that they know more
than they have disclosed.)

All of these preparations by the Boston news outlets seem
fairly innocuous and routine in retrospect. The precise results
of the discussions are hard to pin down, but no one seriously
questions that the Boston media were well prepared to report, interpret, and balance the news they would send out on
the opening day of school, September 12. The antibusing
parents' group ROAR (Restore Our Alienated Rights) called
for a boycott of classes to protest the court ruling. The *Globe*
editors decided to report all that its staff saw or could confirm, and deployed fifty reporters in the field; the assignment sheet shows that twenty-one men and women were
assigned to specific schools and points along the busing
routes. Another dozen reporters were assigned to follow the
buses and specific children (for a white "vignette" story and
a black "vignette"). Another twenty reporters were stationed
at the courts, city hall, the school committee, the governor's
office, police headquarters, and other posts. There was even a
Globe reporter assigned to report on how the story was being
reported—that is, on how the *Globe* knew what it knew.

Other news organizations made different plans. The *Herald
American*, with fewer resources and mixed loyalties—and still
stung by the reaction to the torch murder story—adopted a
straight, low-key approach (one *Herald American* reporter
later said there was "a conscious decision to underplay the
story"). The television news leader in Boston, WBZ-TV, had
all eight of its camera crews out the first morning; the station
disguised its camera people in coveralls and hung Acme
Plumbing signs on the sides of its station wagons. WNAC-TV,
the liveliest news station, organized a pointed editorial com-

mentary; for one week during the fall, WNAC flashed pictures of the city's politicians on the screen while a voice-over asked, "What have you done to save the city today?" The picture was on the screen just ten seconds, but the series appeared, with different faces, every half-hour.

The *Globe* main story on the opening day of school said that city schools were generally calm, although trouble—the stoning of school buses—occurred in one section of South Boston. Attendance figures were given early in the lead story. The story was reported in substantially the same terms by the *Herald American* and by the television stations. At WBZ anchorman Tom Ellis began with a quick news summary saying that the first day of school busing had gone generally well; next came scenes of buses rolling up to schools and Ellis's voice giving the attendance figures. This was followed by videotape of Mayor White praising the city, the schools, and the police for the smooth start of school and referring to the "actions of a few" in South Boston. Ellis then noted: "In South Boston . . . resistance to desegregation resulted in injuries to some children and adults plus six arrests." There was time for a background film report and a live update from the city busing information center. In all WBZ devoted the first forty-six minutes of its one-hour newscast to the school story, with time out only for a sports segment, forty-five seconds for weather, and the commercial breaks. WBZ also returned to the busing story at the end of the hour.

The initial coverage gave attention to the combat guidelines suggested in the Kerner report on civil disorders. The newspapers were comprehensive and careful. Television news directors gave time and thought to their coverage, instead of the usual one minute and thirty seconds of action scenes. There was no sensationalism. In a five-column headline the next morning, the *Boston Globe* proclaimed: "Boston

Schools Desegregated, Opening Day Generally Peaceful."
"When you have forty-eight reporters phone in and forty-
seven of them say all is quiet while one reports trouble,"
recalled Timothy Leland, then an assistant managing editor
of the *Globe*, "what do you think the lead is?"

Although the Boston media initially answered that question
in the way that seemed accurate for the city as a whole, the
national news outlets answered it differently. It was at this
point that the press's technical task of organizing and order-
ing reality shifted to political and moral judgments. Neighborhood leaders had been running against the downtown
Boston press, particularly the *Globe*, for years (John Kerrigan
began a meeting once by asking if "the maggots of the
media" were present). When the fire-and-Belfast scenario
didn't play during the first days of school, the busing story
began to turn on the body counts—first, the success or failure
of the boycott as measured by school attendance, and, second, the success of failure of integration as measured by the
number of fights or disruptions inside the schools. The standard news lead read: "Attendance reached a school-year high
of 77.9 per cent yesterday, the 10th day of the court-ordered
racial balance plan for Boston's public schools. But sporadic
stoning of buses and fighting among students continued in
several areas of the city" (*Globe*, September 26, 1974).

Looking at the daily Boston coverage, the antibusing forces
claimed—or tried to convince themselves—that there was a
deliberate concealment of the facts: school officials and city
hall were not only inflating the daily attendance figures, but
the downtown press was cooperating with them. Racial incidents were not being reported by the big papers or the local
television stations. Every cab driver had a lurid tale that he
claimed had been suppressed by the hated *Globe*, and inex-
plicably, by the once-loved *Herald*, for his passengers. The

fact, never denied, that Boston news organizations had met over the summer with each other and with city hall became an explanation for the great liberal conspiracy of silence.

Time magazine, in its September 30 press section, picked up on this dark theme of collusion and censorship. In an on-the-one-hand, on-the-other-hand kind of piece, *Time* talked about a "well-intentioned agreement," made by the press with Mayor White, to "play it cool." "That most Boston newsmen cooperated in carrying it out," said *Time*, "doubtless helped authorities to maintain a degree of order in a potentially calamitous situation. But there is a danger in self-censorship. In its desire to avoid provocative excesses, the Boston press came perilously close to a kind of news management that can distort coverage just as surely as sensationalism." Tom Winship, however, remembers no such civic commitment. "We agreed that we should be responsible," he wrote *Time* in response to the story, "but all of us view being 'responsible' differently."

The *Globe* view of responsibility translated into more, and more thorough, coverage. In a way the paper became trapped by its own high definition of purpose. Faced with charges of collusion and censorship, the *Globe*, as one editor later explained, "turned itself inside out to double- and triple-check every rumor or tip to be sure we didn't miss anything." Now each high school boy sent home from school and each shoving in the cafeteria line was duly noted in a busing story. When a white crowd chased a passing black motorist and beat him, it became a page one story and picture. When five black youths raped a teenage white girl the next day, it was also page one, with details and quotes from the girl's teenage boy friend filling an inside full column. The *Herald American*'s coverage of the rape was more modest; and the national news outlets didn't report it at all. Some roles had been reversed.

Eventually the busing story came to be seen as more complicated than a listing of attendance figures and violent incidents. No longer concentrating on how many boycotted and who got hurt, the *Globe* reporters began examining the underlying reality of the situation in the city schools. They began to develop baselines for the daily facts; 12 to 20 percent of Boston high school students, by some estimates, are usually absent Tuesdays through Thursdays, and cutting may jump higher on Fridays and Mondays. In some schools the absenteeism was no greater in 1974 and 1975 than in previous years. They found that the boycott figures were apparently all but meaningless for the "terminal" schools, where young men and women complete their education. "There are only three reasons for going to Southie," Tom Hagedorn, an aide to Kevin White and the proprietor of the Plough and Stars pub, told me one night. "You want to be with your friends, have fun, and play football . . . and this year there was no team." Mary Thornton of the *Globe* found a vocal boycotter who had attended the school he was picketing all of six times the previous year.

The same kind of analysis began to be applied to "racial incidents," like the extensively reported "tray-throwing fight" in the South Boston High cafeteria. Wellesley College student Karen Maguire, one of the very few Southie graduates who ever went on to a four-year college, remembered the same thing in her Southie days—and so did her mother, also a Southie graduate.

As reporters and editors began supplying such contextual paragraphs in the busing story, they also began to examine critically the rest of the Boston school day: the outmoded or nonexistent facilities, the nature of the instruction, the teachers' training, the sources of funding, and the alternative forms of control—in short, the wider context of school and society.

"There has been trouble in the Boston school system since the 1830s," says Alan Lupo. "Only back then it was over the teaching of Protestantism to Catholic children." As usual it took the press some time to go beyond the surface of a story.

The fact that South Boston High School was quiet on some autumn days did not deceive anyone into thinking that Boston's desegregation troubles were behind it. As a result of the school committee's decade of bitter resistance, school desegregation arrived practically unplanned. The Southie school year confirmed the observation of Harvard social psychologist Thomas Pettigrew in the *Globe*: "It's no great trick to run a desegregated school that is a living hell." Robert Dentler of Boston University expected three years of "depressed achievement, paralysis, and conflict" in the schools before things would begin to turn around. The politicians, who by their inaction helped bring about this sorry situation, were relatively untouched by criticism. The downtown press, which uncharacteristically planned its actions, became one of the villains of the story. Professors Pettigrew and Dentler proved to be right in their predictions. The opening of the 1975-1976 school year brought more resistance and more drama. The new school year found the press still yoked to its old habits.

During the summer of 1975, the principal planning of the major news organizations was concentrated on the expected troubles in the Boston schools. The Massachusetts State Police had issued over 800 sets of press credentials by early September—316 to national news media people and some 500 to local press people, according to an account in the *Globe.* In part turnout was heavy because the press was looking for trouble. For almost a year, as the expanded second phase of Boston's cross-district busing was being planned, the media shoptalk had been about violence. The truck drivers and longshoremen of Charlestown (an area included in phase two), it was said, were even more insular and angry than the people of South Boston. The 1974-1975 catchphrase among reporters had been "Southie will be another Belfast." In 1975-1976, it was "There'll be urban guerrilla warfare" by the townies. Several news organizations decided to deploy helicopters over the expected trouble spots during the first week of school. "It is a sad sign of the times that covering the opening of school is considered a dangerous breaking news story," observed Sandra Burton, *Time*'s able Boston bureau chief, in the September 22, 1975, issue of the magazine.

The fantasies and fears no more materialized in Boston that year than they had the year before. Charlestown is the home of Bunker Hill and a local antibusing group called itself the Powder Keg; but the longshoremen and mothers of Charlestown didn't blow up the place. The townies chose to make prayer, not war. Processions through the streets ended with women kneeling and saying Hail Marys—asking God for relief from busing, one leader explained. It was a striking image that few picture editors could resist.

The street and airborne overkill aside, the press did perform responsibly in phase two. Everyone in the press agreed on that, although it would seem to be the minimum obligation of a skilled craft. NBC News, for example, matched a "portrait" of white Charlestown with one of black Roxbury. The MIT News Study Group videotaped about two weeks of national and local television coverage of the opening days of Boston's schools. The group found that almost everything that was admirably done by way of background and understanding of desegregation appeared not on the weekday evening network news but on the weekend network news or on the morning news programs ("Today" and the CBS Morning News with Hughes Rudd and Bruce Morton). There, stories can be soft and are allowed to run for four or five minutes.

National readers and viewers did get to "know" Boston, where most of the news people were. They did not get to "know" Jefferson County (Louisville), Kentucky, where almost as many students were involved in busing. The preparations had been as extensive and the racial rhetoric of the opposition as supercharged. And most importantly, the Jefferson County plan was far more significant as a national story because it involved city-suburb busing.

In recent years the white flight to the suburbs has been seen as the final, frustrating obstacle to school integration; if fewer and fewer white children remain within the central city boundaries, then it is hard to see how black children can get the supposed advantages of attending "white" schools. The Jefferson County desegregation plan dealt directly with the situation by treating the Louisville area, city and suburbs, as one integrated, metropolitan political unit.

Some national news organizations were in Louisville before the schools opened, but there was nothing at all like the numbers and attention clustered in Boston. The Louisville media, almost without exception, believed that the opening day trouble—a downtown scuffle between police and demonstrators, another incident at a high school—was minor. ABC and CBS network news, according to the *Louisville Times* television critic Howard Rosenberg, saw it differently, using film and narration about the downtown and high school incidents. NBC portrayed a calm scene; its Chicago crew went home the next morning. That Friday, however, a night of rioting began in Jefferson County. School buses were burned; police and the National Guard moved in, and the NBC crew and others scrambled back. One news organization, caught by surprise, had to send its people to Louisville from Boston.

Is the lesson, then, that it takes violence to get a story into the news flow, and into our consciousness? Not really. We all

realize by now that the news tends to be where the news
people are. We also know that the possibility of dramatic
news—news about events that are highly visible or laden with
emotion—tends to attract news people. But covering violence
is somewhat like violence itself: it is essentially mindless
(although no one wants to detract from the courage of the
street reporters). The violence inside a decaying, urban school
system is less easy to portray. And the interior violence that
rages in many people is hardest of all to approach and to
explain.

Many news organizations are now doing better with these
matters. Among the best reporting to come out of Boston
were the pieces by Jimmy Breslin for the *Boston Globe.*
Breslin wrote about the fundamentals, including the poverty
and ignorance that kept white and black working people at
each other's throats. Breslin covered school desegregation by
describing the educational idyll at an excellent private suburban academy, just a short drive from the Charlestown and
Roxbury tenements, where the affluent send their children.
Breslin is now considered a writer and a novelist who stands
apart from the "objective" tradition of journalists. Even the
better news outlets still shrink from serious discussion of race
and class in America. During the 1960s, the national news
outlets, including the networks and the national papers, supported the civil rights movement; there was a "liberal consensus" that the black struggle deserved help. But now that
black rights seem to clash with the rights of others, the liberal
consensus has broken down. The white ethnics have been
discovered. The clarity of vision of the civil rights 1960s is
gone, replaced by a 1970s ambivalence about desegregation
("the blacks really don't want it themselves"). This ambivalence is apparent in minor matters, such as defining Boston
and Louisville as the "busing story" rather than the "desegrega-

tion story." And it is apparent in the bigger issues. Not too long ago University of Chicago Professor James Coleman, author of the little-read but much discussed *Coleman Report*, appeared to say that "massive" court-ordered desegregation, particularly busing, hastened white flight from the cities. The news that busing caused resegregation—and, not so incidentally, was driving yet another nail in the central city (where so many news organizations do business)—was eagerly swept up and channeled into the national news flow. Busing is bad, was the message; we should forget about it. Coleman later backtracked from any such hard conclusions in an interview with Robert Reinhold of the *New York Times*. The recantation hardly attracted the attention of the original sensation. Similarly, a meticulous study by one of Coleman's colleagues, Professor David Wiley, demonstrated just how important the school day can be to childhood achievement; its message was that schools—even public schools—do make a difference. But the study was almost universally ignored. With everyone's attention on the trouble in the streets and around the schools, an important message about the schools themselves was lost.

When events are sudden, or confirm the convictions of the moment, or happen close to home (or close to where the news people are), they become "big news" in America. When events occur over time, or far away, or stir basic questions, they may not be treated as "big news," or as news at all. I've come to think of this as "Kurdism."

The Kurds used to be good for a few laughs in the years when I worked as a news magazine editor. At the Tuesday editorial conferences, the magazine's foreign editor would give his rundown of the international story list. He would lead with all the big acts ("Japan: Industrial Giant" or

"France after de Gaulle"), and there would be the usual
pitch for the obligatory fun pieces, kinky sex stories out of
London ("The Bishop Who Liked to Spank Saucy Girls") or
Rome ("The Mercedes-Benz Prostitutes of the Via Veneto").
The foreign editor would then ask for a column or so of
"selected short subjects," but the rest of us would howl,
"Ah, the Kurds, the Kurds . . . the fierce tribesmen of the
Kurdistan . . . they're eating their curds and whey." More
hoots, and then we moved on to the real news—Washington,
Wall Street, and Jackie. By Friday most of the "selected
short subjects"—later to become known as the Third World—
had fallen on the cutting-room floor.

I remember the generic Kurds and the ways of the press
when the various annual lists of big stories and the men/
women/persons of the year appear on the wires and on the
newsstand each December. What, I wondered, might a list of
the major neglected stories of the year look like? Who were
the nonmen and nonwomen of the year? I picked one year,
1975. I had some guesses, based on looking at a dozen or so
newspapers and magazines every day and spending at least an
hour nightly watching television news. But I also asked about
twenty other heavy consumers of news for their nominations
for the biggest non-news stories of 1975.

As might be expected, the most frequently cited uncovered
stories were about what the trade dismisses as "room empti-
ers." Stephen Schlesinger, who writes the "Press" department
for *Time*, nominated such heavyweight material as the decline of education in America: "Teachers are being dismissed
all over the country, colleges are shutting down and ending
tenure for their faculties, Ph.D. holders are driving cabs because there are no university jobs, and high-school classrooms
are overcrowded as a result of educational aid cutbacks, but
the press refuses to concentrate on this as a continuing

story." He also nominated the U.S. role in Angola, a "commitment that remained unreported until several senators revealed the CIA's secret funding of the war." Schlesinger wanted to know why, after all of the press's self-criticism about its coverage on Vietnam, the Angola story was missed.

There were several candidates for nonperson of the year. Schlesinger offered the unemployed: "The press has managed to swallow the Ford argument that 8 percent unemployment is inevitable." MIT linguist Noam Chomsky nominated the southern Lebanese living under Israeli jets. Israel's military actions against several of its neighbors have been going on for a long time and in a "brutal" fashion, Chomsky said, but when there is coverage the people involved may be called "Bedouins" in the stories, "perhaps because it is easier to drive them into the desert under that name."

Chomsky also brought up my old friends, the Kurds: "One of the more interesting, and barely mentioned, revelations of the Church committee was that the CIA was financing the Kurdish rebellion. After the Senate had released the facts, Kurdish leaders, considering themselves freed from secrecy, gave details. They reported that they would never have undertaken the rebellion had the CIA not promised to back them, through Iran. Then Kissinger decided, in his wisdom, that it would be better to relieve the Kurdish pressure against Iraq so that the border conflict between Syria and Iraq would be exacerbated. The CIA cut the flow of aid, the Kurdish rebellion was crushed, there was a real threat of genocide (but what is a little genocide between friends?); in fact no one knows what happened."

Not quite. The *San Francisco Examiner* of February 1, 1976, dropped a clue about what did happen. In one sentence in a story on the House Intelligence Committee's suppressed report on CIA activities, it said the committee had found that there may have been more than 100,000 casualties on the Kurdish side. The low news value of 100,000 Kurds shouldn't be too hard to understand. It flows from a traditional method of assigning space for news stories: 10,000 dead in Africa or Asia equals 1,000 dead in Western Europe equals 100 dead in West Virginia equals one dead next door.

There was a surprising amount of agreement among my panel on the biggest neglected story of 1975. The world—free, communist, and Third—has been arming itself to the teeth. "Nonmilitaristic" Japan has everything but the A-bomb. The so-called LDCs—less developed countries—aren't far behind. Countries that can't manage to deliver a letter 200 miles have been buying sophisticated weapons systems from the United States and the Soviet Union. According to figures supplied by Anne Cahn, a research fellow at Harvard, an estimated $18 billion worth of arms were sold in 1975. Most of these weapons were sent to the Middle East and the Persian Gulf; over half of them came from the United States.

My own nomination for the major neglected domestic story of 1975 is easy: corporate political payoffs to Washington politicians. Rich Thomas, the *Newsweek* reporter who did some of the best unnoticed work on this story, remarked to me that there is an unexplored world "awash in boodle and loot" in Washington. This wholesale bribing of the White House and the Congress has been going on for decades. According to a Library of Congress study, American companies publicly admitted making more than $300 million in questionable or illegal political payoffs. Some of the millions that changed hands in recent years—and the hands apparently included, among others, Gulf Oil, the 3M Company, Lockheed, Ashland Oil, Lyndon Johnson, Hubert Humphrey, Hugh Scott, Wilbur Mills, and Russell Long—were reported to have been in the form of "campaign contributions." Admittedly what the giver regards as a bribe the receiver may think of as expenses. At least that is how most of the recipients remember it, when they recall anything at all. The mass amnesia of senators and congressmen about bundles in the $15,000 to $50,000 range rivals that of postwar Germany, where no one could be found who remembered any Nazis. By mid-1977, we all found out that "boodle" was a major neglected story of 1976 as well; only the source of the money was South Korea this time.

How can we account for this performance? The nonjournalists' quick answers are usually wide of the mark. The press isn't "racist," though as the skins of the participants become darker, the lengths of the stories shrink. The press isn't "pro-Israeli," though it is very sensitive to Jewish-American feelings. The press isn't afraid of the "vested interests," though it makes sure Mobil's or Senator Scott's denials appear right along with the charges. The paranoids are wrong: there is no news conspiracy. Instead there are a lot of editors and executives making decisions about what is "the news" while constrained by lack of time, space, money, talent, and understanding from doing the difficult and/or hidden stories. The story of illegal contributions could not be pried out of the usual sources: grand jury testimony, helpful lawyers, or congressional committees armed with the power of subpoena. Reporters had to pore through depositions taken by the Securities and Exchange Commission. There was no zealous prosecutor, no Judge Sirica, and certainly no congressional inquiry. Any possible wrongdoing, like campaign "gifts" not reported for income tax purposes, was, initially at least, a civil matter between the IRS and the politician and therefore secret.

And, of course, there are no completely "missed" stories.

Most of the big media can point to an article or film report about the unemployed or Gulf Oil or the arms race or even the Kurds. The CIA's involvement in Angola was reported by Leslie Gelb in the *New York Times* on September 25, 1975. Two months later Gelb and Walter Pincus of the *Washington Post* both reported that CIA director William Colby and Under Secretary of State Joseph Sisco had briefed a closed session of the Senate Foreign Relations Committee on what the United States was doing in Angola. In fact the CIA has apparently been funding Holden Roberto, an Angolan, since 1962.

The basic problem, as political scientist Ithiel de Sola Pool pointed out, is structural. The *New York Times* gets around to every story eventually. But even the best of the press remains dependent on official sources. Angola got into print, after fourteen years, because some senators wanted it out. Moreover the press lacks any memory; the Holden Roberto story has been around for years; it may have appeared in print, but no one remembered it until the *Times* and the *Post* stories put Angola on the map. Similarly the press hasn't set itself up to show slow evolutions in politics and economics. The columnist George Will remarked that the mass movement of rural southern blacks to the North in the 1940s and 1950s went largely unreported; but if an electric eye had been set up next to some road across the Mason-Dixon line by the Commerce Department, and the two-millionth black to pass it had been given a Chevy station wagon by General Motors, then the press would have amply recorded this media even for readers and viewers. Then the press would walk away from the story: black migration would have been "done."

THE "WATERGATE EFFECT" AND THE FUTURE OF THE NEWS

CHAPTER 17

The future, the comic Mort Sahl used to say, lies ahead. The critic's hope in monitoring the press—watching the watchers as they watch—is to encourage a systematic restructuring of the press institution. There is some evidence that criticism produces a degree of reform, but the critic's main contribution may be in slowly influencing underlying ideas and processes. Meanwhile changes are achieved directly by individual talents, acting and overcoming within the system.

Norman Sandler is part of the future of the press in America. He was graduated from college in 1975. His first full-time job was to cover the Iowa state legislature in Des Moines for United Press International. In the summer of 1977, Sandler spent a great deal of his time on the telephone, calling Washington, Manila, and Hong Kong. The UPI bureau in the American heartland had itself no immediate interest in his enterprise. After Sandler finished his normal nine-to-five duties reporting on the Iowa legislature, he spent his own time on his then current preoccupation—a tortuous, and conceivably dangerous, investigation of the activities of certain foreign intelligence agencies within the United States.

Sandler isn't a journalist anyone very far beyond the city limits of Des Moines is likely to know right now. But he plans to change all that. He doesn't mind working until two in the morning in pursuit of his story or spending his own money to travel 1,500 miles to New York for a rendezvous with a stranger who may or may not be a good source of information about the Korean intelligence service (KCIA) or the Iranian secret police (SAVAK). Like hundreds of other young or unknown reporters around the United States, Sandler sees himself as an investigative reporter in the tradition of Bob Woodward and Carl Bernstein, the two *Washington Post* men who covered the Watergate scandals, and of Seymour Hersh, the *New York Times* reporter whose stories include the revelations about the My Lai massacre in Vietnam and the CIA's ties with Howard Hughes.

The "tradition" Sandler is working in is scarcely five years old, dating back to just about the time when Sandler, an undergraduate with an interest in politics, was trying to decide whether to go into journalism or the law. "Woodstein" decided for him—and for hundreds of other young men and women. The stories of governmental law breaking and the tragedy of the Vietnam War catapulted the obscure, hardworking, "shoe-leather" investigative reporter to star status—to the top ranks of contemporary folk heroes, the stuff of cultural mythology. Alan J. Pakula, the film director who turned Woodward and Bernstein's best-selling account of their work, *All the President's Men*, into an equally popular motion picture, saw the two reporters as the leading players in a modern version of the movie western. Their story, he said, resonated with "that American belief that a person or small group can with perseverance and hard work and obsessiveness take on a far more powerful, impersonal body and win . . . if they have the truth on their side."

There is considerable poetry in this description. Woodward and Bernstein, after all, were employed by the *Washington Post*, less a weak and insubstantial reed than a major corporate institution in the life of Washington. They toppled not the government—the Republicans continued to run the executive branch after Richard Nixon's resignation until the voting public turned them out—but rather a cabal of twenty or so men at the top of an administration. This was hardly lawman Gary Cooper standing alone in the streets at "High Noon" or the solitary figure of Shane riding into town.

But the Woodstein myth does embody an essential truth. Both the Watergate and Vietnam revelations of the early 1970s signified an important break point in the relationship between the American government and the American media, particularly the Washington-based and national media. Before 1972 and 1973, it would be fair to characterize the big media—the three television networks, the wire services Associated Press and UPI, the news magazines *Time* and *Newsweek*, and the leading newspapers like the *Washington Post* and the *New York Times*—as largely pacified members of the press establishment. The big media, in general were, to use the phrases from the Vietnam days, "members of the team" and "with the program." If the symbolic journalistic event of the 1970s was the investigative reporting of Woodstein and Sy Hersh, then the symbolic journalistic event of the 1960s was the *New York Times*'s decision not to print the story its reporters had obtained about the prospective Bay of Pigs invasion. Its editors, in consultation with the White House, feared publication would harm the operation. Douglass

Cater's study of the Washington press in the early 1960s unapologetically called it "the fourth branch" of government.

The experience of Watergate and the Vietnam years seems to place the big media in opposition to big government—the so-called adversary role honored in constitutional textbooks. No less an authority than U.S. Supreme Court Justice Potter Stewart, speaking at the Yale Law School in 1974, declared that "the established press in the last ten years, and particularly in the last two years, has performed precisely the function it was intended to perform by those who wrote the First Amendment to our Constitution." Press "adversaryism" became good business practice. The *Los Angeles Times* syndicate, selling a new column by Jack Cloherty and Bob Owens called "The Investigators," spoke of "the new breed of columnist, post-Vietnam, post-Watergate . . . our dynamic duo will be naming names, exposing exposés, uncovering cover ups."

Not everyone would agree that press practices conform with textbook theory. The writer Tom Bethel, in a long analysis in *Harper's* magazine, suggests that the big media are not an investigative adversary of the government but part of that government. The collective "Washington," as Bethel points out, is not a monolithic entity institutionally inclined toward wickedness and corruption "could it but get away with it." Rather it is a series of middling bureaucracies that are usually at war with each other. The press is not a dispassionately critical adversary, defending the people's right to know, standing watchfully on the ramparts of freedom and democracy, but yet another bureaucracy, dependent upon the real government for leaks, documents, and dissident opinion. This is the "fourth branch" of government theory, updated. In this view Woodward and Bernstein did not break open the Watergate story; bureaucratic institutions did, including the FBI, federal prosecutors, the grand jury, and the congressional committees. Woodstein was dependent upon these governmental sources for leaks and stories. Bethel, unfairly, implies the reporters were as much stenographers as investigators.

What is commonly referred to as the "new" investigative journalism is not actually new, and it is neither as exalted as Justice Stewart pictures it nor as routinized as Bethel suggests. Woodward, Bernstein, Hersh, and their colleagues, including the Norman Sandlers out in small bureaus, take up a style that flourished in America at the turn of the century. They work in the older tradition of the muckrakers—Lincoln Steffens, Upton Sinclair, David Graham Phillips, Ida Tarbell, and Ray Stannard Baker, among others. Perhaps the lineage goes back even earlier to the social writings of Dickens in England as well as Marx and Engels. The American muckrakers (the word came from Bunyan's *Pilgrim's Progress* and the man who could look nowhere but downward to the filth on the floor) focused on the corruption of monopoly capitalism and its venal political machinery and set the characteristic style of investigative reporting. Their goal was not any revelation but an exposé of wrongdoing by authority. The story that migrant workers received starvation wages was not investigative news to anyone over ten years old; the story that public officials connived with that arrangement was.

Most critics would agree that there was no sustained period of journalistic muckraking between, say, 1913 and 1970 (although there were notable major individual scoops and exposés, important in themselves, by Heywood Broun, Clark Mollenhoff, Fred Cook, Drew Pearson, and later, Jack Anderson). Was it because corruption and chicanery had disappeared, and there was no official muck to rake? Not at all. On one level, the notion of objective reporting took over American journalism in the early twentieth century and helped improve much of the news coverage. Reporters were to become professionals and stay sober; they were not to pay for stories; they were not to impersonate law officials or anyone else in the pursuit of the news; they were to forsake sensationalism and cheap thrills. Above all they were not to take sides or slant their stories. Objective journalism had for its model the medical doctors: white-coated specialists describing pathologies as if through microscopes. This model corrected many unsavory practices in the press itself and marked a widely hailed progress from the partisan press of the nineteenth century (a press not unlike that in the majority of countries in the world today).

On another level, however, the decline in muckraking may have been also the result of a certain overarching consensus between media and government. World War I united the country, including the press, in a largely popular cause; the prosperity of the 1920s united the country, and press, in an era of jazz and good times; the depression of the 1930s, the global war, also popular, in the 1940s, the cold war of the 1950s and early 1960s—all closed the majority ranks of American society. Only a few pariahs questioned the general consensus—H. L. Mencken in World War I and I. F. Stone in the 1950s. By the early 1970s, however, much of that unity was gone and, with it, the compliant press.

The new zeal for investigative reporting is probably a cause for more joy than alarm, although some critics fear that the press already is too powerful and all but unaccountable except to public opinion—which the press helps mold in the first instance.[1] But this view overlooks at least three facts of contemporary journalistic life.

First, investigative reporting is still the exception rather than the rule, even among the best and the brightest of the American media. ABC, CBS, and NBC do little regular investigative reporting. Public television's 200 stations do no better. The media conglomerates that own most of the newspapers in small towns in the United States have been, by and large, toothless watchdogs of the public interest. The exceptions have been the Knight-Ridder newspaper chain, especially its outlets in Miami and Philadelphia, and the Times-Mirror Company, publishers of the *Los Angeles Times* and *Newsday*.

Second, there is a long list of things that investigative reporters cannot do. Most newspapers will not as a rule permit reporters to pay for stories, tips, or other information of any kind. Nicholas Gage of the *New York Times* is the investigative reporter of organized crime whose exploits made him the model for the CBS television drama series, "The Andros Targets." As Gage points out, journalists have none of the legal authority of a police officer, district attorney, or FBI agent; the reporter "carries no gun or badge, has no power to issue subpoenas or obtain a search warrant and cannot grant immunity in exchange for information. Anyone who doesn't want to talk to him can slam the door in his face." Gage and other investigative reporters acknowledge that they are dependent for information in part from their contacts within the government bureaucracy. In that sense at least, investigative reporters are not adversaries but accomplices of government.

Third, time, money, and energy set limits on reporting. There is a finite investment that investigative reporters in daily news organizations can make in any given story, no matter how critical the cause. By no means does all investigative reporting feed on tips and government informants. Woodward and Bernstein were not the passive receivers of leaked documents. They labored long hours to produce their own leads. (Anyone who wants to understand how the investigative reporter works should read their account in *All the President's Men*.) The most celebrated case of a so-called passive exposé was the publication of the Pentagon Papers. Daniel Ellsberg, a former government analyst who turned against the war in Vietnam, did indeed hand over classified documents to Neil Sheehan of the *New York Times*. But Sheehan, as a result of his excellent coverage of Indochina as a combat correspondent and his earlier stories of the American involvement in Vietnam, had become well known to every careful reader of the war news. As the French physiologist Claude Bernard once said, "Chance favors the prepared mind."[2]

Distinctions should be made in the styles of investigative reporting. The kind of work done by Woodstein, Hersh, and Gage might generally be called "source" reporting because it is based on wide contacts and the cultivation of insiders. A second type of investigative reporting might be called "cause" reporting, to denote an investigation of exposé intended to serve some specific point of view. Most of this kind of work is not done by daily journalists at all; the canons of objectivity tend to rule against it. Among the most notable cause reporting has been the work of Ralph Nader on automobile safety and the writings of Rachel Carson on the misuse of pesticides. More recent examples include the late writer Paul Jacobs's dispatches on Chile for *Newsday*. A third kind of investigative reporting might be called "analytic" (or "computer-assisted"). The work of reporters Donald L. Bartlett and James B. Steele at the *Philadelphia Inquirer* stand as a model of this type. Leonard Downie tells how the two men spent one whole autumn documenting their investigation of the near-criminal state of the criminal justice system in Philadelphia. Bartlett and Steele, he writes, went through records of 10,000 criminal indictments, police complaints, warrants, arrest sheets, bail applications, and court hearings, 20,000 pages of courtroom testimony, and 1,000 miscellaneous psychiatric evaluations, probation reports, and hospital and prison data. Out of all this material, they culled the completed cases of 1034 criminal defendants charged with murder, rape, robbery, or aggravated assault, and they methodically noted from these records, 42 different pieces of information about each defendant and his case. This information was then coded onto 9618 IBM cards and put into a computer.

From the resulting 4,000 pages of computer printouts, plus their own visits to the criminal courtrooms in city hall and lengthy interviews with defendants, crime victims, prosecutors, defense lawyers, judges, and other court personnel, the two reporters . . . fashioned a portrait of local criminal courts "in far worse shape—practicing subtle, wide-ranging forms of discrimination and routinely dispensing unequal justice—than even their harshest critics would have guessed." These findings were presented to readers of the *Philadelphia Inquirer* in February 1973 in a week-long 25,000 word series of articles, supplemented by graphic charts and tables drawn from the computer-analyzed data.

These three styles of investigative reporting are not pure types. Reporters may work with both their secret sources and the public archives. They may have a point of view, or a cause to advance, although most daily journalists are more interested in the process of competition—the scent, the chase, beating the opposition—than they are in substance ("getting" the Republicans, or Democrats).[3]

To say that there are different kinds of investigative reporting is not to say that one is superior to the other. American journalism—and American society—needs all three kinds. Unhappily there is still much that has to be investigated, and exposed, and not all that many reporters on the assignment. Critics ought not be blinded by the financial success and folklore status of a relative handful of reporters. The high-quality investigative work done by the *New York Times* and the *Washington Post* is not typical of the national media. For that matter the work of Woodstein, Hersh, and Gage is not even typical of the work of the majority of the reporters on their own papers. Most of the rest of us harvest the daily news crop on a nine-to-five basis and then go home.

The commitment to investigative reporting tends to be in direct proportion to the depth of feeling about the inequalities and injustices of American society. Reporters can run with the hounds (their normal "objective" position) or hold with the hares. One day a year the prize committees of editors and publishers meet to honor those few reporters who regard their work as something more than ego or prestige or entertainment or business, who do take seriously the textbook talk about "the ramparts of freedom." Then these proprietors return home to their own offices, where too few of their decisions are aimed at creating the conditions for a truly vigorous, free press the other 364 days of the year.

Investigative journalism has never been, and is not now, a full-time preoccupation of the press. And it is still a duty that the press treats with ambivalence. Early in 1976, Daniel Schorr, then of CBS News, arranged for the publication of a suppressed congressional report on illegal and excessive CIA activities. He gave the report to the *Village Voice* in New York; Schorr himself (rather than the suppressors of the report in the House of Representatives) became the target of criticism. The House Ethics Committee called Schorr to testify. Schorr, an aggressive, abrasive, and controversial journalist, became the center of attention rather than the CIA. "Killer Schorr," the ex-CIA director Richard Helms called him, adding what the bolder newspapers referred to as a "ten-letter vulgarism." Granted Schorr has an ego as wide as Pennsylvania Avenue, but there is nothing in the First

Amendment that says journalists have to be honorable, decent, loyal, responsible, or kind or that they should possess any of the other Boy Scout virtues. We can be a ten-letter vulgarism. The courts, bless them, say we don't have to be likable—just free, and others are free to criticize and condemn us. Journalists don't even have to be young and good looking.

Equally important, there is nothing in the First Amendment saying that only the *New York Times* or one of the other national newspapers has the constitutional right to inform the public of government misdeeds. The *Washington Post*, in particular, became terribly stuffy in its news stories about Schorr's choice of a trendy "left-liberal" New York publication. With journalist friends like that, the First Amendment needs all the help it can get from the courts and from the public.

The courts and the public, for their part, need constantly to be reminded of the importance of the First Amendment. A press that is honorable, decent, responsible, honest—and free—would be an excellent reminder, and endorsement as well, of the founding fathers' wisdom. Critics, in their writings, teachings, and by their own example, ought to keep summoning the press, the courts, and the public to the cause of robust and responsible journalism. In that way the press watchers become part of the future of the press in America as well.

NOTES AND SOURCES

Most of the material in this book comes from interviews and research conducted by me and my associates in the News Study Group in the Political Science Department at MIT. In the few cases where materials come from sources other than our own research and reporting, I have tried to indicate this. There is one problem with the interviews. The news business, and especially television news, is so volatile that presidents, executives, and talent move from job to job—or are removed from jobs—with the blink of a rating point or circulation drop. The titles given most of the men and women quoted reflect the job each had at the time of the interview.

The notes offer further sources and information for those who want to look into some of these matters in more detail. In addition there has been one other invaluable source for our understanding of press and political processes. Since 1972, the News Study Group has been videotape-recording public documents on television—news conferences, special reports, presidential debates, candidates' commercials, congressional hearings, and primary and election night coverage, as well as the appearances of public figures and the coverage of public events within the television news programs. We have over 600 hours of this material available for study, and this videotape library provides the visual evidence and case materials for the analysis and conclusions made here.

Notes to chapter 1

1. When Senator Adlai E. Stevenson III of Illinois announced in early 1976 that he would not run for president of the United States, he seemed to be saying that all the excitement and activity of the campaign—the "high human drama" of which we are constantly being reminded in the newspapers and on television—may not be worth the price paid in time, effort, and sanity. A candidacy launches a thousand skirmishes, Stevenson explained: the candidates become whirling dervishes, all competing for the attention of the media. Commentators gauge the "viability" of candidates on the most superficial grounds, such as "the size of the campaign bankroll and the applause volume at joint appearances."

2. The most thorough of the first general accounts of the 1976 campaign is *Marathon* (Viking, 1977) by veteran political reporter Jules Witcover.

Notes to chapter 2

1. Support for this work came in part from the research group headed by Professor James David Barber of Duke University. His work, in turn, was funded by the Ford and Markle foundations. Barber and his coworkers looked at the role of the media in the 1976 nominating process. His own work is being published separately, and his conclusions and ours may not necessarily coincide.

2. Alexandra Norkin of our News Study Group also found that there were some minor myths being fashioned during the campaign:

● *The myth of momentum*: a candidate who does well in one primary will, by the laws of momentum, do well in the next one. In fact Carter's momentum in New Hampshire did little for his showing in Massachusetts. The same was true for Reagan's primary victories but his loss at the convention.
● *The myth of media*: media coverage means victory. Udall explained his losses by "not being known." Jackson says his message did not get across; more likely the message was not accepted.

• *The big story*: the story today is "there is a new Republican frontrun-- ner this morning." These stories are treated as the definitive word on what is happening in the race and are used to predict future races; it does not seem to matter that at the next primary these stories are by necessity changed.

Notes to chapter 3

1. The "eureka" moment for Jerry Rafshoon, Jimmy Carter's televi- sion expert, did come early. Rafshoon gave this account of a candidates' rally in Manchester, New Hampshire, in September 1975, writing in *Broadcasting* magazine: "I scanned the audience when Jimmy Carter, a 17-hour day of campaigning behind him, took to the podium. And I say to you, in my obviously biased opinion, that what I saw was magic. Not by instantaneous bursts of applause reacting to the tailored message we have become so conditioned to, but by something else; something else— you couldn't put your finger on it because it somehow transcended through. But I can tell you that his Manchester audience saw something they had not expected. It came with the passing of each word, from one minute to two, then three, four and five.

"I knew then that I had to get that something on television. I also knew that I wasn't going to do it in 30 or 60 seconds. So I suppose it was that moment when I decided to go with our five-minute format. I was sure that it was the only vehicle short of personally introducing Jimmy Carter to 113 million Americans that would reveal the depth of my candidate."

2. Ronald Reagan's March 31 broadcast was carried by NBC-TV. He attracted almost the same audience as the entertainment program, "Mc- Naughton's Daughter," shown in the same time period one week earlier.

3. The cumulative figures indicate that NBC News's coverage of the nationally televised presidential primaries was seen by 56.7 million people, according to an NBC Research estimate based on Nielsen televi- sion index data. CBS attracted 40.8 million people with its primary coverage and ABC, 30 million.

4. There is no doubt that polling will play a major part in the 1980 presidential coverage. At a meeting of the National Association of Broadcasters in March 1976, NBC News president Richard Wald pre- dicted that television news was entering a "period of instantaneous polling." It now takes two or three days to do a Louis Harris style national poll and a full day to do the exit polling NBC and CBS did in 1976. But within ten years, Wald forecasts, "There will be a mechanism by which some anchorman, sitting somewhere, can say: 'And what do you think of Henry Kissinger's plan to whatever-it-is?' And he'll push a button and within ten minutes a national poll sample will have been taken, and people will say what they think. I think it's a horrendous

idea. But we'll do it." A few weeks after Wald's remarks, WNEW-TV in New York tried an "instantaneous response poll" of New Yorkers' presidential preferences. Viewers were asked to phone the station with their "votes," which would be handled by a Votrak Information System, described as a "high-speed polling device capable of handling 100,000 phone calls in an hour and tallying the results." Though there were bugs, the system worked reasonably well.

Notes to chapter 4

1. While we can thank the League of Women Voters for bringing this vitality to the 1976 campaign, the Aspen Institute, also a private group, deserves our gratitude as well. The institute pushed the FCC to change its rules about allowing debates restricted to major party candidates (in the past the fear of demands from minor candidates for equal time had effectively blocked debates in the 1968 and 1972 presidential elections). However, in September 1975, the FCC handed down a decision in a case commonly known as the CBS-Aspen case. This ruling allows the networks and/or individual stations to broadcast debates between candidates for public office and not have these debates fall under the equal time ruling (Section 315 of the Federal Communications Act) if the following conditions are met:
A. The networks or stations broadcast the debates live and in their entirety.
B. The debates are held by an independent third party, i.e., not the networks, not the candidates, and not the national committees of the two major parties.
C. The debates must be held outside of television studios.
In a subsequent decision in March 1976, in a case popularly known as the WTTW case, the FCC clarified its earlier decision by stating that networks or stations could have no editorial control over the content of the debates. Network commentary and analysis prior to or subsequent to the debates was permitted under this formula.

2. For a good first-hand account of the 1960 Kennedy-Nixon debates, see Douglass Cater's Op-Ed article in the *Washington Post*, July 6, 1976. Cater was an interrogator in the third of the four encounters. "I had entertained Walter Mitty notions of posing questions so trenchant that they would get to the heart of the issues," he writes. "But the format was neither fish nor fowl, not permitting follow-up of 'Meet the Press' variety nor a truly unrehearsed clash of ideas. Both Kennedy and Nixon proved remarkably adept at this art form. Quickly mastering its peculiar gamesmanship, they knew how to appear to extemporize, yet waste none of their precious media time in reflective pauses, never grasping for an elusive word. In the swift alternation of reply and rebuttal, they managed to ration each subject to the allotted two-and-a-half minutes

for reply and one-and-a-half for rejoinder. No matter how narrow or broad the question, each extracted his last second of image projection. The interrogator's role proved barely more than to designate category— animal, vegetable, or mineral—on which the two would take off in their own directions."

Notes to chapter 5

1. The Syracuse findings were published in book form under the title *The Unseeing Eye*, Patterson and McClure, Putnam, 1975.

2. According to Rafshoon, "We spent about $2.3 million on the primary advertising campaign of Jimmy Carter. About 95% of this went toward broadcast. Of this figure, television took the bulk, 80%, with the remainder going toward radio. We spent approximately $1 million in production and collateral." In the general election Carter and Ford had a mandated $21.3 million for the entire campaign, including staffing, travel, paperwork, telephones and so on. Of that, about $10 million was used by Carter for advertising, including production by Rafshoon. He noted: "That would make a fine regional campaign, but we had to use the same selective buying we did in the primaries—only to a greater extent. We only had about 20% of the budget that George McGovern had in 1972—in a losing effort." The figures for the Ford campaign on television were $11.12 million compared to perhaps $25 million spent by Richard Nixon before the campaign finance law.

3. Jordan served as an unpaid volunteer (BBD&O does not handle political accounts). He was brought into the campaign at the urging of Don Penny, a former comedian and comedy writer who was then a White House consultant, and of David Kennerly, the president's photographer.

Notes to chapter 6

1. Just as the technocrats looked and sounded alike, so did their products, as the discussion in the previous chapter attempted to show.

2. In addition to the Barber study of press-candidate "interactions," Professors Patterson and McClure reported their findings on the presentation of the campaign on television. Professor Gilbert E. Scharfenberger of Salem (Massachusetts) State College has already reported on a study that downgrades the role of television coverage. His study during the last ten days of the Massachusetts campaign indicates that the primary voters made their decisions based on some other factor, such as print media, radio, or contact with campaign workers. The survey was based on full-time monitoring of the three commercial stations in Boston from 5 P.M. Friday, February 20—the weekend before the New Hampshire primary—to 2 A.M. Tuesday, March 2, the day Massachusetts voters went to the polls. It showed that:

• Former Georgia governor Jimmy Carter was on television by far the most of any of the Democrats—both in news coverage and in advertising—yet he was disappointed by coming in fourth.
• Senator Birch Bayh of Indiana was the third most heavily covered Democrat by the television newsmen, yet he came in seventh.
• Congressman Morris Udall of Arizona, who tied for second in news coverage and was eighth in paid advertising, ran second in the primary.

Notes to chapter 7

1. The latest version of this nonsensical view comes from Professor Michael Robinson of Catholic University in the summer 1977 issue of *The Public Interest.* According to Robinson, "In the 1950s television was a *reflection* of our social and political opinions, but by the 1960s it was an important *cause* of them." Robinson's post hoc, ergo propter hoc fallacies are thoroughly taken apart by the estimable George F. Will in his column in *Newsweek*, August 8, 1977, p. 84.

2. This cause is slowly making converts. The commonsense observation that the viewer has become more selective has been discovered at last by McHugh and Hoffman, the broadcasting consultants. In 1977, with the aid of a firm of social psychologists and a polling organization, McHugh and Hoffman published a monograph called *The TV Viewer Comes of Age.* It was distributed mainly to clients.

Notes to chapter 8

1. The article, "Sex on TV: A Content Analysis," was researched and written by Susan Franzblau, a doctoral candidate at the State University of New York at Stony Brook, and by Joyce N. Sprafkin and Eli A. Rubinstein, faculty members there. It was one of six appearing in a special *Journal of Communications* symposium, "Sex, Violence and the Rules of the Game," in the spring 1977 issue.

2. "TV's Sex Drive: Turning on the Ratings," *Newsday*, July 3, 1977. Nicholas Johnson, the director of the National Citizens Committee for Better Broadcasting, Washington, D.C., has also been keeping track of sex on television.

3. The search goes on for scientific ways to package, then project, and, finally, measure sexuality on television. When the AT&T Long Distance Division wanted to promote direct telephone dialing, it decided it needed the right "charismatic" spokesperson. It narrowed the field to three well-known sports figures—dark-eyed, moustached Mark Spitz, the Olympic swimmer; lithe, French-accented Jean-Claude Killy, the skier; and tall, bearded Bill Russell, the ex-Boston Celtic. It then went to the West Coast and the audience testing firm of Walt Wesley Com-

pany. Wesley uses a twenty-five-person jury and a psychogalvanometer to measure a performer's or a program's "arousal" index. The psychogalvanometer is similar to the traditional lie detector machine; it uses finger sensors to register the changes in electric resistance in the palms of the respondent when presented with "emotional" materials (the so-called GSR, or galvanic skin response phenomenon). The higher the index, the sweatier the respondent's palms and the greater the response. Normally a good arousal index score is considered .300. Spitz scored a .180; Killy scored a .312. Russell practically broke the electrodes with a .500. His strong showing got him the job of appearing in those well-done television commercials that open with him talking about the advantages of direct dialing and other long-distance services. When Russell starts talking, women's palms respond; when he sinks the basket—"to make his point" about direct dialing—men get aroused.

Notes to chapter 9

1. When the television news ratings begin to plummet, critic Jack Gould of the *New York Times* once observed, they bring on the carpenters. The time when a new studio set, say something looking like an American Airlines ticket counter, could shore up the audience for the evening news has long since passed.

2. Despite this record, Kavanau is highly regarded by his peers. Gabe Pressman, the star reporter of channel 5 in New York, called Kavanau "the best news director" he has ever worked with.

3. NBC in Los Angeles was the first major market station to offer two hours of local early evening news.

4. I regard WTOP-TV's news as the best local news operation in the country. I ought to point out that I am an on-air commentator for the station. The first statement may be influenced by the second statement, but I still believe it is objectively true.

5. The work was done at the University of Pennsylvania under Dr. George Gerbner.

Notes to chapter 10

1. Altman has since left the firm to head his own marketing company. A number of such popularity measuring firms have come into existence around the country to rate local newscasters.

2. The best guess is that small home appliances like toasters, blenders, and electric can openers are involved.

3. The founding fathers' project never made it in bicentennial '76—or in 1977, for that matter.

Notes to chapter 11

1. Here are sample questions from the survey: *Which of the following statements about shield laws is true?*

● The reporters' privilege case of 1972 invalidated all the state statutes allowing reporters to protect confidential sources.
● In general, state shield laws provide almost absolute protection against disclosure of news sources, but at the federal level, the congressional statute provides only qualified protection.
● In general, state shield laws apply to the source as well as the reporter, and the courts have consistently ruled that the source can legally prevent the reporter from disclosing his or her identity or the information he or she gave the reporter.

Which of the following statements about the First Amendment is true?

● It was written and ratified as a direct result of Andrew Hamilton's defense of John Peter Zenger.
● It intended to limit the power of the clergy to villify the press.
● It was intended to limit the power of both the Senate and the House of Representatives to engage in censorship of expression.
● All constitutional historians agree that it had clear priority over all other amendments in the Bill of Rights.

A reporter is held in contempt of court in a federal district court proceeding and fined $500 for disobeying a gag order. The court order is subsequently held to be unconstitutional by a federal court of appeals. Under current federal law, a reporter may

● Be ordered by the federal district court to obey the gag but not pay the fine until the Supreme Court decides the case.
● Be ordered by the federal district court to obey the gag and pay the fine until the Supreme Court decides the case.
● Disregard the gag order and the fine because the gag order has been voided based upon its patent unconstitutionality.

2. WTOP-TV, in a letter filed with the FCC, said it would provide free time to proponents of oil company divestiture in response to the FCC's ruling that Texaco advertisements carried by the station had advocated the antidivestiture viewpoint. However, the letter from WTOP-TV Vice-President and General Manager James T. Lynagh argued that the FCC, in arriving at its decision, failed to deal with its previously stated policy that the fairness doctrine should be invoked only if such advertising "obviously addresses, and advocates a point of view on, a controversial issue of public importance." WTOP-TV contended that the Texaco spot did not meet this test.

3. Friendly's book was published by Random House in 1976. It should

be read in its entirety. For a review of his arguments, see Edwin Diamond, *Columbia Law Review*, 76, no. 8 (December 1976):1314.

4. Tornillo was executive director of Classroom Teachers' Association and was a candidate for the Florida House of Representatives. The *Miami Herald* printed several editorials against Tornillo's candidacy, calling him "Czar Tornillo," and accusing him of leading an illegal teachers' strike in 1968. One editorial said, "For years he has been kicking the public shin to call attention to his shakedown statesmanship."

Notes to chapter 12

1. Some ABC executives believe one factor in their move from third to first has been market research. They used questionnaires and surveys to determine that their best hope to win over viewers would be to program for younger adults whose tastes in programming were not yet fixed.

2. A rough rule of thumb is that one ratings point equals 729,000 households equals about $1 million in advertising revenues.

3. Whatever Wald achieved with the new nightly news format, it wasn't enough in the eyes of his superiors at NBC. After a wide range of disagreements on substantive matters with NBC network president Herbert Schlosser, Wald left the network at the end of 1977. He was succeeded by Lester Crystal, whose journalistic experience has been almost solely in broadcasting. Schlosser himself has since been fired.

Notes to chapter 13

1. The *Journal* article, one of seven appearing in a special *Journal* symposium entitled "Gossip as Social Interaction," was written by Jack Levin, a faculty member at Northeastern University, and Allan J. Kimmel, a graduate student at Temple University. Some other findings:

● Celebrities' families and friends appeared three times more often in 1975 than they did in 1955.
● By 1975, the celebrities' personal lives accounted for 59 percent of all gossip, a "dramatic reversal" from 1965, when their professional activities were accorded that same amount of space.
● In 1975, columnists were 18 percent more likely to judge a celebrity's behavior than they were twenty years before—but 77 percent of all opinions were positive.

2. The *Washington Post* started a feature "Gossip Column" in 1977 but abandoned the idea after a few months. Most of the material was appearing already in various parts of the "Style" section.

3. CBS News offered its video version of *People* magazine in the form

of the program "Who's Who" starting in early 1977. "Who's Who" was abandoned in the summer of 1977. A series of internal problems at CBS, rather than the idea of the program itself, caused cancellation.

4. After leaving office, Kissinger accepted a high-paying consultancy with NBC News. He was asked to advise on foreign coverage and appear on camera in a number of specials—effortlessly making the transition from diplomat to performer.

5. Shortly after Hamilton Jordan moved into the White House as President Carter's chief political adviser, the "Gossip Column" in the *Washington Post* actually reported that Jordan didn't wear underwear. He replied that the writer of the column, Nancy Collins, would be the last to know whether her story was true. "Everybody" talked about it for days in Washington.

Notes to chapter 14

1. I was once one of these editors. Between 1962 and 1970, I was senior editor of *Newsweek* (from 1958 to 1962, I was the magazine's science editor). No one can spend twelve years in such an engaging activity without developing extremely strong feelings about his or her work.

2. Ray Cave took over Grunwald's job in the late summer of 1977.

3. The real future of magazines may be in publishing every two weeks. The fortnightly might be an old idea whose time has come. The pace of a monthly is too leisurely. The newsweeklies are always out of breath. But fortnightlies are beginning to flourish: *Rolling Stone, Fortune, Forbes, New Times,* and *Esquire,* under new publisher Clay Felker.

Notes to chapter 15

1. The De Francos, as far as I can determine, have not been heard from again.

2. The press lord is a recurring type—the uncommon man, usually born rich, who claims to have a sense of what the common man (and woman) wants. Others were William Randolph Hearst, Colonel R.R. McCormick, and Captain Joseph Patterson.

3. In the first year of his ownership, Murdoch followed a hands-off policy at his other acquisitions. The *Post* kept him quite busy.

4. Paul Weaver did a scholarly study of the *Daily News* while working on his doctorate at Harvard. He called the changes the embourgeoisement of the paper.

Notes to chapter 16

1. Judging by the picture coverage of the first week of school in Boston in September 1975, the local papers picked photographs that reflected the "larger picture" the papers were trying to convey. Out-of-town papers, on the other hand, worried less about balance and their impact on the community. According to an analysis by Alexandra Norkin of MIT's News Study Group, the two major Boston papers ran ten photos of violent action out of seventy-six. Comparable figures for out-of-town papers were four of seven in the *New York Times* and three of six in the *Washington Post*. In Boston the *Globe* chose a crowd shot of its page-one coverage of the opening day of school. The picture is not dramatic: it is impersonal, the faces are distant, and there is no compelling center of attention. But to the *Globe* editors it was a representative photo of a large mass of whites peaceably protesting. The *Washington Post*, however, chose an action photo of three scuffling men taking away a bullhorn from a fourth. (The scuffle was a sidelight to the school story—the man was a street-corner evangelist.) Two days later much the same contrast between home and out of town was evident. The *Globe* and the *Boston Herald American* ran a picture of Charlestown mothers kneeling and praying. The photo may have its visual drawbacks—static, dull, vague—but the message conveyed is unmistakable. The *New York Times*, on the other hand, chose a different picture of the same women, one taken before they prayed. The *Times* picture has "drama." The women stride toward the policeman, giving the photo immediacy and impact. In a visual sense it is a better picture, but one with quite another message.

Notes to chapter 17

1. In the spring of 1976, the general manager of the Associated Press, Wes Gallagher, chose the annual convention of the American Newspaper Publishers Association to complain that the U.S. press had taken off on "an investigative reporting binge" that is causing many readers to look upon it "as a multivoiced shrew nitpicking through the debris of government decisions for scandals, but not solutions. . . . The First Amendment is no hunting license, as some seem to think," Gallagher concluded.

2. Limited resources do not mean that small-town papers are prevented from doing investigative reporting. In 1976, the *Anchorage* (Alaska) *Daily News*, with a circulation of 16,000 and a staff of 20, won a Pulitzer Prize for uncovering abuses in the powerful Teamsters Union of Alaska. Year in and year out, the Pulitzer committee finds similar work to honor.

3. Those who never worked in the news business tend to think of it as

ideological or, the other extreme, professional. There are elements of these attributes in the press, but neither "explains" the press. A good working explanation was offered by Eric Sevareid at the convention of the National Association of Broadcasters in March 1977. Sevareid said, "I don't know, quite, whether I'm in the news end of the broadcasting business or in the broadcasting end of the news business. But I do represent news, the hasty, often improvised and unstructured, often agonizing attempt to give the world a little glimpse of itself every day. It is not a profession in any strict sense, not exactly a business or a trade. It is a calling. We have to try to live at the growing points of human society, at the cutting edges of history. Wits and resourcefulness play a bigger role than learning or intellectual disciplines. We are pinch hitters every other inning. All one can hope for is a respectable batting average."

INDEX